Touching Others
With Your Words

ALSO BY CHARLES SWINDOLL

The Church Awakening

Available wherever books are sold.

Touching Others With Your Words

CHARLES R.
SWINDOLL

New York   Boston   Nashville

FaithWords
Hachette Book Group
237 Park Avenue
New York, NY 10017

www.faithwords.com

Printed in the United States of America

RRD-C

Originally published in hardcover by Hachette Book Group.

First trade edition: April 2013
10 9 8 7 6 5 4 3 2 1

FaithWords is a division of Hachette Book Group, Inc.
The FaithWords name and logo are trademarks of Hachette Book Group, Inc.

The Hachette Speakers Bureau provides a wide range of authors for speaking events. To find out more, go to www.hachettespeakersbureau.com or call (866) 376-6591.

The publisher is not responsible for websites (or their content) that are not owned by the publisher.

The Library of Congress has cataloged the hardcover edition as follows:

Swindoll, Charles R.
  Saying it well : touching others with your words / Charles R. Swindoll.—1st ed.
    p. cm.
  ISBN 978-0-89296-831-2 (regular edition)—ISBN 978-1-4555-0737-5 (large print edition)   1. Oral communication—Religious aspects—Christianity.   2. Persuasion (Psychology)   I. Title.
  BV4597.53.C64S95 2012
  253'.2—dc23
                                                                        2011029395

ISBN 978-0-89296-832-9 (pbk.)

Dedication

Learning how to do things well takes time…a lot of time.

*It took me a lot of time to learn how to relate well—
to care about others in deep, sincere, and meaningful
ways. I have my marriage and my family to thank for that.*

*It took me a lot of time to learn how to lead well—
to stand firm and not cave in when life is difficult,
demanding, and exhausting. I have my training in the
Marine Corps to thank for that.*

*It took me a lot of time to learn how to think well—
to study diligently, to pursue the truth, to be faithful to my
calling, and to be disciplined with my time. I have many of
my teachers to thank for that.*

*It took me a lot of time to learn how to communicate well—
to put thoughts into mental pictures, and then to shape
those pictures into words so that I might connect clearly
with others. I have my former professor, my model, my
mentor, and my dear friend for more than fifty years to
thank for that.*

Dr. Howard G. Hendricks *means more to me than I'm
able to express. In many ways, I am the man I am today
because of his contributions to my life. Therefore, it is
with great delight and genuine gratitude I dedicate this
volume to him. Due to his personal investment in me, I
now know the joy and the benefits of saying it well.*

Contents

Introduction

I am a preacher. I'm involved in many other things, but, mainly, I preach. And I love it!

As a child, I never would have imagined myself saying that. The last place I wanted to be was standing in front of other people to speak. While I was raised around churches and had gotten to know a few preachers fairly well, the thought never entered my head that I would one day stand and deliver.

Not only was I not interested, I lived with a major struggle: I stuttered. Who knows why? All I can tell you is it only got worse during my early teenage years. By the time I entered high school, speaking in front of a group was my least favorite place to be. Obviously, God's plans aren't hindered by our fears or limitations. For reasons I will never understand, He decided a hopelessly tongue-tied stutterer would someday devote his life to preparing and then delivering a fresh message from His Word at least forty times each year (often more). That in addition to fulfilling the role of shepherd.

The journey from stuttering to "saying it well" took a lot of time. It was neither easy nor quick. The process required the help of others who saw potential in me that I could not. My journey carried me halfway around the world and back before I would even *consider* any kind of role involving public speaking. This journey also required years of formal education, and several more under a series of mentors, each with something specific to offer that I really needed. Finally, I had to endure a few turbulent years of flying solo before I began to feel comfortable fulfilling my calling: preaching.

After all these years (soon to be five decades) of speaking, teaching, and preaching, I feel that I'm finally ready to put into print much of what now works for me. I'd like to communicate everything, but that's unrealistic. Some things—let's face it—can't be put into words on a page; they must come naturally from within. Each of us has an inimitable "style" that is ours and ours alone. God has gifted each person like no one else. It is essential that you discover your own "put together," as my dad would say. Once you find out what that consists of, you need to cultivate being YOU. I'll be careful to keep that in mind as I write this book. The last thing you need to be is another me. One is certainly enough! But there are some things I will mention that might be of value to you; I hope so.

Before we go any further, let's go back to what I called "essential"...your being YOU. I want to pass along three simple yet extremely significant insights that I've mentioned to individuals and groups over the years. These three, if remembered and cultivated, will not only enable you to keep being YOU, they will make a world of difference in your verbal communication skills when you stand and speak to others.

- Know who you are.
- Accept who you are.
- Be who you are.

Not only is each one essential, the order is important. At first glance they may seem so elementary you want to yawn. But wait. Look again. In order for you to stand and deliver with any measure of confidence and ease, discovering and applying each one is invaluable.

Know who you are. Truth be told, most folks I meet have never made a study of themselves. Therefore, they do not know themselves—not deeply. For whatever reason, the lack of in-depth self-awareness is widespread. Most do not know their giftedness and skills, their unique temperament and personality, their strengths and weaknesses, or how they come across when they are with others. I'm underscoring this because knowing ourselves is basic to delivering a clear message to others. The better we know who we are, the greater will be our effectiveness and ease of delivery ... and the less we'll attempt to be someone we're not. That, by the way, is a major plague among preachers.

Accept who you are. As we discover who we are, the next all-important decision is to accept the truth of that discovery. The by-product is wonderfully relieving—you become free. Remember, it's the truth that sets us free. Rather than acting otherwise, the one who accepts himself or herself, lives in the wonderful world of reality, not make-believe fantasyland. This doesn't mean, however, that we like everything about ourselves; it only means we understand our makeup. We are aware of our identity, we are willing to live with it, and we won't attempt to act otherwise. Good communicators don't fake it. This leads us to the third and crowning realization.

Be who you are. I know of nothing more valuable, when it comes to the all-important virtue of authenticity, than simply being who you are. When you become comfortable inside your own skin, you'll experience a natural flow from your lips. Furthermore, you will have far less difficulty arriving at two invaluable accomplishments: "finding your voice" and "becoming the message." Unfortunately, this "being who you are" doesn't come as naturally as you might think, it's not something you can sit down and decide—although it begins with a decision—and you don't suddenly arrive. It's a process of growing in which you willingly allow God to make you increasingly more YOU, in life first, and then on your two feet before an audience.

I'll write much more about that in the course of this book because it is so crucial to "saying it well." Unfortunately, in trying to explain how one "finds his or her voice" and "becomes the message" quickly becomes either too esoteric to be practical or too pedantic to be interesting. So, I decided to use my own journey as an example of how the Lord accomplished that in my own life. I rarely prefer to talk about myself, but it's easier to show the transformation in my own life than to tell about it in the lives of others.

That is, after all, the method used by the Bible. Think about various people featured in the pages of God's Word. Most were effective in their communication because they acknowledged the truth about themselves, came to terms with that truth, allowed the Lord to do His work in and through them, and then—finally— spoke with a voice of authenticity. To name only a few, consider these fourteen individuals:

- Moses, by age eighty, couldn't speak with ease and he admitted it.
- Amos was a rough, unsophisticated prophet and he didn't hide it.
- Jeremiah was so brokenhearted his tears frequently flowed.
- The Baptizer refused to waste his time trying to be the Messiah.
- David never forgot the humble roots of his early years.
- Paul saw himself as "chief of sinners" and "a wretched man."
- Joseph forgave his brothers, but never denied their wrongdoing.
- Esther knew that what she said to the king was a huge risk.
- Luke was a physician and his scholarly vocabulary shows it.
- Once the Virgin Mary understood her role, she accepted it with humility.
- When Elijah fell into a depression, he acknowledged it.

- Nehemiah refused to let Sanballat intimidate him.
- Job openly expressed his grief and confessed his confusion.
- John wrote of his own fear in witnessing the future judgments.

Even Jesus, though not hindered by sin or personal issues, had to grow into His identity as the Messiah. He grew from infancy into a full knowledge of His deity, and then at age thirty-three identified Himself as "the way, the truth, and the life."

Each one of these individuals delivered messages that were meaningful and influential. Though they lived centuries ago, what they said (and in some cases, wrote) continues to reach deep into hearts and touch lives. It's still going on. When we analyze each one, we realize how different those people were, but each person's inimitable "style" penetrated the minds of those who heard them. In some cases, life was never the same as a result of what they communicated. A major reason for their effectiveness was their self-awareness, their willingness to accept reality, and their determination to be who they were.

I wanted to cover these bases early on, lest anyone who picks up this book thinks that by reading what I've written you can escape the reality of who you are. On the contrary! It is who you are that will play a major role in your proclaiming your message with passion and effectiveness. Because God gave you your makeup and superintended every moment of your past, including all the hardship, pain, and struggles, He wants to use your words in a unique manner. No one else can speak through your vocal cords, and, equally important, no one else has your story. When all of that is blended into a message He wants proclaimed, it is nothing short of remarkable. Perhaps you're not ready to believe that right now—as I wasn't able to see past my own stuttering—and so I would ask that you simply "take it by faith" for now. It will take a while for you to get everything into focus. It took me decades.

For the sake of clarification, let me assure you that what follows is not a slick set of techniques that will turn you overnight into an outstanding communicator. While I will do my best to explain the things I've learned which have become invaluable to me, please don't think that when you put them into action, you'll have the persuasive ability of Winston Churchill or the colorful eloquence of Charles Haddon Spurgeon or the commanding presence and voice of the late President Ronald Reagan. That's not only impossible, it's nonsense. Instead, view them as tips from a fellow traveler, one who has already made most of the wrong turns and stumbled over the hazards that lie before you. No amount of technique will ever replace authenticity, but when you speak from a place of authenticity, the techniques will enhance your message.

I hope through this book to encourage you to know and then accept and then become the real YOU, warts and all. As you get more comfortable with that, you will have less interest in trying to be (or sound like) somebody else. Since God made you YOU, He expects the message that you communicate to flow out of YOU and no one else. The only thing you and I have in common with every other individual is humanity. Whatever we speak flows through similar human vocal cords that every other human being possesses. Other than that anatomical fact, we're absolutely distinct individuals.

It is that which makes our message compelling and our delivery unique—our own individuality. Let's never forget that. From this point on, it's important that you release yourself from the straitjacket of others' expectations. Furthermore, you must determine to overcome your fear of not sounding like some other person you admire. You can certainly learn from them...but don't waste your time trying to be them—or acting a little like them. That's phony. Until you free yourself from that trap, you'll not find your own voice. I repeat: you are YOU and none other. From here on out, seek to glean whatever you can use from this book, never forgetting that each insight or principle or suggestion must be fitted into YOUR style and YOUR way of expressing yourself when YOU speak or preach.

How I wish someone in my formal education had told me these things! Because no one did, I spent far too much time trying to look like or sound like someone I wasn't. Thankfully, all that is behind me—and I hope the same will someday be true of you.

It is appropriate for me to pause long enough to express my gratitude for several individuals who have encouraged me in the writing of this book. My faithful publishing friends, Rolf Zettersten and Joey Paul of FaithWords, not only believed in this project, they urged me to write it after they published my previous work, *The Church Awakening*. Their excitement has motivated me to stay at it and to keep "saying it well." My longtime personal friend, Sealy Yates, has remained an excellent sounding board for me as we have talked at length about the value of and need for this book. His excellent assistance as my literary agent has been invaluable. And, of course, my editor, Mark Gaither, has provided outstanding ideas and suggestions along the way. Being my son-in-law along with being so creative and talented with his pen has led to hours of meaningful interaction together. How often we spanned the extremes in our numerous dialogues—from quiet and deeply serious discussions to outbursts of hilarious fun and loud laughter. Without Mark, I simply could not have written my words so clearly or expressed them so well.

That's enough to get us started. In the pages that follow, I want to take you through a process that's like a flow chart of my own life as a public speaker and preacher. To help me focus on one important segment after another, I've given a one-word title to each section.

Because everything began with what I often refer to as my "calling," that's the best place to start.

Touching Others
With Your Words

CHAPTER ONE

Calling

[God's call] had everything to do with living one's life in obedience...through action. It did not merely require a mind, but a body too. It was God's call to be fully human, to live as human beings obedient to the one who had made us, which was the fulfillment of our destiny. It was not a cramped, compromised, circumspect life, but a life lived in a kind of wild, joyful, full-throated freedom—that was what it was to obey God.

—*Dietrich Bonhoeffer*[1]

Do you think you could be happy and fulfilled doing anything else, in any vocation other than ministry?"

The question set me back in my chair for a moment. Dr. Donald K. Campbell, the registrar (and future president) of Dallas Theological Seminary, looked intently across his desk, perhaps gauging my reaction. His question found its way to my heart and probed its true intentions. Fresh out of the Marine Corps, wearing a flattop haircut and the only dark suit I owned, I sat at rigid attention as my mind retraced the steps that led me to Dallas, Texas, that morning in May 1959.

Two years earlier, I had very different plans for my life. After graduating from Milby High School in Houston, I took a job as an apprentice in the machine shop of the Reed Roller Bit Company. My ultimate goal was to become a mechanical engineer. By the time I finished that program, which included attending night school at the University of Houston, Cynthia and I had met, fallen in love, married, purchased a little frame house in the Houston suburb of Channelview. We also began serving in a local church in that small community—she played the piano while I led the singing. My childhood roots ran deep in Houston soil and we felt sure the same would be true of our children someday. Only one small matter stood between me and the ideal future I had imagined for myself: The Reserve Forces Act of 1955. This required at least two years of active military service followed by four years in active reserve duty. Rather than face the uncertainty of the draft, I spoke to a Marine Corps recruiter. After he assured me that I would be given a state-side assignment—no overseas deployment—I signed the enlistment contract and breathed a sigh of relief. We might have to live some-where other than Houston for a while, but Cynthia and I would be back soon enough, and, most importantly, *we would be together.*

After completing recruit training in San Diego and advanced infantry training at Camp Pendleton, I received orders to report to 100 Harrison Street in San Francisco—Pacific Headquarters—an assignment marines hoped for. Cynthia and I were elated. We bought a new car and set out for our temporary home on the California pen-insula. We found a tiny studio apartment in Daly City. Cynthia found a good job, I filled an enviable post near the waterfront, and we enjoyed a kind of extended honeymoon in that beautiful and roman-tic city. Then…a slip of paper bearing the president's seal changed everything.

I had seen this kind of envelope before and it almost never con-tained good news, so I stuffed it into my pocket resolving to open it later, when my courage returned. That afternoon, I sat in our car outside the electronics firm where Cynthia worked, fingering the unopened envelope and staring across the Bay at Alcatraz, that miserable island abode of the nation's most dangerous prisoners. Finally, I sliced open the speed letter. I was shocked to read the official order for me to transfer to the tiny Japanese island of Okinawa—nearly seven thousand miles from my new bride. In that state of mind, Alcatraz seemed more attractive to me. Our idyllic world came tumbling down.

Cynthia and I wept late into the night until exhaustion carried us to bed. I will admit that the circumstances felt like a stroke of divine cruelty. God knew my plans and that my desires were honorable. I wanted to cherish my wife, work hard in a fine company with good pay, rear godly children, and glorify God with the days given me on earth. I couldn't understand why He would allow circumstances to destroy something so good and so right. Eventually, my bewilderment turned into disillusionment, which gave way to bitterness.

> I couldn't understand why He would allow circumstances to destroy something so good and so right.

I left Cynthia in Houston to live with her mother and dad and reported to the staging regiment at Camp Pendleton for a month before shipping out from San Diego. My older brother, Orville, was living in Pasadena at the time preparing for a future in cross-cultural missions, which eventually took him to Argentina for more than thirty years. I had a few days of liberty before embarking, so I visited him. My disillusionment was all too obvious. Just before I boarded the bus to return to Pendleton, he pressed a book into my hands, saying, "Here's a book I want you to read on your way overseas."

I looked at the title: *Through Gates of Splendor*. I had not read the book, but I knew what it was about. Everyone did. Just a couple of years earlier, every newspaper in the United States—and many others around the world—carried the story of five missionaries who were brutally killed by a remote tribe of Indians—then known as the Auca—deep in the jungles of Ecuador. The book I held in my hands was written by Elisabeth Elliot, one of the five widows.

I handed the book back to my brother and said, "I'm not interested in reading this."

He pushed it back. "I want you to read this book."

"I'm not interested in reading this book. I'm not going overseas to be a missionary."

"*Take* the *book!*" he said firmly. "Read it!"

We exchanged some unpleasant words, but I boarded the bus with the book in hand and two hours of free time. As heavy clouds hung low and rain splashed against the window of that lonely bus, I opened the book and started reading:

Chapter 1: "I Dare Not Stay Home"

I was riveted by the story. Before I knew it, the bus arrived at the base... but I couldn't stop reading. I found the only place where the lights stayed on all night, in the hallway leading to the head (the men's room). Sitting on the floor, I finished the book by dawn. By the last line, the stubborn, selfish bitterness that had seized my heart started to release its grip. I had entered the world of five young men who entered college and then language school to prepare for a lifetime of missionary service. I learned that, not long after graduation, all five lay dead in the Curaray River, some with spears in their bodies. That impressed me. Still, while these men came to a tragic end, they were not the first missionaries to give their lives in the course of following their calling. My heart softened because Elisabeth Elliot, in cooperation with the other four widows, told the story with complete confidence in the providence of God. Her words dripped with grace toward the savages who had killed her mate. Life had handed this young woman every reason to become disillusioned, every right to grow bitter; instead, she strengthened her resolve to follow her original calling. Rather than dismiss her circumstances as senseless, or perhaps an indication the mission had been folly, Elisabeth Elliot continued working in Ecuador. In fact, after publication of the book, Elisabeth, her three-year-old daughter, Valerie, and Rachel Saint

> Life had handed this young woman every reason to become disillusioned.

successfully entered that village, won the trust of their husbands' murderers, and completed the work their martyred mates had begun.

Why? How could they do that? Circumstances didn't change their calling.

Not only did that book break the hold of bitterness on my heart, it opened my mind to the possibility that my boarding a troop ship for the far side of the earth—seven thousand miles from the life I had envisioned for myself—might be something more than the whim of circumstance. I thought, *Maybe...* No earth-moving revelations. No sudden epiphany. No dramatic moment of clarity. I simply entertained the remote possibility that I should be doing something that counted for eternity. But that was all.

A couple of days later, along with thirty-five hundred other marines, I boarded a transport to Okinawa. Four days out, a storm churned the Pacific into a tempest that tossed our ship like a toothpick. The driving rain and fifty-foot swells mirrored the chaos that had become my spirit. With two more weeks to go before reaching the other side of the world, I read the book again. Only this time, I didn't see just Elisabeth's account of the events leading to January 8, 1955, on the Curaray River; I saw God's hand at work in the lives of each of those five men. Each in a different way, He brought them all together and led them to the right place at the right time to accomplish something profound. In retrospect, their deaths inspired *thousands* of men and women to devote their lives to teaching and preaching the Bible, serving Christ all over the world. While it didn't answer my questions or even dispel my confusion, I began to accept as fact that God had a purpose in my transfer to Okinawa. His calling on my life was now in its infant stage.

By the time I reached Yokohama and finally my Marine Corps base on that tiny South Pacific island, I felt a sense of destiny. I had no clue how valuable that time would be, but I had some sense that my unexpected "calamity" was not an accident. Disappointment with God yielded to acceptance of His wisdom beyond my understanding. Bitterness slowly gave way to submission.

Soon after arriving, I found myself in a dangerous environment not unfamiliar to military bases. Camp Courtney was a volatile mixture of red-blooded young men, boredom, and unaccountability. I knew right away, I needed the support of other Christian men. Fortunately, I heard about a ministry called "GIs for Christ" meeting somewhere between my base and the capital city of Naha. That first Friday night, I sat among a group of uniformed men as GIs put on a little skit, led the singing, and offered a short message. As the meeting closed, I moved toward the door to leave and noticed a man sitting near the back wearing a dark overcoat. His five o'clock shadow and gruff appearance convinced me he was a man off the street, perhaps curious about the meeting. So, I engaged him in conversation and before long, spoke openly of Christ as I explained the gospel to him. Having finished my presentation of the fundamentals of the faith, he responded, "That was very well done."

The man turned out to be Bob Newkirk, a missionary serving with The Navigators. He said, "Any guy who's got the guts to walk up to a stranger and do what you did, I want to know more about him." That began a friendship that turned out to be life changing.

I got to know Bob and his family as he poured his life into mine.

I completed The Navigators Scripture memory program, continued as part of the "GIs for Christ" program, and eventually led the group. Throughout that time, Bob became a mentor. He and his wife, Norma, allowed me to spend my days on liberty and numerous holidays with them. Bob let me tag along when he ran ministry errands and fulfilled his duties on Okinawa. As I look back, I clearly see that my time with him not only kept me out of trouble and strengthened my spiritual life, it gave me greater opportunity to give further thought to my calling. Of course, I couldn't see that at the time; nevertheless, if awareness of my calling were a seed, it began to germinate during those early months.

Part of Bob's ministry included street meetings—sometimes on the back of a flatbed truck—which included leading the crowd in some singing and delivering a short gospel message. Before long, Bob had me taking a lead role in those street meetings. I struggled at first, but my confidence grew over time. When you begin to learn the Word of God, and really begin to believe its promises, and make them personal, it gives you courage and galvanizes you against other people's rejection—not only when speaking publicly, but in your personal relationships.

When I first arrived on Okinawa, the company sergeant learned of my Christian faith and dubbed me "Friar Chuck." That troubled me at first. I wasn't ashamed of my worldview; I just resented being singled out and mocked. As the Scriptures became more a part of my life, I paid less attention to the ribbing. I liked being known as "the Christian guy," a designation that gave me the opportunity to lead a few of my fellow marines to Christ.

As my confidence grew, I discussed my growing interest in

spiritual things with Bob. He affirmed me along the way. Late one evening, after one particular street meeting, I said to Bob, "I think God may be calling me to ministry."

Bob smiled and said, "As I have observed you, that makes a lot of sense, frankly." He never pushed. In fact, he deliberately steered clear of interfering with God's activity in my life. People in positions of great influence need to be careful; their impact can sometimes cause confusion rather than clarity when someone in their care is in the process of discovering his or her calling.

We discussed my growth as a leader over the previous several months. I had completed every part of The Navigator program and I was leading other men. I had led several men in my Quonset hut to Christ. I was comfortable leading the "GIs for Christ" gatherings and speaking at public meetings. Bob affirmed me and agreed to pray with me over the matter. Before long, the feeling of vague possibility solidified into a firm conviction. I wrote Cynthia and she immediately affirmed my calling, enthusiastically pledging to follow me anywhere the Lord might lead us.

As I reflect on that time when my calling to ministry became clear, several truths about a "calling" emerge.

Support of Spouse

When you're married, the calling is *yours*—God didn't call Cynthia to ministry; He called me—yet the support of one's spouse is essential. If a husband or wife is reluctant or tentative, either the timing is wrong or the calling needs to be reexamined. You need to move forward as one, in complete unity. And that can sometimes be a difficult matter to resolve. If your spouse isn't completely on board, *wait.*

If your spouse isn't completely on-board, *wait.*

Resolve to take the pressure off your mate to see your call as clearly as you do. Resist the urge to manipulate, coerce, or convince him or her. Reject any feelings of resentment toward your spouse, choosing instead to regard your mate's reluctance as the Lord's signal to slow down and to examine the issue *together*. And, by all means, pray—individually and together—asking God to bring clarity to both of your minds.

As I have helped other men and women discover their calling, I have found the reluctance of a mate to be an invaluable source of wisdom. Sometimes it's simply a matter of timing; the call was genuine, but other issues needed to be resolved first. Other times, the marriage needed work before moving forward. There have been situations in which the calling needed refinement. In every case, when the couple resolved to wait until both could proceed in complete unity, they avoided disaster. I have observed over many years that when one dragged the other, the couple struggled for years.

In my case, Cynthia affirmed my thinking and excitedly asked, "What's next? Where do we go from here?"

The Affirmation of Peers

When a calling is authentic, you don't need the approval of others. In fact, some may resist your calling because they have a personal interest in your staying put. Yet it's not a good sign if impartial people who know you well express doubts. As the proverb says, "Without consultation, plans are frustrated, but with many counselors they succeed" (Prov. 15:22). The general consensus among wise, impartial people you trust should be "That makes good sense; I can see your doing that."

In my case, Bob saw in my past clear indications of future success.

Other Christian friends on Okinawa were not at all surprised when I spoke of my calling and explained my plans for the future.

The Appraisal of Challenges

Every calling involves sacrifice. There's no such thing as a decision without a downside. On occasion, what you have to give up is significant. In my case, I would be giving up my original plans to put down roots in Houston, near family and all that I had known and loved. I would be trading a stable, well-paying job as a mechanical engineer for the uncertainty of becoming a seminary student. The investment of my previous employment would yield no financial fruit. I was, in fact, starting over. Furthermore, I was entering a whole new world with no guarantees and zero financial stability.

When a calling is genuine, you count the cost but none of the sacrifices feel like a hindrance. On the contrary, the challenges become invigorating. I no longer had any interest in mechanical engineering. As I embraced my new calling, the unknowns both scared me and thrilled me; and the thought of returning to the stability of my old job—which I had once enjoyed and was familiar with—now felt like a prison sentence.

> When a calling is genuine, you count the cost but none of the sacrifices feel like a hindrance.

No Specifics

When I first spoke to Cynthia about my calling to ministry, I said, "You realize, of course, that I have no idea what this means exactly." A calling rarely includes a detailed picture of what you'll be doing, where you will go, or even how you will fulfill your purpose. That can feel troubling because many have the mistaken notion that a calling comes with a supernatural, clear vision of the future. It doesn't. All I could tell anyone at that point was that I would be devoting myself to a vocation in Christian ministry. Missionary to China? Traveling evangelist? Serving some role in a local church? Teaching? Writing? Chaplaincy? I honestly had no clue.

A clear sense of calling rarely comes with a detailed plan. In most cases, God supplies only one detail: the next step. I've noticed that's where a lot of people become paralyzed. They refuse to release what they have or walk away from where they are without first receiving a detailed vision of their destination. They want the entire journey handed to them in a mental map before committing to the first step. Consequently, some never fulfill their calling. Those who do embrace their calling as more than a pipe dream sometimes fail to take the first step because they do not trust their own instincts, or they do not receive encouragement from their loved ones, or they do not trust God to sustain them along their journey through the unknown. Initially, we do not know where the calling will take us, but the first step flashes like a bright neon sign.

For me, the first step was training. I didn't know for certain where I would receive instruction, but I knew I needed to be better equipped. I would return home to my job at the Reed Roller Bit Company to put food on the table, but I would waste no time submitting an application for admission to my first choice: Dallas Theological Seminary.

A Sense of Destiny

With a genuine calling comes a settled assurance. A conviction that's hard to describe takes root in the deep, quiet depth of your soul. While tempests churn your conscious mind into fifty-foot swells, down in the ocean depths of your being, beyond the reach of circumstances, you *know* what you should be doing and you *know* that you can find no satisfaction in any other pursuit. In fact, as you embrace your calling, you begin to recognize a profound sense of destiny. Not only were you created to fulfill a divine purpose, you acknowledge that the events of your life have prepared you for the next step in fulfilling your calling.

> Not only were you created to fulfill a divine purpose, you acknowledge that the events of your life have prepared you for the next step in fulfilling your calling.

There in the crucible of Okinawa, I awakened to the calling of God to proclaim the truths of Scripture. I finally realized that it was necessary for me to be there. God *had* to interrupt my life plan—as good and as godly as it was—to get my attention. God *had* to remove me from the distractions of what I thought was an idyllic life to show me something greater. God *had* to isolate me from all other voices and all outside influences so that, in the solitude of that remote South Pacific island, my reason for being would become obvious. Once I accepted that difficult truth, my past made more sense. I recognized that my path thus far could have led nowhere else and that it was leading me toward a God-ordained future.

For example, I first began to consider ministry because of the success I enjoyed as a leader. When I entered the ranks of the Marine Corps, I didn't know I had the qualities necessary for leadership until one day, while on the rifle range, my drill instructor shouted my name. As I stood at attention before him, he handed me a red armband, designating me the "right guide," that is, the company leader. He said, "Take this. You're a leader." I was stunned. He could have told me, "You're Chinese," and I would not have been less surprised.

I also entertained the idea of ministry because I had developed a measure of confidence in public speaking. I felt at ease in front of an audience. I could think and speak fairly well on my feet, and with preparation, I had the ability to express myself with even greater ease. But this ability was anything but natural.

While I was growing up I never thought of myself as a public speaker, and I certainly would never have imagined myself a preacher. I was raised around churches and had gotten to know a few preachers, but the thought never entered my head that I would one day stand and deliver. Not only was I not interested, I lived with a major struggle: I stuttered. Who knows why? All I can tell you is it grew steadily worse during my early teenage years. By the time I entered high school, speaking in front of a group was the last place I wanted to be.

All that changed the day I met Richard Nieme.

Mr. Nieme (pronounced "Nee-mee") was the drama and speech teacher at Milby High School. For some reason unknown to me he determined to get me into at least one of his courses. I've often wondered if my sister, Luci, tipped him off, since she used to endure my strutting around the house q-q-q-q-quoting lines f-f-f-from various p-p-p-poems I'd m-m-m-memorized. I've always loved great poetry. I found that memorizing the lines came easily, but delivering them was another story. But I didn't let that stop me from committing poetic lines to memory—I loved doing that! My problem was punching out those lines smoothly. I could see them in my head, but my tongue and lips didn't cooperate. Trying to impress my family as the poet laureate of the Swindoll clan while quoting several of Coleridge's moving lines from "The Rime of the Ancient Mariner" or a passionate section of Tennyson's "The Charge of the Light Brigade," I sounded more like Porky Pig on a bad day.

That explains why I looked down and backed away when Mr. Nieme first approached me in the hallway. I was convinced he was talking to the guy at the next locker. That kid had everything; he was muscular, handsome, and popular. He had a harem of girls hanging around him before every class. It made all the sense in the world for Mr. Nieme to recruit him, not me. But that clearly wasn't his plan. He didn't seem to realize that I was already well on my way to winning the "Least Likely to Succeed" award at that school. When he pressed me for an answer, all I could squeeze out was, "M-m-m-m-me? Are y-y-you t-t-talking to m-m-m-me?"

He flashed a big, toothy smile and responded, "Of course! You belong on our debate team and in my drama class!"

That made absolutely no sense to me and I told him so—or I tried to. But he wouldn't give up. He said strange stuff like, "You've got what it takes—you really do. I'm convinced that you will one day star in the leading role of one of our plays." By then I was stunned. Those words seemed incredible to me. I couldn't believe he used the word "convinced." The only thing I was convinced of was that he thought I was somebody else. But he didn't let up. I couldn't believe what he said next: "After you and I have spent some time together, you'll be as convinced as I am."

Now, that intrigued me. What could he possibly do or say that would enable me to punch out my words like other kids? Did he do magic? Could he really help me speak without stuttering and stammering?

> Could he really help me speak without stuttering and stammering?

Nieme was smart. He never pushed too hard...never shamed me or tried to force me. He would drop the bait in subtle ways each time he saw me, always reassuring me that (1) I had what it takes (whatever "it" was) and (2) he would show me how. His blend of enthusiasm, affirmation, and confidence finally broke through my resistance and doubt. I signed on. His beginning drama course became one of my electives. Little did I know the difference that decision would make, not only for the rest of my high school years, but for the rest of my life.

He didn't waste any time. He and I met regularly that summer, just the two of us, as he mentored me in the basic rudiments of speech therapy. He took his time helping me picture in my mind all those words that I had previously rushed into. He gave me exercises that encouraged me to "pace" my words, each time very deliberately. We would go over all the exercises again and again as he patiently instructed me... always encouraging me. He helped me see that my mind was running ahead of my mouth (I now have the opposite problem!). I needed to slow the process and think about what I was saying in order to coordinate the flow of words. He emphasized the value of enunciation. He underscored the importance of projection. Slowly, I began to get the hang of it. In fact, before school started that next fall, I was making real progress conquering a habit that had embarrassed me for years.

No one was more excited than Mr. Nieme! He couldn't wait to cast me in a minor role in the first of four plays we did that year. I found his enthusiasm contagious, so I threw myself into the part with gusto. I not only said each one of my lines, I stuttered only a time or two. He was elated. In fact, he made sure I had a part in each of the other three plays that year. Believe it or not, by my senior year, we did a three-act play, *George Washington Slept Here,* and I played the leading role. As the final curtain closed on the last act, guess who was first on his feet yelling and whistling and screaming for a curtain call?

Sadly, Richard Nieme died several years ago. I grieved his passing. Though I wasn't able to attend his memorial service, I was asked to write the eulogy, which I was honored to do. Tears ran as I sat all alone, remembering the man who accepted me and loved me and believed in

Tears ran as I sat all alone, remembering the man who accepted me and loved me and believed in me long before I could ever believe in myself.

me long before I could ever believe in myself. He passed along some of the most helpful principles I've learned. Thanks to him, I discovered how to communicate with ease and authenticity before an audience. I still use some of those principles he taught me each time I speak or preach publicly. Admittedly, there are times I still find myself almost stuttering on certain words, but thanks to those summer days he patiently worked with me, I rarely stumble badly. My gratitude for the investment Richard Nieme made in my young life knows no bounds. And, were it not for his dedication to a stammering nobody in the halls of Milby High School, my days on Okinawa would have passed without consequence. I never would have taken a lead role in Bob Newkirk's ministry and would not have been prepared to recognize my calling, much less respond to it.

This growing sense of destiny not only brought the realization that God had been systematically removing barriers to fulfilling my purpose—the terrible speech impediment being the most significant—I also saw His hand at work very early in my life. I recall one particular moment when I was eleven years old. As I raced through the kitchen toward the back door, eager to join my friends in a game of sandlot football, my mother stopped me. "Come here, Charles, I want to show you a Bible verse I am claiming for you."

At that moment in time, I had one objective in life: to get to the sandlot before they chose up sides. That was very important to me because I wanted to be on Bruce's team. Either Bruce had flunked a couple of grades or he was the biggest kid in the history of the sixth grade. So, the formula for winning was simple. If you had Bruce on your team, you won. I liked winning, so I had no interest in Mom's Bible verse. But she insisted, "Come here!"

She showed me a proverb:

A man's gift makes room for him,
And brings him before great men. (Prov. 18:16)

She said again, "Charles, I'm claiming that for you."

"Gee, Mom, that's great. Can I go now?"

Fast-forward to the early 1980s. A group known as Christian Embassy invited me to speak at their annual event, which was held at The Homestead, a historic retreat center in central Virginia, not far from the Capitol. I arrived the day before to settle in, finish preparing my talk, and attend their evening reception. That's when I discovered the audience would include two members of the president's cabinet, numerous high-ranking officers serving at the Pentagon, more than one ambassador, and administrators representing several levels of government. It was one impressive group of people!

The next morning, I went for an early run on the grounds of that historic inn, which had been welcoming guests since 1766. On the advice of another guest, I followed a particular path through those Allegheny old-growth woods until I reached an enormous oak said to have been familiar to Ben Franklin. I doubt five men could have joined hands around the base of that tree and it towered above all its neighbors. As I paused before that historic tree, I was overcome with a sense of history and the gravity of what I was about to do became unmistakably clear. As I ran my hand over the bark of that tree, touching that living witness to history, my mother's words suddenly returned and washed over my mind, bathing my memories in the warm assurance of my call. That night, I would indeed stand before great men. Though not a prophetess, her prophecy would be fulfilled. She had spoken as a mother expressing great hope for her son... but that day I realized the Lord had woven her words into His purpose for my life.

I knew I had nothing to fear standing before those men and women holding positions of immense power. God made me for this. He had prepared me. He guided my footsteps from my mother's kitchen, to the Marine Corps, to Okinawa, to Bob Newkirk, and from there to Dallas Theological Seminary.

And so…as I sat with my wife before Dr. Campbell that May morning in 1959, his question resonated in the hollows of my heart.

I knew where I had been and I had a strong sense of where I was going.

"Could I be happy and fulfilled doing anything else, in any vocation other than ministry?" I knew where I had been and I had a strong sense of where I was going. If there were any doubts before I walked into his office, his question convinced me that I would be a frustrated shell of a man pursuing any other endeavor. I raised my eyes to meet his and I replied, "No, sir, I could not be happy or fulfilled doing anything else."

Calling and Speaking

So, what does this have to do with public speaking? Why did I devote an entire chapter to exploring the topic of "calling"? The answer is simple. One's calling—knowing who you are and for what purpose you have been selected and equipped—is foundational to success in all areas of life, not the least of which is public speaking. A clear sense of calling transforms good public speakers into great communicators. There are two powerful reasons for this.

Great communicators speak with passion.

One writer noted that the most effective sermons are preached on tip-toe. In an article written nearly a century ago, he compared two evangelists who had been invited to address soldiers at a military base.

One preached a wonderful sermon full of spiritual truth and intellectual food for thought. It would have been welcomed in the pulpit of any great evangelical church in America. But there were no results among the soldier boys. It lacked heart and warmth. The preacher kept his facts with his feet on solid ground and I enjoyed it, but the soldiers were bored and left him by scores until he did not have half an audience.

The sermon of the other preacher was not half as good in material or in intellectual or spiritual insight. In fact, the next morning one of the army chaplains told me that he would not like to see in print such a common sort of talk and call it a sermon. It was rather weak in logic and in spiritual discernment. But it got the boys and led literally hundreds of them to confess Christ. Why? He preached with the deepest heart earnestness and longing for the lives of the men before him. He was possessed with a passion which put his soul on tip-toe in his anxiety to lead men to God. And they felt it and they responded to that appeal.[2]

Any reasonably intelligent person can gather relevant facts; that's simply a matter of knowing how to search the Internet or utilize a library. Most any person with average critical thinking skills can arrange those facts into a logical sequence to prove a point or present new information. In fact, I can say with confidence that given sufficient time, I can prepare a talk on just about any subject. Dentistry, stamp collecting, astronomy, flying an airplane—it really doesn't matter. It is doubtful, however, that many will stay around long enough to hear what I have to say. Not because the subject is boring or because I didn't spend enough time preparing, but for the simple fact that I don't find any of those topics all that interesting. And if *I* don't find them riveting, my audience won't either. Great speeches and life-changing sermons begin with good material, but it's the speaker's passion that seizes an audience and compels their attention.

Great communicators know their calling. They joyfully sacrifice anything that distracts them from fulfilling their purpose. They relentlessly devote themselves to the pursuit of more knowledge and greater expertise. They delight to know the latest developments, the most current methods, and the secrets of emerging leaders in their field.

Great communicators
know their calling.

They have strong opinions about their realm of expertise—what has worked in the past, what needs to happen next, and what must change in the future. Consequently, all of that dedication and the full measure of the communicator's passion set him "on tip-toe" when speaking. When you give someone who knows her calling a stage and a microphone, her enthusiasm invariably holds her audience in rapt attention long enough to transform their thinking until she's ready to let them go.

Those who do not know their purpose in life and who have not given passionate pursuit to their calling may become competent in the craft of public speaking, but they will never achieve anywhere near their full potential, to say nothing of greatness. They can try to manufacture enthusiasm, but bigger gestures and more shouting won't fool audiences for long.

Great communicators stay in the zone.

A great speech

- Serves the audience.
- Honors the occasion.
- Utilizes the venue.
- Acknowledges the times.

We'll develop these points later on, but for now, I want to focus on the effect of knowing one's calling. Accomplished public speakers eventually develop the skills to achieve all four goals, regardless of the circumstances, even when called upon to speak extemporaneously. However, great communicators carefully screen their invitations, accepting only those that offer the greatest opportunity for success in all four endeavors. When you know your calling, you know your audience intimately and you gain a keen sense of what they need. Furthermore, knowing your purpose in life will sharpen your instincts to a razor-fine edge. You will know which occasions are ripe for your perspective, you will learn how to make the best use of a venue, and your timing will become borderline impeccable.

Great communicators know their calling and they learn to stay in "the zone." Those who haven't come to terms with their calling can become competent speakers but, without a clear life focus, their speeches lack that certain "something" and they just can't figure out what's missing.

What about you?

People most naturally associate the idea of "calling" with ministry. And rightly so. God does select a handful of men and women from each generation to lay aside other pursuits in order to serve Him full-time in vocational ministry. Our culture also uses the term "calling" in conjunction with vocations our society has deemed lofty or noble. For example, one might say he is called to the field of medicine. Another may follow her calling in the fields of law or social work. That's because the concept of a

> The concept of a "calling" envisions the sovereign work of God.

"calling" envisions the sovereign work of God in the selection and preparation of an individual to fulfill a particular role or accomplish a specific task. He or she is divinely selected and then systematically prepared to fulfill his or her purpose in life.

I don't want to diminish the high and holy calling of service to God in ministry, and I don't intend to cheapen other noble professions. Nevertheless, I do believe each person has a calling upon his or her life to fulfill a special purpose. This calling may or may not affect one's vocation; not all callings demand a career change. In fact, many people make their living at one vocation in order to finance their calling. Artists, musicians, and other gifted individuals commonly do this. Even Paul the Apostle used his trade in tent making to finance his evangelistic efforts (Acts 18:3; 1 Thess. 2:9; 2 Thess. 3:8).

I draw my conviction from my understanding of the Bible, a perspective that can be summarized nicely with two proverbs:

> *The mind of man plans his way,*
> *But the Lord directs his steps. (Prov. 16:9)*

> *Man's steps are ordained by the Lord,*
> *How then can man understand his way? (Prov. 20:24)*

Both proverbs affirm that each person has a divinely ordained purpose. When the Creator fashioned the universe out of nothing, He had *you* in mind—among a great many other things, of course. Nevertheless, you factored into His idea of how the world should work. He gave you specific gifts and He ordered certain events to help nurture those abilities. In my case, He gave me a teacher named Richard Nieme, who cleared away a speech impediment in order to release my gift of public speaking. He provided a mentor named Bob Newkirk, who gave me many opportunities to speak and to lead. I suspect that if you review your own history, you'll discover the imprint of God's design on your life as well.

Even so, these two proverbs dispel any notion of fatalism. While God has given each individual a unique purpose to fulfill, a personalized path to follow, He also grants us the freedom to choose whether or not to walk in His way. In other words, the Lord has prepared a plan for your life, but you are not compelled to follow His design. He has gifted you and has nurtured you, but you don't have to follow His plan. You can shape your life as you please; you have a range of freedom in which you can ignore your design and make your own way. If God designed you to be a screwdriver, you can try to hammer nails if you want. But I don't recommend it. The price you pay in terms of frustration and mediocrity is too high.

> If God designed you to be a screwdriver, you can try to hammer nails if you want. But I don't recommend it.

For now, set aside any thoughts of public speaking. Don't worry; I'll come back to it soon enough. But for the time being, focus instead on discovering your calling, your purpose in life. Don't move on to the next chapters until you have come to terms with this foundational issue. Otherwise, they will hold little value for you. Indeed, excellence in public speaking will elude you like quicksilver.

CHAPTER TWO

Preparing

The world is waiting to hear an authentic voice, a voice from God—not an echo of what others are doing and saying, but an authentic voice.

—A. W. Tozer[3]

"Saying it well" has everything to do with preparing well. Poor preparation—weak message. There is no exception.

I didn't go to seminary to learn how to preach; I committed myself to training so I'd have something to say. Once I discovered my calling, I found direction, but I had a long, long way to go before I was ready to stand before an audience and deliver the goods. At the time, I could not have known how long that journey would last, but I knew my first priority was preparation.

This might seem obvious, but I think before you speak to others, you should have something to say. And, for sure, you should know what you're talking about.

You laugh? How many times have you heard someone stand before a crowd and then say nothing eloquently? How many well-executed speeches or sermons have you heard that offered no fresh information, no creative insights, no stimulating motivation, no passionate call-to-action? I can't speak for you, but I've heard more than I care to remember...usually from a pulpit. I call them "longhorn sermons"—a point here, a point there, and a lot o' bull in between.

I didn't want that to be true of me. I loathed the thought of clothing the riches of truth in rags. I had been called to proclaim the truths of Scripture and to urge women and men to apply its principles. But before I could do that, I needed knowledge and skills. I needed to know what the Bible was all about. Admittedly, I lacked the skills necessary to dig practical, relevant answers out of the Scriptures when faced with the ever-changing needs of those who listened. Following my growth in biblical knowledge and the cultivation of my theological understanding, I then made the mechanics of public speaking my focus.

While on Okinawa, I took on more responsibility in the leadership of "GIs for Christ" and accepted greater participation in street meetings with Bob Newkirk, all the while growing more comfortable before others. That, as I explained, led to a realization that I had been called to full-time, vocational ministry. In what capacity, I didn't know. To what part of the world, I hadn't a clue. But the next step could not have been clearer. In fact, when Cynthia responded to my letter telling her of my call, her next sentence was, "What about training? Where will you go to prepare?"

Any worthwhile calling demands preparation. Instruction. Guidance. Knowledge. Skills. Training. Natural talent may be sufficient to do an adequate job, but it's not enough to get anywhere near excellence. Those who rush into their calling without adequate preparation invariably make mistakes. Most of those mistakes could have been avoided with the advice of someone more experienced. Moreover, they learn the hard way what a mentor could have taught in a brief period of time. How often I have seen God-given talent run amuck by human pride.

> Any worthwhile calling demands preparation.

Cynthia and I agreed that any work done for God was worth the investment of preparation. It was just a matter of choosing the right place, sitting at the feet of the right people.

Just a couple of years earlier, any distance to prepare for a lifetime of ministry would have been a daunting prospect, but my perspective of geography changed while on Okinawa. I was willing to go anywhere. So, when deciding on a seminary, I thought about my most significant influences. I recalled a pastor in Houston who whetted my appetite for theology and the deeper truths of Scripture. He was a Dallas Theological Seminary graduate. I reflected on my brief encounter with Ray Stedman while stationed in San Francisco, also a product of DTS. I scanned my bookshelf and saw a distinct pattern in my reading habits: *Salvation* and *True Evangelism* by Lewis Sperry Chafer, *Things to Come* by J. Dwight Pentecost, even some works by W. H. Griffith Thomas. I also respected a few notable names, including J. Vernon McGee and Jim Rayburn, the founder of Young Life. Each author had prepared at that same school.

It didn't take me long to set my sights on Dallas Theological Seminary. If forced to consider another school, I would find training somewhere...but DTS quickly became my first choice. Unfortunately, the seminary offered master's-level degrees and, therefore, might not accept my limited academic background and practical years of apprenticeship in lieu of a traditional bachelor's degree. To make matters worse, they had far more applicants than available seats. Still, I had to try.

On Probation

In April 1959, after another seventeen-day transport across the Pacific—this time much smoother, in more ways than one—I mustered out of the Marine Corps on Treasure Island, not far from where I began active duty. I boarded a flight for Houston, where Cynthia and I stole away for a second honeymoon. Within a couple of weeks after returning home, I began the application process. Much sooner than I expected, an invitation came from the registrar to visit the campus and allow him to interview the two of us in person. So, one spring morning, Cynthia and I made the four-hour-plus drive to Dallas...I freely confess I was more nervous than a witch in church.

While we waited to see the registrar, Cynthia and I held hands and prayed, which helped calm my nerves. That is, until my name was called. I stood at attention before the desk of a very severe-looking woman who stared at me over the top of her glasses. She glanced at my file and then back at me with an expression that said, "Good luck, buddy. You haven't the slightest chance with this background." I thought she was the registrar until Dr. Donald K. Campbell emerged from his office to greet me. As it turns out, she was merely the gate-keeper. I had yet to face the decision maker.

> "Good luck, buddy. You haven't the slightest chance with this background."

Initially, Dr. Campbell seemed stern, to me, but he quickly warmed up. He asked us to tell our story, so I gave a brief history of our marriage and my call, and explained how I arrived in Dallas from Houston by way of Okinawa.

After asking several penetrating questions about my call to ministry, He expressed his reservations in unguarded terms. "This is master's-level work and you don't have an academic record to demonstrate you can handle it. I want you to complete a couple of exams before we go any further." He handed me a packet and said, "Complete these at home and return them by mail. We'll proceed from there."

"Thank you, sir," I said. "I'll do my best."

"If we accept you as a student, you'll be on probation for a year. Do you understand?"

I nodded. "Yes, sir. I accept those conditions, and I'm grateful you'll even consider that."

"And you'll need to give this your all. One hundred percent."

I assured him, "I promise to give it my best."

"Because," he pressed further, "two other candidates who want your slot will be receiving a disappointing letter."

I suppose that should have made me more nervous, but for reasons I can't explain, the overwhelming odds against my admission gave me great peace. If accepted, it would be a clear affirmation of God's desire that I attend Dallas Seminary and nowhere else. If I were denied admission, He obviously had other plans. Regardless, the challenge cemented my resolve, and, somewhere beneath the doubts and fears I felt a settled confidence that my next four years of preparation would be spent at that institution. I completed the exams, returned them as promised, and then received a letter inviting me to begin my studies in August. The letter reiterated that I would be enrolled as a "special student" on probationary status. I was expected to meet with Dr. Campbell two or three times each semester to review my progress. Fine with me...grace abounded...I was in!

In late July, Cynthia and I began preparing campus apartment No. 9 for move-in. I don't want to say the place was old and unkempt, but it came with hot-and-cold-running rats. We scrubbed the entire apartment as clean as a surgical suite—we even painted the walls "aqua." Then, while Cynthia cleaned the stove with hammer and chisel, I machine-stripped the hardwood floors and put down a first-class finish. After several fuses went up in smoke, the maintenance superintendent stepped inside and said, "What on earth are you doing? You aren't allowed to make changes to this property!" He looked at the floor, the machine, and then me. "Who do you think you are?"

He looked at the floor, the machine, and then me. "Who do you think you are?"

I shrugged and said with a guilty smile, "Well...the floors were terrible, so thought I'd...Hey, you want me to do the hall?" I smiled. He didn't.

"No! No, just finish up and don't make any more changes!"

We got along great after that. He couldn't argue with the improvements and I made sure to help out whenever I could. I later hired on as the DTS groundskeeper, and, by the end of the summer, I had the place blooming in brightly colored flowers.

Ours was one tiny apartment! At the most, 650 square feet. Two rooms, a little kitchen, and a bathroom so small someone sitting on the toilet would have to stand up to close the door. The units were packed tightly, the walls were thin, and with no air-conditioning, everyone kept their windows open during hot weather. So, you got to know your neighbors really well! Even so, we remember that little place fondly. Moving into apartment No. 9 began four of the greatest years of my life. At last my preparation was officially under way.

Not long after we got settled into our little place, classes began around the middle of August. It was at that point I encountered my first crisis: syllabus shock. I had not been to a university—at least with a traditional classroom setting that would prepare me for master's-level work. So, I felt intimidated by the young scholars around me and especially by the sheer volume of assigned reading. All put together, I had hundreds of pages to read each day and, soon, papers and projects to complete. At the end of that first week, I sorted through the assignments, put them in chronological order, and said to myself, "All right, Chuck, stick your butt in that chair, stay at that desk, and dig in. Other guys have been here and made the grade. Some were smarter, but none can work harder. If they could do it, so can you."

Disciplined for Study

My dad was a hard worker, which was an excellent influence. My mother had impressed upon all of us the value of learning. My older brother and sister were excellent students, which gave me a good model to follow, although not at first. Orville made straight A's, which I thought made for a very boring report card. Mine, on the other hand, had variety; my marks were much more interesting to look at. But now, I had to get serious. Fortunately, by the time I began to pursue my calling, I discovered all those positive influences helped prepare me for seminary. This included the hands-on training I received as an apprentice and, for sure, the discipline of my Marine Corps training.

My years in the military gave me a regimented, can-do mind-set that helped me power through lots of personal obstacles. So, by the time I began classes, I had all the tools I needed to succeed. It was just a matter of "want to." And I wanted nothing more than to squeeze out of that experience everything I could absorb. I sat in the front row of every class, I interacted with my professors, I kept a book with me wherever I went, and I made each assignment a priority. I made *preparation* my sole focus (outside of marriage, of course).

> I made *preparation* my sole focus.

Other guys made the mistake of thinking they were in ministry already, taking pastorates and devoting themselves to para-church ministries or evangelism or chaplaincies. Not so much for the sake of earning a living, which is often necessary, but because they couldn't wait to get started. Some felt they had a *duty* to serve in ministry positions while in seminary, sometimes without pay. I, on the other hand, followed the advice of a seasoned pastor who said, "Chuck, you aren't in ministry yet; you're *preparing* for ministry. Don't let anything distract you from the disciplines of preparation. When you complete your training, you'll have a lifetime of ministry ahead of you."

His advice proved invaluable. In fact, it resonated with what I heard several times during boot camp: "You're not a marine; you're a recruit!" And Dallas Seminary in those days was inflexibly regimented, so there were some similarities! I said to Cynthia on several occasions, I don't know if I could have done this if I hadn't been conditioned for discipline by the marines. Other guys made it through on their "smarts" alone—brilliant men with unbelievable capacity for memorization and learning with almost no effort. Not me. Mine was a day-in-day-out application of discipline and determination.

In the years since my time in seminary, I have found the words of Howard Hendricks to have been prophetic. He said, "As you are now, you will be then. The discipline you cultivate now, you will carry with you into ministry. The poor habits you develop here will dog your steps throughout your career." He was right. If you are a person who dashes off papers at the last minute and crams for exams, you'll be a pastor who whips up your message on Saturday and unloads a "longhorn sermon" on Sunday.

Margin

Preparation, of course, had to leave enough room for real life: illnesses, romance, family, trips to see our parents in Houston, holidays. I quickly learned the value of maintaining a balanced life. I had to develop the discipline of laying aside work as an investment in my well-being. No one can work 24-7, and, because I was married, I had someone else to think about. So, Friday night became our date night.

I quickly learned the value of maintaining a balanced life.

I would clean the apartment on Friday afternoons so Cynthia could come home from work and simply relax. Then, we usually ate at a little place called Heath's Steakhouse, a tiny restaurant where you sat at a counter and watched the cook prepare your steak and baked potato. What it lacked in ambience it more than compensated in value. We enjoyed two thick steaks with all the trimmings for seven dollars, including the tip. It wasn't much, but it was what we could afford. We entered seminary knowing those four years would be lean, so we learned to take pleasure in the small things. Frankly, we loved it!

When you're preparing for the future, you can't forget about the present. I saw a lot of guys fall prey to burnout. Some literally worked themselves sick. Others saw those four years as a grueling test of endurance, after which life would reward them with a stable income and plenty of time for R & R. Typically, those guys either washed out before the end or they carried that same attitude with them into ministry. Those who survived their four-year marathon were miserable in school and became just as miserable in ministry.

The demands of seminary did become overwhelming and I was, at times, stretched to my limits, but I had learned how to avoid burnout from boot camp. The physical demands of those twelve weeks could be grueling and the program pushed every recruit to the point of exhaustion—and beyond. Still, I noticed that each period of intense physical demand was followed by a balanced meal and adequate time for rest. It didn't *feel* adequate at the time. Rolling out of our racks at 05:00—well before sunup and sore to the bone— felt like torture. But the Marine Corps has been training men for combat for well over two centuries; they have the system down to a science...so don't mess with it! Each block of time was—and still is—devoted to a specific activity.

Time	Activity	Description
05:00	Reveille	Wake up, brush, shave, dress, make bed
05:10	Fall-in	Line up in assigned area for morning calisthenics and running (Monday, Wednesday, Friday)
06:30	Morning Chow	A balanced meal, heavy on protein
08:30	Training	Combat exercises and classroom instruction
12:00	Noon Chow	A balanced meal, heavy on protein
13:00	Training	Combat exercises and classroom instruction
17:00	Evening Chow	A balanced meal, heavy on protein
18:00	D.I. Time	Time when drill instructors address the recruits about any issues they deem important, and distribute mail
20:30	Personal Time	Time to write letters, do laundry, shine boots, clean the barracks, etc.
21:30	Lights-out	Time for sleep

Sunday mornings began with chapel and the rest of the day was given to classroom instruction, discussion of core values, and preparation of your gear—spit-shined shoes, clothes properly folded, brass polished, etc., etc.,...etc.

This regimen prepared me to accomplish a lot of work at Dallas Seminary without sacrificing my marriage or my health. I devoted generous blocks of time for reading assigned texts, writing papers, memorizing Greek and Hebrew vocabulary, practicing translation, and carefully preparing for exams. I ruthlessly protected those blocks of time from outside intrusion. I also set aside time to take care of practical matters, such as cleaning the apartment, maintaining our car, and keeping my wardrobe in good shape. (I spit shine my shoes to this day.) Back then, the dress code called for dress slacks, jacket, and tie, so all that needed to be maintained. And, just as important, I set aside and protected blocks of time for rest and to enjoy relaxation with Cynthia. Our Friday night dates were just one way we set aside time to cultivate our romance and enjoy the process of preparation. As my mother would say, "We made it work."

Preparation, while intense, must leave room for real life to take place. I had that fairly well in hand until my third year. During my second year, I found the groove and was able to keep pace with the course load, while finding time to be a husband and take care of life outside of schoolwork. Then, in January 1961, second semester of my second year, we were delighted to learn Cynthia was pregnant with our first child. She continued to work that semester, but it was clear that, by summer, I would have to replace her income. We prayed a summer job would lead to full-time employment that not only met our financial needs but allowed me to continue my classes.

> Preparation, while intense, must leave room for real life to take place.

That summer, Howard Hendricks put me in contact with Ray Stedman, the pastor near San Francisco I so admired when we lived there. They had been classmates and remained good friends, so he put in a good word for me. Not long after that, Ray invited me to serve as an intern that summer, so Cynthia and I drove to Palo Alto to lead the high school and college ministries at Peninsula Bible Church. (I'll come back to that experience later.) What great preparation, learning alongside Ray Stedman!

When we returned to Dallas to resume classes in August, Cynthia was due to deliver in early September. By the grace and provision of God, Dr. Pentecost asked me to become his pastoral assistant at Grace Bible Church, which was a huge answer to our prayers. I could serve there, earn enough to keep us going, receive practical training from a seasoned pastor, and continue classes. As I stated before, I had developed a good rhythm, so the added burdens were manageable. Cynthia took over the daily responsibilities of maintaining our home and taking good care of our son, Curt, while I earned our living and continued my commitment to a thorough period of preparation.

Those were changes made necessary by normal life circumstances. But I didn't respond wisely my third year at DTS. To those unavoidable responsibilities, I added twenty-one credit hours and audited two other courses, if you can believe it. To put this in perspective, sixteen credit hours in one semester was considered a "full load." If the courses were light enough, you could take eighteen with a good deal of extra effort. Registering for twenty-one hours, plus two audited courses with a ministry job and a baby in the crib was somewhere between maddening and insane.

I had no idea just how much a baby would change everything, not just our workload and schedules, but our very selves. I also failed to realize that the classes I had begun would be some of the most difficult in the entire course of study. Third-year Greek. Second-year Hebrew under Dr. Bruce Waltke, fresh from Harvard University. Eschatology, taught by Dr. John Walvoord, the president of the seminary at that time. I had no less than nineteen papers and a mini-thesis that semester. After Cynthia gave birth to our firstborn, Curt, she not only took care of his needs, she typed all my papers, which I wrote out longhand. (No computers back then!)

Clearly, I had taken on too much. They were the longest, most difficult months of my academic life. Preparing for ministry is one thing; torturing oneself is quite another. I never forgot it and I learned important lessons about maintaining a balanced life and the importance of planning. In terms of balance, you can't continually sacrifice today on the altar of tomorrow or you'll never enjoy life; contentment will always lie somewhere just over the horizon and you'll never enjoy the blessings God has given you in the here and now. Furthermore, all that affects your attitude. Yet, preparing for the future does require the sacrifice of short-term pleasure in the present. Hardship is the investment we make today in order to reap greater rewards tomorrow. Keeping those two truths in balance is a continual struggle for all who want to pursue excellence in their calling. Amazingly, I maintained good grades, but I almost broke my emotional back under the load.

> Hardship is the investment we make today in order to reap greater rewards tomorrow.

I also learned the hard way about a concept later described by Dr. Richard Swenson as "margin." If you think of your life as a glass, and your responsibilities as the liquid it contains, margin is the empty space between the surface of the liquid and the rim of the glass. Margin—that all-important empty space—is the place of residence for your patience, your creativity, your feelings of contentment, your ability to cope with stress... including your ability to learn. Information goes in easier and it stays longer when you have margin. And, in many ways, that's where learning has the greatest opportunity to become life changing. Preparing properly requires sufficient room to think, to relax, to pray, to breathe.

I also discovered that excellence demands margin. I survived that semester and even managed to retain much of what I had learned only because I hadn't begun that period of intense pressure already exhausted. I knew I couldn't continue such a maddening pace and turn in excellent work. So, I made a conscious decision in my next semester to slow down and reduce my load. You can get by when you're stretched to your limits, but to become excellent in any given area—to rise to your own potential consistently—you must be healthy, rested, and focused, not preoccupied with stress, or rushed with deadlines, or ruled by the tyranny of the urgent.

Prepare for Unforeseen Challenges

After that terrible semester, I learned my lesson...only to discover another profound truth about life and margin: nature abhors a vacuum.

Babies neither understand nor care about the concept of margin! They don't care about whether Mom or Dad maintains a balanced life. Sleep? Forget it. Spare time? In your dreams (when you can sleep). Money? It's amazing how much it takes to feed a baby and then keep the other end clean. Then, around that time, Cynthia's mother was dying with cancer. I passed two kidney stones. And, that semester, we conceived a second time, only to miscarry five months into the pregnancy. I thought the grief would wipe both of us out. Times of preparation are great opportunities to get ready for what's ahead.

> Times of preparation are great opportunities to get ready for what's ahead.

That dreadful season of sadness gave way to the joyful news we were expecting another child, which we learned near the end of the first semester of my fourth and final year in seminary. Between my first and second semesters, we were visiting our parents in Houston. Following church on Sunday, a drunk driver slammed into us. The collision totaled our car, broke Curt's jaw, and caused Cynthia to begin hemorrhaging. She spent the balance of that pregnancy on bed rest to keep the bleeding from going out of control. So, we lived for several weeks under the constant anxiety of losing another baby. To our delight, our very healthy Charissa was born in August 1963.

Normally, the last year of a master of theology program is devoted to writing a master's thesis, a copiously researched "miniature book." And that's on top of a regular slate of classes. I was determined to avoid the self-inflicted pain of my third year by getting ahead. So, instead of using the previous summer as an extended holiday, I researched and almost completed my thesis. When I handed the final draft to Dr. Hendricks in October, he looked dumbfounded. "What is this?" he asked.

I said, "It's my thesis, 'The Teaching Ministry of the Pastor-Teacher.'"

He looked at the stack of paper like it had fallen out of a flying saucer. "Ooookay."

"Is that unusual?" I asked.

"Uh...yeah! *Very* unusual."

At the time, I could have guessed the majority of students didn't even begin their theses until the beginning of school in August, but I didn't realize how rarely they utilize the summer. It was unheard of, apparently. Still is, from what I hear professors say. I found it difficult to believe then, and I don't understand it now. Why *wouldn't* a last-year student use the extra time during summer? Why postpone the work until a time you *know* will be filled to overflowing by other mind-stretching assignments?

As I stated before, nature abhors a vacuum. I simply would not have survived my fourth year, with class work, earning a living, caring for Curt, cultivating a marriage, and then the series of difficulties we encountered as well. I cannot imagine finishing on time if I had not created margin by completing my thesis early. That taught me a lesson I never forgot. If you can get it done now, *do it*; the future comes with no guarantee you'll have the time or

> If you can get it done now, *do it*; the future comes with no guarantee you'll have the time or opportunities available to you today.

opportunities available to you today. I cannot number the times that principle has come to my rescue during the past fifty years of ministry.

Preparing for the Real World

From a practical point of view, Curt's arrival at the beginning of my third year in seminary could be regarded as a distraction from my training. From the sovereign view of Providence, however, the timing could not have been better. Because Cynthia could no longer work, breadwinning became my responsibility again. That practical need pushed me to seek an internship, which then qualified me to serve as an assistant pastor. Both of those experiences provided crucial training I didn't know I needed at the time. Preparation, if it is to be complete, must include real-world experience under the guidance of wise mentors.

After I explained my situation to Howard Hendricks, he wrote his friend, Ray Stedman, and that summer I became one of two students invited to serve at Peninsula Bible Church in Palo Alto, not far from San Francisco. The other man was Gib Martin, a former Jesuit priest. Ray put me in charge of "The Pow-Wow," a ministry for high school students, and I also led the college ministry. Being a risk taker, Ray also let me preach a time or two. And while I gained good experience fulfilling those roles, the real benefit of my time in Palo Alto came from Ray's personal investment in the two of us.

What a mentor! He died in 1992, and, to this day, I think about him at least once a week. I would love to pick up the phone and ask his advice or hear his perspective on some of the issues I am facing.

What I learned from Ray that summer can't be found in a textbook. As I watched him lead others, and teach the Bible, and work alongside elders, and engage the members of his congregation, and interact with leery politicians, and respond to counterculture critics—day in and day out, through every circumstance—I observed that Ray Stedman was absolutely and always Ray Stedman. He never tried to be anyone else, including what he thought you might like to see. I learned from him that authenticity is the only way to do ministry. It's not merely a good way, or even the best way; it's the *only* way. (The same is true of any vocation.) Understand. Ray didn't tell me this. I learned it by watching him one day after another. What a model of authenticity!

> I learned from him that authenticity is the only way to do ministry. It's not merely a good way, or even the best way; it's the only way.

When I pointed this out to Ray one time, he asked, "Why would you want to be anyone else?"

I answered, "Because I admire other people, especially men who have succeeded where I want to succeed."

He replied, "Good! Admire them. There's nothing wrong with admiring others. Study their methods; learn from their mistakes; take note of what made them who they are. You can even emulate a few of their qualities. But never attempt to *be* them." His words still ring in my ears.

Ray practiced what he preached. He brought his authentic self to every encounter and hid nothing. If he didn't have the answer, he said, "I don't know." If he struggled with something, he admitted he was struggling. If he had a shortcoming, he asked for help. He also knew his strengths and he concentrated on doing what he did well. And throughout his ministry, as many other pastoral interns came and went, his openly displayed humanity inspired each of us to seek help from the Savior he proclaimed. To do otherwise merely pushes people away; they know a phony when they see one. By your silence, you claim to be above the things that others struggle to overcome. Those in ministry can be the worst at that!

Of course, I wrestled with how far to carry this. Too much authenticity can get a little weird. You can't say to someone in your congregation, "Yeah, last week I lusted four times. By the way, your wife's gorgeous!" But you can say, "I understand the struggle everyone has with lust; it's a fight for me too." In fact, I've found it helpful to bring that authenticity into the pulpit when I preach. I don't turn a sermon into a grand mea culpa; that would be distracting. But I do admit my shortcomings. Over the years, I have found that people readily accept a speaker who doesn't pretend to have mastered every detail of the message.

> Over the years, I have found that people readily accept a speaker who doesn't pretend to have mastered every detail of the message.

Ray's authenticity extended to the church as well. He was willing to admit when a talk he gave didn't go well, and he was just as ready to acknowledge failures in the church. Without casting blame, he would simply point out the obvious. When he began his study, Body Life, he said, "Our church is virtually empty on Sunday nights. We're not doing something right." And that "we" included himself! He didn't point a finger at the elders; he didn't harangue the congregation for not showing up; he didn't shake up the staff with backbreaking demands. Instead, he acknowledged the problem and led a brainstorming session on how to fix it.

He put forward an unusual idea that probably wouldn't work in any other location or at any other time. This was San Francisco in 1961, the fertile seedbed of the counterculture hippie movement. He said, "We should have a service where everybody's very comfortable. Let's take the chairs out and let everyone sit on the floor."

A polite silence filled the room as everyone tried not to look at each other. Finally, someone said, "You mean like literally, remove all the chairs?"

"Yep!"

"And have everyone sit on the floor?"

"Right."

When people pushed back on an idea without offering a good reason other than "That's crazy. It'll never work," it just made him want to do it all the more. Shades of Walt Disney. He didn't mind standing alone on an issue because he knew who he was. And because he had a clear understanding of his own identity, he could get past what anyone thought of him and focus on the topic of discussion. If he backed down from an idea, it was because the idea lacked merit, not because he felt intimidated by the majority opinion. I should also add he had a terrific sense of humor. He was fun to be with.

As it turned out, he was right. People flooded into the auditorium on Sunday nights. They sat comfortably on the floor and took part in a relaxed, on-the-floor kind of service. Peninsula Bible Church drew hundreds of students from the Stanford campus for a couple of hours each Sunday evening. But even if it had been a failure, Ray would have asked the tough questions, challenged conventional thinking, found a creative idea, and then put it into action. And he certainly would have had fun in the process. What a guy! I loved him dearly.

Know Thyself

Watching Ray operate added a new dimension to my preparation. Seminary provided knowledge and taught me how to think theologically. On-the-job training under the watchful eye of a seasoned mentor helped me develop the necessary skills to apply what I had been learning. But my time with Ray made me aware of something I lacked: I didn't have a strong sense of identity. I then set out to achieve a threefold objective that would guide the rest of my career:

Know who you are.
Accept who you are.
Be who you are.

Please read the following *very* carefully. It's life changing.

When you start preparing for your calling, you begin by gaining the crucial knowledge you lack. You build on that foundation by acquiring the necessary skills to apply what you have learned. But most people stop there. Most don't take the next essential step in their preparation. Too many leave the crucible of education without a clear understanding of their own identity. And let me assure you, standing before a large group of people to speak on any subject—the Bible, sales-and-marketing strategies, politics, electronics, parenting, relationships—requires a strong sense of self. If you don't know who you are, and if you haven't come to terms with your own identity, then you cannot be yourself while speaking. Your lack of self-awareness will begin to show. Audiences instinctively pick up on that fundamental weakness and they remain suspicious of whatever that person has to say.

> If you don't know who you are, and if you haven't come to terms with your own identity, then you cannot be yourself while speaking.

In many ways, the quest to know yourself, accept yourself, and then be yourself is a lifelong journey; it never really ends. But, over time, you can reach a place of reasonable confidence from which you can speak from the heart with relative ease. For me, that wouldn't come for another eight to ten years after seminary. But I determined in Palo Alto to begin laying that foundation as a part of my preparation.

While I continued to gain knowledge in seminary over the next two years, I applied my education to real-life ministry at Grace Bible Church as Dr. Pentecost's assistant. I also made a careful study of this scholar-pastor. I greatly admired his intellect and how diligently he prepared each sermon; yet he was himself. He was not at all like Ray Stedman...or Howie Hendricks. He was...well... Dwight Pentecost. He carefully wrapped his biblical, theological, and linguistic research in the muscle and sinew of humanity. The blood of his own struggles coursed through many illustrations and most of his applications. He was himself in the pulpit—humble, forthright, intelligent, and authentic. Though different from Ray Stedman, he chose to draw his audience *into* the message as Ray always did—with authenticity rather than repel them with factoids and platitudes.

I was ordained after graduation, a process not unlike a doctoral dissertation. Candidates must write a copiously researched position paper on all the major doctrines: God, the Trinity, Christ, the Holy Spirit, sin, salvation, sanctification, the church, etc. Then the candidate must face an ordination council and endure several hours of oral examination. I sat alone before Dr. Dwight Pentecost, Dr. Charles Ryrie, Dr. Stan Toussaint, two other local pastors, another professor of theology from Dallas Seminary, and three elders in the church. I still remember some of their test questions.

- "From memory, outline the Book of Ezekiel and describe how you would preach through that prophetic work for a modern audience."
- "What are the most significant literary differences between the Synoptic Gospels and the Gospel of John?"
- "How does the Gospel of Matthew present the kingdom of God and how does it develop the identity of Jesus in relation to the kingdom?"
- "What is the overall message in the book of Jonah? Why would God use a prophet that rebellious?"

- "Compare and contrast the ministry of John the Baptizer and the ministry of Jesus."
- "How would you use the Book of Proverbs to counsel the parents of a rebellious teen?"
- "What is your position on divorce? Please support it with several Scriptures."

The ordination council was strong but kind. I came away from that three-hour session feeling like a dishrag thoroughly wrung out and hung up to dry. Thankfully, I passed. By God's grace they ordained me without reservation, which affirmed my intellectual readiness for ministry, but I didn't feel ready to fly solo. Not by a long shot.

Prior to graduating, I received no fewer than four offers from churches to consider: a church in Dayton, Ohio; another in Castro Valley out in California; another in Chattanooga, Tennessee; and the opportunity to remain at Grace Bible Church as Dr. Pentecost's full-time assistant pastor. While the other offers were appealing to some degree, I felt a strong need for further preparation. By then, I knew many of my strengths and weaknesses. I had gained a basic grasp of the academic requirements related to being a pastor, and I could somewhat hold my own in the pulpit—I won the "Harry A. Ironside Award for Expository Preaching"—but I recognized a need for more development in the practical matters of running a church. I also needed to hone my gifts as a preacher. So, I decided to remain there until I had gained the additional qualifications I lacked.

It's not enough to be a good preacher. Lots of great preachers have failed to make a significant impact because they lack personal character traits and the necessary leadership skills to develop a respected platform from which to speak. How much credibility would you give a magnificent

It's not enough to be a good preacher.

orator whose church is known for its lack of concern for the poor? Probably very little. Preachers—all public speakers, for that matter—must also be good leaders. After all, public speaking *is* leadership!

For two more years under the mentoring of Dr. Pentecost, I learned how to run an elder's meeting effectively. I discovered how to cultivate an atmosphere of cooperation without abdicating my role as the leader. I cultivated many of the skills needed to stimulate conversation—constructive talk that brings difficult issues to the surface and invites creative ideas—yet without turning the group into a committee. I developed the ability to connect with various ages and work with diverse backgrounds without losing my own identity or trying to become someone I'm not. I gained crucial communication skills outside the public speaking context—skills for both listening and encouraging. This dimension of learning not only helped me later, in the leadership of a church, it kept me closely connected to people of all kinds, from mechanic to mogul, from strong Christians to cynical critics, so they were never far from my mind when I spoke to large groups.

One of the compliments I receive from listeners never fails to encourage me: "I listen to you because I know you live in the same world I live in." I have my years of preparation to thank for the cultivation of that ability.

Preparation and Speaking

This chapter's title may have been misleading. Perhaps you were expecting information on how to prepare a speech or sermon. We will, in due time, examine the process of getting a talk ready for presentation, but excellence begins long before the days leading up to a speaking engagement. I cannot write a book that pretends to offer shortcuts that work. They don't. The fact is public speaking requires a significant lifelong investment in preparation. Here's why:

Excellent communicators know who they are.

Many books on public speaking attempt to teach the reader how to craft an "image mask" and how to wear it convincingly. That's not their stated intent, but the effect is the same. Even though this is popular—and even though you can get away with it on occasion—it's phony. The more you speak, the more you will have to wear that mask in public. That's how people in the public eye lose themselves. You don't want that.

Others examine the style and habits of great communicators in order to find keys to success in public speaking, but imitating the style of someone you admire will grow tiresome, for both you and your audiences. Still others describe the mechanics of public speaking—diction, posture, eye contact, gesturing, organization, illustration—and they can help the speaker eliminate distracting habits or overcome shortcomings in style. But nothing can compensate for a lack of authenticity. Knowing who you are and speaking passionately about what truly matters to you will cover a multitude of public-speaking sins. When you speak from the heart, the mechanics of public speaking become as natural as breathing with just a little fine tuning.

> Nothing can compensate for a lack of authenticity.

Without coming to terms with your own identity and without sufficient preparation in pursuit of your calling, you must wear a mask whenever you stand before others to communicate. Preparation is crucial to knowing who you are, what's important to you, and what you should be saying. Preparation, then, gives you a central theme around which all of your communication revolves.

To become an excellent communicator, choose a realm of expertise and become an expert.

Excellent communicators speak with authority.

You can't fake authority. People have tried to *appear* authoritative by altering their mannerisms or assuming an impressive posture, or increasing their volume or intensity, usually to compensate for their lack of knowledge or experience. But audiences see right through all that. Trying to speak with authority on a subject in which you have little specialized knowledge or experience will only backfire in the end. Authenticity is the key. Either gain the authority to speak in some realm of expertise, or limit your talks to those subjects on which you have something of value to offer your audience. When you operate over your head, you'll soon look foolish. Or you'll turn to gimmicks. I recently read of one pastor who was vulnerable enough to admit it. Relying on 3-D videos to enhance his messages, he acknowledged, "It's a little cheesy, but cheese works."

One gains the authority to "say it well" by preparing well. Preparing is not the same as research. Research is the study one does in preparation for a specific speech or sermon, which we will examine later. Preparing begins with specialized education followed by real-world experience. Seminary prepared me to do serious research on biblical and theological subjects. My internship with Ray Stedman and nearly five years as an assistant pastor with Dwight Pentecost prepared me to deal with congregations, week in and week out, with some measure of authority.

> One gains the authority to "say it well" by preparing well.

During those early years, I was significantly younger than the people I served. Moreover, many of them came from social classes far above my station; some were quite wealthy with household servants. Others were hard-charging entrepreneurs to whom hundreds of employees reported. I will admit, I often felt intimidated by their intelligence and impressed with their worldly knowledge. One time, I stood in front of a group of very wealthy men and women and read aloud a note card with the word "vermouth," which I pronounced "vur-mowth" instead of "vur-mooth." And they burst into laughter. But it wasn't derisive laughter. Their laughing was filled with affection for me because I didn't pretend to know things I did not; I spoke with authority only on the things I had devoted years to learning.

Preparation gave me the confidence to stand and deliver something of value to people who had more experience, more money, more power, and, in many cases, far greater intelligence. Whereas they were leaders in their areas of expertise, I offered something they lacked and, therefore, found helpful. I spoke with authority and authenticity, and my audiences loved me for it.

Excellent communicators never stop preparing.

Audiences need insightful and workable solutions to the problems they face today. They will respect you for the credentials you have earned; they will admire you for the problems you have solved or the innovations you have pioneered; but audiences are quick to *listen* to those who struggle as they do and have answers to their most pressing problems. Therefore, any speaker worth an audience's investment of time or money should maintain perpetual enrollment in the school of hard knocks. So, don't cut classes when you attend that school.

> Any speaker worth an audience's investment of time or money should maintain perpetual enrollment in the school of hard knocks.

Like a calling, preparation is a lifetime pursuit, fueled by curiosity and made necessary by challenges. Those who "say it well" continually grow in their fields of expertise, not only because they love to learn but because the needs of their community demand the latest knowledge and most innovative techniques. Those who "say it well" have paid the price of preparation by staying on the cutting edge of their discipline. Such well-prepared speakers will never lack an audience.

You and Your Calling

If you have taken the time to discover your calling, then you have undoubtedly discovered a field of expertise demanding additional training. If you haven't begun this process, it's time to go there! In order to "say it well," you need a deep well of knowledge from which to draw. If, on the other hand, you do have sufficient preparation in a particular realm, then communicating with excellence requires two initial decisions.

The first decision is whether or not to seek or accept an invitation to speak at a particular event. To make a wise choice, it's important to know who you are *not*. For all the study I have given to the Bible and theology, I do not accept most invitations to speak on eschatology (the study of the end times), and I rarely lecture on prophetic topics.

> It's important to know who you are *not*.

Dallas Theological Seminary became known for those subjects, so people sometimes expect me to be an expert in that realm. They might have known Dr. John Walvoord, the president of the seminary for thirty-four years. At the height of his career, he became a walking compendium of knowledge in that field of study and could stand before the world's leading experts in the field with complete confidence. I studied under that scholar, but I am not Dr. Walvoord. I didn't make eschatology a focus of intense study. I am able to provide my church with competent instruction, but I will never be considered an expert on prophetic themes. That isn't my comfort zone.

If, however, I receive an invitation to speak on marriage, the family, or the home, then I'm your man. Or, if you want a presentation on the practical application of the spiritual disciplines or the church or some other aspect of Christian living, I have enough confidence in my preparation to place my thoughts alongside those of any other expert. Furthermore, I can take you through most of the books of the Bible with a fair amount of ease. I know the topics on which I have something valuable or important to say, and yet I remain realistic about my limitations. By knowing who I am *not*, I have avoided almost certain failure by declining certain invitations.

If you have already given significant time and energy to preparation in a given field, limit your speaking opportunities to that domain. Politely decline invitations that do not give you the opportunity to speak passionately in your area of expertise. This will help you build a good reputation as an excellent speaker, which will encourage future opportunities. If you venture too far outside your realm of preparation, you will have left a roomful of potential referrals with a negative impression of your abilities as a speaker. Stay realistic. Know who you're *not*.

The second decision is the subject of your presentation. Excellent communicators draw upon their expertise to discern the needs of their audience and then they craft a speech or sermon to suggest practical solutions. Preparation helps you find the area of overlap between your expertise and their needs so you can choose the most appropriate invitations to accept and then sharpen the focus of your presentation to provide the information your audience needs and will most appreciate.

You may have detected a pattern emerging from the first two chapters. "Calling" and "Preparing" have to do with identity. Public speaking is an expression of who you are. What you have to say to audiences must be the overflow of a healthy person devoted to something important and adequately prepared to lead others through speech. There are no shortcuts to knowing who you are and then preparing yourself to make changes in the world. Nevertheless,

> Public speaking is an expression of who you are.

I can assure you that the time and effort you invest in discovering your calling and preparing to pursue it will reap lifelong dividends.

Once the issues of calling and preparation have been settled, you are ready to be fashioned by God into something useful. He does this like a potter molds clay. As wet, malleable material, scooped from the ground, moves within the Lord's hands, He expertly applies pressure to create something altogether unique. This is His method of molding those who "say it well"—movement and pressure—a process I describe as "Going."

CHAPTER THREE

Going

> *We shall not cease from exploration*
> *And the end of all our exploring*
> *Will be to arrive where we started*
> *And know the place for the first time.*
> —*T. S. Eliot*[4]

There's a danger in writing a book like this. Many marketing professionals in the publishing world would like to convince you that buying a book will provide you all the information you need to become an overnight success as a (fill in the blank). For those looking for shortcuts to becoming a compelling, highly-sought-after public speaker or a riveting, admired preacher who packs in the crowds, the first two chapters may have been disappointing. By now, those who purchased this book for get-famous-quick strategies haven't found what they were looking for and have moved on to something more cogent and clever. So, I will assume that you're different. You continue to read because public speaking is, for you, a means to a more significant end. If you're a pastor, then preaching is a primary means of caring for the people you shepherd. If you're an educator, then standing in front of a class is a principle tool for learning. If you're a company executive, a community leader, a politician, or an officer of a professional team, then public speaking is how you move your agenda, keep it interesting, and inspire positive and progressive change.

Thank you for continuing to read. Pride is a poor motive for public speaking, so I not only admire your desire to keep the speaker's platform in perspective, I applaud your good intentions.

I wish I had the secrets to overnight success. If I had any shortcuts to share, I can assure you I wouldn't have kept them to myself all these years. But the truth is, there are none. I have no tips or tricks to make you an effective communicator in a day or two. Saying it well, like any craft, requires dedication (a calling), training (preparation), and then seasoning (time—lots of time). Preaching—the high and holy task of faithfully proclaiming divine truth, God's Word—is an especially demanding duty, not merely for its subject matter, but for the immense stakes involved: the souls of men and women. So, when I completed my seminary training, I committed myself to continual studies in the Scriptures...I became a journeyman in the craft of communication. I determined back then never to lower my standard.

In the world of trades and crafts, a person who completes his or her apprenticeship is called a "journeyman." He or she is not yet a "master." To become a master of a trade, the journeyman must hone his or her skills through years of practical experience. In the middle ages, a tradesman moved—or journeyed—from one workshop to another, or from one construction site to another, to gain a broad spectrum of experience under several masters. Once you have identified your calling (chapter 1) and you have devoted yourself to preparation (chapter 2), you're ready to begin your journey, as it were, to becoming a master at saying it well. And, like any successful journey, arriving at your destination—becoming an expert at

> I wish I had the secrets to overnight success.

saying it well—requires knowing when to leave where you are, where to go next, and how long you should remain before going again. This journey is a continual pursuit of your calling and a perpetual extension of your preparation. And it is in the process of *going* that God seasons you as a communicator to say what must be said and, ultimately, to say it well. This seasoning through the broad experiences of life gives you depth and insight, which will set you apart whenever you speak in public. After all, there's no market for a speaker who will tell you the obvious.

> This journey is a continual pursuit of your calling and a perpetual extension of your preparation.

Knowing When to Stay

When I came to the end of my seminary education, several people encouraged me to take on the role of senior pastor at one of several churches recruiting at the seminary. They had heard me preach, they had seen me at work in campus leadership, they knew of my two years under the mentoring of Dr. Pentecost at Grace Bible Church and my pastoral internship with Ray Stedman. So, they pushed me to aim high for my first ministry position. But two things held me back. First, I didn't want to approach ministry like one who climbs a corporate ladder. The conventional thinking was to leap for the highest rung possible on your first post after seminary and then start climbing from there. Second, I knew in my heart I wasn't ready. I needed to learn the mechanics of church ministry: how to run a productive staff meeting, how to work with elders and deacons effectively, how to structure a church program and then implement it with complete buy-in from the congregation, how to meet the emotional needs of parishioners at their highest and lowest points, how to handle criticism, and how to endure through times of hardship. I didn't suffer from insecurity; this was a realistic assessment of my skills—or lack of them in certain areas. So, after graduation, I remained in Dallas and joined Grace Bible Church's full-time staff as Dr. Pentecost's assistant pastor.

Don't get me wrong. I never lacked for eagerness or opportunity to minister elsewhere. While serving at Grace Bible Church, before and after graduation, I received several attractive invitations, which I brought to the attention of Dr. Pentecost. He looked at them as seriously as I did, and he would say, "You could certainly go there, and you might be a good fit, but this may not be the right time for you. Ultimately, you need to be sure about where you should be serving and when; so, if you think this is the right time to go, I'll support you all the way." Despite those offers, I kept my ambition in check.

As I served alongside this seasoned man of God, I watched ministry in action without the pressure of public exposure. I got the chance to see the inner workings of a church. I learned to appreciate the cyclical nature of ministry. I enjoyed the passing of one season to the next, not only on the calendar but in people's lives. I liked being a part of baby dedications, and educating children, and then baptizing those young people when they gave themselves to Christ, and celebrating their graduations, and officiating at their weddings, and then holding *their* babies in my arms. I saw the incredible potential for the church to impact the lives of people during those special seasons. And, as I preached and taught in his absence, I became attuned to the varying needs of people in different seasons and how to tailor my words accordingly.

About a year or so after working with Dr. Pentecost full-time,

I began to feel more confident about leading a church, so I entertained the possibility of going elsewhere. A church in Fort Worth asked me to consider being a pastor there. In pastoral ministry, a casual interview is the first step toward making a move. There's no offer of a position, just an invitation by the church elders or a special committee to submit a résumé and begin discussions. Neither the church nor the prospect commits to anything official and there's no obligation by either party. If the discussions go well and both are in agreement—and *only* under those circumstances—the prospective pastor is put before the entire congregation as a "candidate." The "candidating" process usually involves some preaching at regular services and several informal opportunities to mingle with families in the congregation. Following all of that, if both the church leadership and the candidate agree, the church issues a formal "call," which in secular terms is a written job offer stating the expectations, benefits, salary, and other pertinent details. In the case of this church, a formal "call" required a congregational vote.

I told Dr. Pentecost about the invitation and began the process. He promised to pray for me. Cynthia and I visited the church and met with the elders. I preached the morning and evening services and we felt right at home; the people were wonderful and the church culture was very familiar to us. We felt unusually comfortable. The elders and their wives welcomed us graciously and they felt strongly that, though we were young (both still in our twenties), we were a great fit for their ministry. After a short time, they called and said, "We'd like you to consider our church voting on a call. Would you like to take this next step?" I agreed. The following Sunday, the church voted. If the vote was not unanimous, it was mighty close. So, from their perspective, I belonged in Fort Worth, serving that church as senior pastor; nothing could have been more obvious to them.

I was excited. Cynthia was excited. I shared the outcome with

Dr. Pentecost and he congratulated me. We visited the church that Sunday evening and great excitement filled the room! We were warmly welcomed as their new pastor and his wife. While driving back to our home in Dallas, neither Cynthia nor I said a word. We drove in virtual silence, deep in our thoughts. Our initial excitement gave way to a pensive, somber mood, which confused me. We should have been brimming with enthusiasm about our new future and eager to explore the wonderful opportunities for ministry that lay before us. The church was filled with excitement...why weren't we?

I lay awake all night, churning and turning. The next day, when I telephoned Dr. Pentecost to tell him that I had accepted the church's call, he congratulated me. He said, "That's wonderful, Chuck, I'm very happy for you. We'll put together a nice farewell for you at Grace so everyone will know where you're going and what you'll be doing. They'll miss you—as will I—but we all want to express our support for you and Cynthia."

I remember a strange feeling of uneasiness or misgiving that washed over me as I dialed his number...it persisted throughout our brief conversation. And I felt especially uneasy as I placed the receiver down. Finally, I confessed to Cynthia, "I can't do it."

Cynthia had been thinking about preparing our Dallas home for sale, where we would live near the new church in Fort Worth, and what her role would be as we settled in. The church was putting helium in the balloons for a big welcome celebration. Things were moving very, very quickly, so, as much as I wanted to put off that phone call, I had to make it soon. I called the chairman of the elders immediately and said, "I'm sorry, but I can't come."

Of course, that was the last thing he expected me to say. He invited me to lunch that same day and I explained everything. Every embarrassing, confusing detail. He pressed me to explain what was wrong. Was it the church? Salary? Benefits? My duties? Something someone said or did? But I stated no to every question he asked. I assured him nothing was "wrong," yet everything within me was now saying it wasn't right. I had been presumptuous. I had pushed my plans through, but I had failed to make it a focus of my prayers.

Oh, I prayed about it. But, looking back, I realized that my prayers followed in the wake of my decisions. I failed to lead my decision with a sincere questioning of God's mind on the issue.

I had been presumptuous. I had pushed my plans through, but I had failed to make it a focus of my prayers.

When it became clear that I was not, indeed, coming to be their pastor, the head elder said, "Our church will have had the distinct privilege of having Chuck Swindoll as our pastor for twenty-four hours!" And, for years to come, he never let me forget it! He was a gracious gentleman about the whole mess and we remained great friends in the many years that followed.

Immediately after I communicated my change in plans to the elder and to Dr. Pentecost, I felt instant relief. While nothing specific made the move "wrong," and while I could point to nothing specific that made my staying at Grace Bible Church "right," I could not ignore my gut. The incredible misgivings at my going and the overwhelming relief at my staying where I was spoke volumes to me. While the events left everyone confused—no one more than me—I had made the right decision. That night, I slept like a newborn baby.

I tell you about this period of my history and that embarrassing episode to underscore a couple of thoughts.

First, ambition is not necessarily a bad thing, but it should never serve oneself. In fact, it should be kept low on the list of priorities when deciding where to stay and when to go. Don't let ambition

Don't let ambition cloud your judgment and rob you of the opportunity to gain valuable life experience where you are.

cloud your judgment and rob you of the opportunity to gain valuable life experience where you are. You might feel limited in your current position, like your talents are going to waste or you could be accomplishing so much more if only given a broader opportunity elsewhere. Those negative feelings are proof positive that you're growing. Your frustration, however, is not good enough reason to go elsewhere. Not by itself, anyway.

When considering the church in Fort Worth, my immaturity took over. I found it reassuring that a sizable congregation with a fully developed ministry actually wanted me. I thought about all the good stuff that comes with being a senior pastor in a healthy, respected church, but I didn't wrestle with the many responsibilities that the position entailed. I think that was the source of my uneasiness. In the drive back to Dallas, when misgivings first overshadowed my excitement, I was probably in the frame of mind I should have been in ten days earlier. I looked at the future objectively for the first time and realized that I could probably do the job, but not with the confidence I would later gain by staying where I was.

A second thought: pay close attention to your gut instincts. Intuition is a powerful, yet underutilized tool in decision making. I'm a facts-and-figures guy by nature. I list pros and cons. I weigh the evidence when charting the future. I'm not wired to rely on something so subjective and intangible as my feelings when making life decisions. Some people are and they do it well, but not me. Even so, I have learned to slow down when all the objective facts point in one direction yet my insides remain in turmoil. A churning gut is announcing, "Apply the brakes!"

Third, you must be convinced of your decision to stay or go, regardless of outside pressures. The telephone call to the chairman of elders was one of the most agonizing I have ever made. I had given every indication that I was coming despite many opportunities to back out. My decision affected so many people at two churches and plans had been set in motion in both ministries. No objective reason kept me from following through with the initial decision. Still, I could not quell my uneasiness. Regardless of the inconveniences to others and the agony of my own embarrassment, I remained where I was until I was sure the time had come for me to go.

Knowing When to Leave

The journey is, unfortunately, a tedious trial-and-error process. The path can be a wandering one. Sometimes, God takes us on excursions that feel like a waste of time when we reflect on them soon afterward. Years later, however, we come to see them as a necessary part of the journey. The middle third of Moses' life comes to mind as a notable example. He began life in the court of Pharaoh, presumably groomed for leadership in that great civilization.

> Sometimes, God takes us on excursions that feel like a waste of time when we reflect on them soon afterward.

However, at the age of forty, a crime of passion suddenly changed the course of his life. The result? He spent the next forty years at the far end of nowhere, tending sheep for his father-in-law, accomplishing nothing of significance and impacting no one to speak of. It must have been a disillusioning and confusing time for him, certainly in the beginning. Yet, as we see now, his time wandering in the wilderness was a necessary part of his journey. While he accomplished nothing publicly, God accomplished much within the future leader of the Hebrews.

I also think of King David, hand selected by God and anointed by the Lord's prophet, yet forced to live in the dusty, barren wasteland of Judea for a dozen or more years. Meanwhile, a madman filled with murderous jealousy ruled from his throne and sent armies to hunt him down. We have a record of David's thoughts during that time, a number of psalms expressing his anger, and confusion, paralyzing doubt, and trembling fear. Throughout these troubled years, we see a desperate longing to fulfill his divine purpose. What felt like a waste of time to David was, in fact, a crucial time of character development. His detour in life made him the greatest king ever to sit on Israel's throne.

My first detour was, of course, to Okinawa, where God changed the course of my life. As I mentioned earlier, I didn't go willingly. My second detour was entirely voluntary, and it took my little family and me to a small town near Boston. If you can imagine the discomfort of Moses, a palace-pampered prince among the flocks of Midian, and if you can identify with David, the anointed King of Israel living among the caves of Engedi, then you just might be prepared to appreciate the difficulty of a Texan among Yankees in Waltham, Massachusetts!

Many months after my embarrassing episode with the church in Fort Worth, I began to feel restless, which is a sign to observe. Unlike the frustration I described above, this is a different sort of discontent. I was happy in Dallas. I enjoyed the people and the ministry of Grace Bible Church. Cynthia and I had built a lovely little home and we enjoyed the community; it was a wonderful place to rear our two small children. I had experienced the blessings of ministry as an assistant pastor, and I could have continued with equal, if not greater, success. Everything was right. Everything was good. Except, I had become restless within. That restlessness refused to go away.

Pay attention to that. In my experience, a restless feeling that has no identifiable source is the first indication that God has begun to prepare your heart for a change. It's too early to act on it. You don't have any information about the future yet, so you don't want to start making decisions. On the contrary, this is the time to stay put. Rather than allow that restlessness to spur more or different activity, let it be your cue to be quiet and stay still. And in that stillness, pray for wisdom as

A restless feeling that has no identifiable source is the first indication that God has begun to prepare your heart for a change.

you become keenly observant. Pray for wisdom and keep in touch with a few wise counselors as circumstances take on potentially heightened meaning.

One of my professors, Dr. Haddon Robinson, informed me that he had spoken at a church in Waltham and had given them my name as someone they should consider. Later, Dr. Bruce Waltke visited there and affirmed Haddon's earlier recommendation. So, the little church did their due diligence and then called me. Unfortunately, I made another mistake. When I visited the church, I didn't take Cynthia with me. Our two children were small, so travel was difficult. We kept in constant contact throughout my stay, I described everything I saw and experienced, and we discussed the situation thoroughly, but, believe me, that was no substitute for her being there.

I thought everything through and finally accepted their call. We had a nice farewell at Grace Bible Church, sold the house, packed up our belongings, and in the fall of 1965, we drove to New England. As we drove into Waltham and down the main street, Cynthia quietly said, "This is it?"

Not a good beginning.

We moved into the manse across the street from the church, and...there I was. On my own. Not only geographically, but culturally displaced. I didn't fit, and if I had stayed twenty-five years, I don't know that I ever would have fit. Now, if you ask the dear people who attended that church during those two years I was there, they didn't have any complaints. They loved me. Actually, we formed some deep friendships. But no one from that community ever asked, "Should you really be here?"

I did have a few run-ins with the local denomination leaders with the Evangelical Free Church of America. They wanted to do things the way they had always been done and had seldom heard the word "no." I preferred a more indigenous leadership style in the church, so my methods were not always to their liking. That particular denomination can be a little soft on the doctrine of eternal security while I'm very strong on that issue. In addition to that, the church had a tradition of pulpit swapping on certain Sundays, where all the pastors in the region guest preached in the church of another pastor in the denomination. That seemed weird, so I didn't participate in that. There were a couple of missionaries whose doctrines made me uneasy, so I sent a couple of questionnaires to clarify their positions. My probing upset the area superintendent who told me that it was his job to check on missionaries and that the denomination had approved these servants of Christ, so who was I to be second-guessing their decision? All that to say, I had a few skirmishes with the denomination, but no huge conflicts. Through it all, the church always appreciated my candor.

> All that to say, I had a few skirmishes with the denomination, but no huge conflicts.

In terms of ministry, they graciously affirmed my preaching. The Bible studies I led were always well attended and the people appreciated the written pieces I produced for our classes. But for the lack of a better analogy, I felt like I was wearing a poorly fitted suit. No matter how good it looked to others, I was always tugging or fidgeting, never quite able to get comfortable.

At the time, and for years afterward, I thought, *Man, I really blew it; I made some huge blunders in the decision-making process and I arrived at a poor decision. I should have* never *gone to New England.*

Eventually, however, I came to see things much more objectively. Cynthia and I had prayed for wisdom. We faithfully sought the Lord's mind on the move. I should have taken Cynthia to visit the church and to view the area when I was presented as a candidate. I didn't coerce her; she went with me enthusiastically. And there certainly was nothing "terrible" about our experience in New England (although Cynthia says she didn't feel warm for two years). Despite the poor fit, we had made a good decision with the facts available to us at the time. We did begin family camping, and that was a blast!

Was it a mistake to go? Absolutely not. We needed what that experience would bring to us. Life is slower there, unlike the urban mushroom that is the Dallas–Fort Worth area or Southern California. The church didn't expect me to grow their numbers or to expand their facilities. They wanted a pastor who would be a shepherd of the families. So, their expectations left Cynthia and me enough space to work on our marriage, which had suffered some setbacks. Cynthia endured some personal struggles there, and, instead of making a big issue of the situation, the church loved us. And we had time to enjoy our young children—we bought a little pop-up camper and used it regularly, especially during spring and fall. There are no more beautiful places to camp than in the New England states.

> The church didn't expect me to grow their numbers or to expand their facilities.

After two years of wearing an ill-fitted suit, I knew we had to go. Admittedly, I struggled with enormous guilt. They had spent $1,600 to move us from Dallas! I wondered, *After all they've done for us, how can I possibly explain that we shouldn't stay?* But I couldn't continue. So, one morning, I visited the chairman of the deacons where he worked. I entered the store and he said, "Well, Pastah Chock, what brings you down heeyah so uh-ley?"

I told him I needed to talk with him in private, so he took me to the back room. We sat down and I got straight to the point. "I simply can't stay; I have to go."

He immediately asked the question everyone asks in that kind of situation. "What's wrong?"

"Nothing's wrong," I replied. Of course, my mind flew back to a similar conversation with a church elder in Fort Worth. Though separated by two years and over a thousand miles, both men wore the same confused expression. Here I was, again, trying to explain how I've got something going that's not wrong, yet I can't keep doing it. It was bewildering.

After reassuring him several times that nothing specific prompted my leaving, he said, "If God doesn't want you here then neither do we. We love you and want you to be where God wants you." What a model response!

I received a call from Irving Bible Church back in Texas. When we left Waltham, I carried with me valuable lessons that helped guide the rest of my ministry, and even today I go back to those two years with great understanding of many things. We drove away full of relief... and with a brand-new baby in our arms.

Knowing When to Go

If New England was an ill-fitted suit, the bedroom community of Irving near Dallas felt like a pair of broken-in jeans and a sweatshirt. No place on earth could have been more comfortable. The congregation at Irving Bible Church spoke Texan. I understood their culture and could meet their needs before they knew they had them. Many of them were students, even a few faculty at Dallas Seminary, so we had no theological differences. And without a denominational structure, I was free... and I had one less hat to wear. Moreover, I had lots of friends in the area. As the church began to grow, Cynthia and I sank our roots deeper. After just a few months, I thought, *I could do this for the rest of my life.* Those were fruitful, joyful years. While there, God

> I could do this for the rest of my life.

graciously provided yet another baby, our fourth and final child.

Four years later, in February 1971, my mother died. After spending the afternoon with my father I returned home thinking about the funeral service I would preach. My mind flitted between past and present as I absent-mindedly opened the mail. Among the other letters, I noticed an envelope from the First Evangelical Free Church of Fullerton, California. Intrigued, I sliced open the letter and began reading. They had been without a pastor for almost two years and wanted me to visit their church and preach one Sunday. That, as you may recall, is an invitation to consider serving there as pastor. In this case, there were no obligations on either side. No expectations. Just a casual Sunday with a possible future. But I was so content in Irving, I saw no reason even to consider visiting some other church—especially one in Southern California. Besides that, with my mother's death and my father's grief, I had zero desire to go anywhere. So, in the quiet that followed my mother's funeral, I wrote a brief reply, telling them no, thanking them for their kind invitation, and expressing my immense satisfaction at Irving Bible Church.

Not long after that, another letter came, apologizing for the ill-timed letter, and then asking, in effect, "Could you just come and preach? Could you come and bring your family? Or just your wife? Could you come alone? Could you come and candidate? Or not candidate? Or just come for a little getaway, visit Disneyland, and simply look at the area?" They offered every possible option. And I thought, *What on earth is this?* To be candid, it seemed a little desperate, which made me wonder what they weren't telling me.

As I learned later, there was nothing wrong; they were simply eager to find a pastor. Their interim pastor and denominational superintendent Wally Norling, had done a wonderful job preparing the church for another's leadership. He had heard a tape recording of one of my sermons and passed it along to the search committee, which prompted their contacting me.

Once more, I graciously declined the invitation. *But they wrote again!*

Around that time, Bill Gothard had just begun his youth-conflict seminars and I wanted to attend one myself before sending any of our church members at Irving. Unfortunately, to attend an event that started on Thursday and ended on Saturday morning would prevent my being ready with a message on Sunday. So, I arranged to have someone preach in my place in Irving while I traveled to Southern California to attend that seminar. Because I was going to be in the area, I agreed to preach a couple of my familiar sermons on Sunday. I would be what churches call "pulpit supply." *And that was all!* I emphasized that I was not candidating; I merely offered to be one of their many guest preachers that year.

> Once more, I graciously declined the invitation. *But they wrote again!*

As I prepared to leave, Cynthia said, "You might not be looking at them, but you can be sure they'll be looking at you!"

I shrugged and assured her that I had no interest in moving... this was no different from any other time I've preached for a church without a pastor. The arrangement freed me from the burden of preparing a new message, the small stipend would defray some of the cost of travel, I would attend the seminar, and they would have a preacher for Sunday. The circumstances benefited everyone. Cynthia simply smiled and nodded. She, of course, had a sense of destiny that I didn't entertain for a split second.

When Sunday came, I preached their morning service. I felt very comfortable and the congregation seemed to appreciate the sermon.

Afterward, the people who had originally invited me asked if I would meet with them after lunch that afternoon. I agreed, and we later gathered in the empty pastor's study. Soon after sitting down, Dr. Irv Ahlquist said, "Well, we've found our man."

I said, "Really? Who is it?" (Talk about clueless!)

They all laughed like I had said something funny and then they realized that I had asked an innocent question. "Why, it's you."

"No, I'm really not the man. Dr. Ahlquist, with all due respect, I didn't come as a candidate. I'm very happy where I am. I could give you the names of several fine men that would be a great fit here and…"

He said, "I know. I know. And just as you were candid with us, we have to be straightforward with you. We met for about an hour before you arrived and we feel strongly that you're the right man to serve as our senior pastor."

We exchanged pleasantries and left the meeting with no resolution. I had agreed to lead the evening service, so I prepared for that. And in the quiet moments I had to myself, I remember an unwelcome feeling creeping over me, an unexpected sense of rightness to my being there. "Unwelcome" because it complicated the contentment I felt in Irving, and "unexpected" because I came with no desire to pursue this position. Nevertheless, my soul resonated with the prospect of being their pastor.

Nevertheless, my soul resonated with the prospect of being their pastor.

To make things worse, the evening service was absolutely outstanding. A packed youth choir sang beautifully. The musicians and congregation played and sang as one. My message fit perfectly with the needs of that flock, and the congregation responded beautifully. And, by the end of the evening, I couldn't deny what Cynthia had sensed from the beginning. I now had to fly home and face her with the bad news: she was right.

Further consideration would likely confirm what I already knew in my heart. We belonged in Fullerton, California.

Before I left for home, the church stated their intention to put me before the congregation as a candidate. But I said, "Hold on. I want Cynthia to be a part of this decision. She needs to meet you, and visit the church, and see the area." I had learned from my previous mistake in New England.

When I returned home, Cynthia met me at the airport with her hands over her ears and a smile on her face. Like me, she didn't want to hear anything that would pull us away from Irving. Like me, she saw no reason to leave; we loved our life and ministry in Texas. Our kids were healthy and happy. Why leave all this? Once we were in the car, however, she took a deep breath. "Okay, I want to hear all about it."

I said, "I don't know how to explain this. The situation in Irving is good. We've tripled in size, we just completed our new sanctuary and we need to pay for it—not a great time for a pastor to leave—and I could see us serving here indefinitely. I can't think of a reason not to remain here. Yet, *everything inside me* says it's the right time to go."

Again, I'm not one who makes decisions based on intuition. I'm a facts-'n'-figures guy. But I had since learned to listen to my instincts. If I may, my gut shouted, "Go!"

We later made another trip together to visit Fullerton, to get a sense of what life would be like there, and to get better acquainted with the congregation. Soon after arriving, Cynthia began to see what I had observed. The population would soon mushroom and the church was poised for rapid growth. I provided what they lacked and they strengthened my weaknesses. Leadership and programs had been formed and had made good progress, but they desperately wanted leadership and, of course, someone strong to fill the pulpit. The more we questioned and investigated, the greater our sense of calling to Fullerton.

By the end of our time there, we agreed to have the leadership put me before congregation as a candidate. In the Evangelical Free Church denomination, churches are led democratically by the congregation. A vote of the church members would determine whether they would extend a call. The search committee warned ahead of time that the church rarely if ever voted unanimously on anything.

But, without telling anyone, I had already prayed, "Lord, if it's not unanimous, I will remain where I am." I thought, *This is a good way to know if I'm making the right decision.*

"Lord, if it's not unanimous, I will remain where I am."

By the next Wednesday, I received a call from the leading elder. The church had voted *unanimously* to call me as their senior pastor. As I hung up the phone, I wept. Tears of joy for our future in Fullerton, tears of sorrow over the heartbreak of leaving Irving.

I dreaded having to call Bo Hoskins, the chairmen of the elders at Irving Bible Church. I didn't like trying to explain the unexplainable. I've never been one to put off unpleasant tasks; they cause less anxiety when they're behind you. So I met Bo at the church early the next week. I got straight to the point. "I'm going to be leaving Irving Bible Church, but I will give you a full ninety days here to make the transition easier."

"What's wrong?" he asked. (Familiar question.)

"Nothing's wrong. I am not leaving because things are bad in Irving. In fact, I find every reason to stay, except one: I really think the Lord would have me elsewhere. I didn't go looking for something different. When the opportunity came to me, I rejected it several times. But, in the end, I cannot resist what God has made so clear."

He sighed, then graciously accepted my decision. Experience has taught me that more information and fuller explanations don't make difficult news easier to hear. There was a time I would have kept explaining myself to assure others—even try to convince them—that my leaving is what's best. But that never works. You can't soothe aching emotions with logic. You can't talk people out of disappointment.

You can't soothe aching emotions with logic.

Bo leaned back, his eyes filled with tears. He said, almost to himself, "It's going to be a long summer." After a few moments, he said—almost to himself—"How we regret this, Chuck...but if God wants you there, we don't want you here."

I remember thinking how eerily his words echoed those of the man in Waltham, almost verbatim. I said, "That's a very unselfish thing for you to say."

"It's a very *difficult* thing for me to say. But when God makes a move, you have to move with Him."

If I had it to do over again, I wouldn't have given a ninety-day notice. Three months is too long. Much too long! Thirty to forty-five days would have been plenty. Perhaps a couple of months if I had been there more than a decade. But by the end, I had become the lamest of lame ducks. After about four weeks, any congregation begins to look past you to see potential successors. And, no matter how much I encouraged them to bring in candidates, my presence made the process awkward for them.

When the day came for us to drive to Fullerton, some people came by to say a final farewell. Tears and hugs and promises to stay in touch were exchanged as Cynthia, the children, and I took our places in the car. Just before we pulled out of the driveway, one woman bent down, looked through Cynthia's window at the four kids, then Cynthia, and then me. "You keep saying the Lord is in this," she said. "But the Lord gets blamed for a lot of things He has nothing to do with." She held my confused gaze for a moment, and then walked away. Tough words to hear.

> "But the Lord gets blamed for a lot of things He has nothing to do with."

As I pulled out of the driveway, I said, "That's a rough final memory." Cynthia didn't say anything; she just cried as we drove down Finley Road. One of the children asked, "Was that mean?" I replied, "Oh, it doesn't matter." But the woman's words rang in my ears all the way to Abilene. Not because I doubted our decision. I asked the Lord to grant a few other requests on behalf of the church and He had fulfilled them in remarkable fashion. Any doubts I had were washed away by these tangible assurances the Lord would take care of Irving Bible Church. Her words stung because I didn't want to leave with anyone thinking anything but the best. But that's unrealistic. I've learned that when people lose a pastor, they often say things they later regret. I refused to let those words cloud the four great years of ministry in Irving.

This is a good place to note that if you move when God has led you to move—you didn't delay too long—*parting should be a sorrow for everyone.* When a relationship is good, parting sorrow indicates that you have left on good terms. You don't feel relief because you're running away from responsibilities. The people you leave don't sigh with relief that you're gone. When the mourning of separation has passed, sweet memories fill the place

> When the mourning of separation has passed, sweet memories fill the place grief once occupied.

grief once occupied. In the meantime, endure the awkwardness and allow unpleasantness to exist as you help those left behind to grieve.

I share all of this to help anyone who reads these words. These experiences are part of the journey that enables you to be a better communicator. Saying it well stems from handling the transitions of life well—those difficult times when you must leave where you no longer belong—even when the circumstances seem very favorable where you are—to venture out to a place God will show you.

Camelot

From our very first days in Fullerton, ministry was a dream come true. By the time I arrived, the entire staff had stepped aside so I could begin with a clean slate. I begged a couple of them to stay, including Buck Buchanan (who later returned to join our staff). But they insisted that I should select my own staff and build a cohesive team from the ground up. I think their unselfish decision and their wise counsel set the stage for something truly remarkable.

That first Sunday, attendance jumped dramatically. I believed most of the visitors were simply curious tire kickers, there for a Sunday, then off to another church. But the second Sunday, the sanctuary filled almost to capacity. Before long, we had to add a second morning service. That merely proved the church had all the working parts in place, they just needed what I had to offer to make the machinery work. Music, education, outreach... you name it, the programs sprang to life when more and more people started coming. Furthermore, the church understood my strengths and weaknesses. They encouraged my closing the door to my study during certain hours of the day. They never complained about my being too bookish or overly studious. They didn't try to micromanage my preaching. They understood that Cynthia was a

> They understood that Cynthia was a mother to small children, not an assistant pastor who works for free.

mother to small children, not an assistant pastor who works for free. They trusted me to hand-pick my staff, which gave me the freedom to assemble a tight knit, cohesive team of individuals, not only qualified for their roles but compatible with one another. We were off and running... and my preaching took on new dimensions of effectiveness. I felt free! Free to be me, free to dig into God's Word, free to try new things and to speak with greater authority. *I loved it!*

No one can argue with the results. The impact we had as a church on the Fullerton area was dramatic. The lay leadership, the pastoral staff, the congregation, and their senior pastor moved as one. The camaraderie among the pastors made going to the church a joy. My twenty-three years at the Evangelical Free Church of Fullerton felt like a touch of Camelot. We began our broadcast ministry, and my publishing ministry while there. Ministers spend their entire careers hoping to find a winning combination like we enjoyed and few ever find it. Trust me, we had our challenges and more than a few major setbacks, but our forward momentum couldn't be stopped. God's hand was clearly on it all. Our satisfaction and feeling of fulfillment knew no bounds! Nevertheless...

When to Let a Good Thing Go

Every summer, I took the entire month of August away from the pulpit. We arranged for guests to fill in and I used that time for relaxation and refreshment. Some of that time I would take off completely as vacation. I often used those weeks to write or, occasionally, to speak at conferences. And I allowed the freedom from my preaching responsibilities to think about the coming year. Every summer, by the end of August, I had a

> Every summer, I took the entire month of August away from the pulpit.

fairly clear vision for the coming year: our direction, the primary emphasis for the staff, our guiding theme, specific objectives for each department. That always became the centerpiece of our fall leaders' retreat and the pastoral team would run with it. As the summer of 1993 came to a close, however, I could not put a vision together. Normally, I could see the coming year as clearly as I could remember yesterday. But, with the end of summer approaching, I honestly had nothing on my heart. It felt strange.

Around that same time, I received a call from Jack Turpin, Chairman of the Dallas Seminary Board, and Dr. Don Campbell, at that time the president of the school. By that time, I had served on the DTS board for several years, so it wasn't unusual to get a call from either of them...but both? They asked me if I would let them put my name on the short list for the next president.

I said, "President of what?"

"President of Dallas Theological Seminary, of course."

After what felt like a long silence, I said, "Are you two guys in the back office? Is this a phony call?" But they didn't laugh. (I learned later they didn't laugh much back then at the seminary.) The idea of a practical joke wouldn't even cross their minds.

> "President of Dallas Theological Seminary, of course."

"Chuck, this is no joke. We really want you to give this serious consideration."

I replied, "I don't have to think long. No, I'm not your guy. I'm not qualified to lead a bunch of academicians."

After we concluded our conversation, I just sat there limp in stunned silence. I couldn't believe what had just happened. And my mind retraced the path that had led me to Fullerton. While Waltham wasn't a mistake—I made a good decision with the information I had at hand—I didn't want to repeat the experience. My move to Irving made good sense, but just four years later, I found myself driving to Fullerton, a move that could have been as ill fated as going to New England. Many of our Texas friends warned us, "You're gonna lose your family when you go to California." They talked of gangs and made jokes about California being "the granola state," full of fruits and nuts. That scared us. And, out of nowhere, came the memory of those parting words: "The Lord gets blamed for a lot of things He has nothing to do with."

That afternoon, I told Cynthia about the call and what the two men had asked of me.

She said, in a matter-of-fact tone, "Sounds like a good idea to me."

I looked at her incredulously. "What's wrong with you?"

"There's nothing wrong with me. What's wrong with *you*? Why'd you say no so quickly?"

"Because I'm not going to do that. That's not who I am. You don't understand."

"I *do* understand," she replied. "They need you."

"Honey...now you're a little enamored."

She said with an affectionate chuckle, "I'm not at all enamored of you. It's just that I know them, and I know you, and I know you could do things that others can't do."

"But I'm not a scholar," I protested.

"They don't want a scholar. They know who they're calling."

I said, "I'm not talking to you anymore! You're not helping. I need you to help me say no!" I walked out.

Looking back on that conversation, I now understand that Cynthia had a unique perspective. Over the past twenty-three years, she had watched me become who I was. She knew that the man I had become would have something valuable to contribute

"They don't want a scholar. They know who they're calling."

that a true academician did not. And, during several of our visits to Dallas for board meetings, we used to joke about "bringing the school into the twentieth century" sometime before that century closed. I had remarked several times that the place could use some fresh ideas. But I thought I could encourage progress as a board member, and I was too intimidated to think about the demands of the presidency.

I later told Cynthia, "I'm not going. So, you can just put that little thought right out of your mind." And that effectively shut down the conversation. At least until the two men called again. Jack and Don asked if I had given it any more thought. I told them I had, but that the answer was still no. So, they asked if I would serve on the search committee. I gladly accepted the invitation, thinking it would be a good opportunity to serve the school and let the board know I was a team player. In the meantime, I continued to struggle with a vision for the Fullerton church the coming year. As much as I looked forward to the end of summer and getting back into the rhythms of church life, the future lay shrouded in a thick fog. Zero visibility. All of that troubled me deeply.

Paul Sailhamer, our senior associate pastor, called me, saying, "Hey, Chuck, we're getting ready to plan our retreat; we need to get your vision for the upcoming year and I haven't heard anything from you."

Trying to conceal my embarrassment, I said, "I don't have a vision for the new year."

Paul pressed me further. "We're gonna need that in a week or so for our pastor's retreat."

"I know when it is! I know the schedule. I plan these sessions!"

"Then you gotta have a vision!"

I said, "Paul, I can't just whip one up for the sake of a schedule. A lame vision

> "Then you gotta have a vision!"

won't do any of us any good." And we had a few words, which was a little uncommon. We occasionally butted heads without losing mutual respect. It made for some honest exchanges at times, and I accepted the trade-off for the sake of honest communication.

He paused for a few moments and then probed deeper, "What's going on?"

I said, flatly, "Nothing." Perhaps too flatly. But there really was nothing going on. I felt affirmed by the phone call from Dallas, but I had never changed my plans to remain a pastor in Fullerton and I had put the issue out of my mind.

"Why don't I believe you?" he asked in the way only close friends can. "Something's eating at you. What is it?"

Paul knew me too well. He never failed to shoot straight with me, which is one of the reasons I love the man as I do. We have remained close friends to this day. In those few moments, he knew me better than I knew myself. Denial can be like that. I had rejected the notion of being a seminary president, I refused to talk about it further with Cynthia, I put the whole matter behind me, and I tried to reset my mind to leading the church. But I have to admit, a subtle, nagging, persistent question buzzed in my ear like a hungry mosquito at night: *What if?*

In time, I could no longer ignore the question I had so desperately tried to dismiss. You have to understand the weight of leading that seminary. This was like asking someone who had never sailed to take command of a seventy-five-foot sloop. The exhilaration of commanding that magnificent yet complicated ship could, very likely, end with the sails underwater and drowning the entire crew. I was content with the honor of having been asked. In my mind, taking that position could only confirm for everyone else what I already knew: I hadn't the

> I could no longer ignore the question I had so desperately tried to dismiss.

slightest clue about how to be a seminary president. But something happened that I could not dismiss. As one of the first steps in the search process, the committee sent out a questionnaire to students, faculty, and alumni. To my amazement, virtually every list returned with my name at or near the top. When it was revealed to the chair of the search committee and then to me, my stomach churned.

I said to the chairman, "I need to resign from the search committee." I returned home early, recognizing the need for reliable advice and protracted soul-searching prayer. I didn't feel comfortable talking to anyone on the church staff yet about this because I still felt the chances of my leaving were infinitesimal. It didn't make sense to upset anyone unnecessarily, and I didn't want to disrupt the harmony we had enjoyed or the comfortable rhythm we had developed. We were incredibly close. When I breathed in, they breathed out. I sang melody; they sang harmony. I gave a theme; they ran with it. I preached on Sunday; they made that church run like a finely tuned sports car. So, I spoke to a few of our leaders at Insight for Living. My reason for sharing with them was because it would involve our moving everyone in that ministry to Texas, whereas the church staff would not be leaving. It made sense to me at the time to speak only with them.

Nevertheless, the word leaked.

Don't be fooled. Confidentiality is rare. I can find purity among people much easier than discretion. That breech of confidence began an extremely difficult time for us and the people we loved when all I wanted to do was explore the possibility with the very sincere hope of putting it to rest. Admittedly, I should have taken those closest to me into my confidence, but I didn't... and I now regret that.

Eventually, I invited eight or nine people I highly respected, people from all over the country to come to our home to discuss this decision I was facing. I also included our children at this meeting. I told all of them my honest feelings ... that I didn't want the position, but I needed wise and objective counsel because I couldn't get it out of my mind. I wanted their unfiltered, unedited input. By the end of the evening, they stood in unanimous agreement: I should let the candidating process go forward with my name included. My knees buckled as we said good-bye.

By the time I finally accepted the search committee's decision to call me as their president, I knew the rumor mill had most likely informed some in the church. But before I made my official announcement, I met with my closest circle of men on the church staff to inform them of my decision. They were disappointed that I would go through the entire decision-making process, even to the point of asking for input from a broad spectrum of other friends without including at least one or two of them. How I went about my deliberations caused them to question our closeness. In retrospect, I can see why they felt that way. Finding out via the grapevine rather than straight from me didn't sit well, which upon looking back is understandable. Probably like learning about your best friend's wedding from the newspaper. But what was done was done. I was leaving and they were willing to accept it, but it wasn't easy.

> How I went about my deliberations caused them to question our closeness.

Bottom line: no one wanted to see our Camelot come to an end. Certainly, no one less than I.

In the end, our gracious congregation celebrated my decision with many tears, which Cynthia and I shed with them. My Sunday morning announcement that I had accepted the honor of becoming the president of Dallas Theological Seminary received a standing ovation. Our church family, along with our Insight for Living staff, supported our decision and unexpected adventure.

The Continuing Journey

As we continue our journey through life, we carry with us a fantasy that the next place will be our final destination, that we can some-day discard our tents for a permanent dwelling. We're unconsciously driven from one place to the next by the prospect of finding our own Camelot, the perfect location with stimulating work, harmonious people, abundant provisions, long life, and glorious success. Such a place does, indeed, exist...but not on earth. I know this for a fact because, up to that point in my life, I had found the nearest thing to Camelot a pastor could hope for, yet I was discerning enough to know that as long as we remain this side of heaven, Camelot is, at best, only a season. Trying to preserve the ideal is no less futile or pathetic than trying to delay autumn.

> We're unconsciously driven from one place to the next by the prospect of finding our own Camelot.

Leaving a good thing is hard. Going toward the unknown requires trust in a sovereign God who leads you there. It demands sacrifice, a willingness to accept uncertainty, loss of position, mis-understanding among a few friends, and outright hardship at times. The heights to which our ministry climbed came at the great cost of having that much further to descend when the time came for me to move on. In fact, a purely human perspective would regard the move from Fullerton to Dallas as the epitome of foolishness. A critic could have pointed to the next couple of years as proof that I had made a terrible mistake. I left the near-ideal and exciting minis-try of our church for the unfamiliar and sometimes stoic culture of academia. I left the pleasant weather of California for the searing summers, bleak winters, and turbulent skies of Texas. I left a home filled with twenty-three years of our fondest memories, where all four of our children grew to adulthood, to live in an apartment over the garage of a board member's house for the next two years. Moving Insight for Living from Anaheim to Plano was also a lengthy, monumental, and financially stretching undertaking that amounted to starting over virtually from scratch. During that time, Cynthia and I had to spend many of our weeks apart. None of our family members moved with us. Loneliness was our frequent companion. And, most difficult of all, I was a pastor without a church... a shepherd without a flock.

But make no mistake, in terms of ministry, I was exactly where God wanted me. From the very beginning of my time at Dallas Seminary, I loved what I was doing. I was stretched and challenged. What I began to accomplish gave me deep satisfaction and my colleagues at the school gave their enthusiastic support to the changes I implemented. Ultimately, I realized that I had, indeed, made the correct decision. Those first two years, however, became a private crucible, a time of personal refining that could have happened only in the loneliness of that little garage apartment, with Camelot fading in the mists of memory and Cynthia almost fifteen hundred miles away during most of that time, struggling with all the challenges of a worldwide broadcast ministry in transition. What a heartrending journey.

Continuing Education

I tell you the story of my journey hoping you will see your journey more clearly. Who you are and who you're becoming is a product of this leaving-going cycle. God crafts the character of a person using his or her experiences as tools for shaping. He

> Who you are and who you're becoming is a product of this leaving-going cycle.

will do the work regardless, but He invites us to take part in our own shaping. Our responsibility calls for us to be where we should be, and to do what we should be doing. If we neglect this duty, we reject God's design for our lives and we miss His best as we embrace mediocrity. If we, instead, follow the path God has called us to walk, we not only live a life worth living, we have something profound to say that others cannot afford to ignore. I firmly believe that learning to "say it well" is directly linked to going where He sends, to staying where you're supposed to be, and to be doing what He has charged you to do.

As I stated from the beginning, I have no shortcuts to offer. I can, however, offer a few tips from one traveler to another.

Those who "say it well" talk about the past only as a means of charting the future.

A "has-been" is someone who looks in the rearview mirror to see his best days. Has-beens receive lots of invitations to speak, but find few opportunities to return. That's because people who have chosen to disengage from their own journey in order make their living as professional speakers soon run out of things to say. They have interesting stories of past struggles and they offer helpful insights gained from hands-on experience, but, as time passes, the relevance of their message fades. Moreover, audiences don't care about the past nearly as much as they desire wisdom and need insight in facing the future.

> *Those who "say it well" savor sweet memories of past successes, but they see their best days lying somewhere in the future.*

If you want to entertain a crowd, reminisce about the past. If you want to *impact* an audience, use past experiences to chart a course for the kind of future we all want to share. If you do that well, they will then determine what part of that future they can help to shape.

Those who "say it well" savor sweet

memories of past successes, but they see their best days lying some-where in the future.

They continue the leaving-going process, not because discontent drives them, but because they understand that life is a journey...to stop moving is to stop living. In all but one of the moves I made, I left perfectly good situations because I could not deny the leading of God to pursue my calling, to fulfill my purpose, in some other place. Consequently, I have stories to tell and insights to share that will, hopefully, inspire others to continue their own journeys and then equip them for the challenges they'll face. If you want to be an effective communicator, the same will be true of you.

Those who "say it well" got where they are because they came from somewhere else.

Invariably, that "somewhere else" included dark passages through sleepless nights. We tend to judge great lives of the past in the same way we might view a mountain range from the foot-hills. From our viewpoint on a low plain, the hero's towering peaks command our respect while his smaller summits and dark valleys remain hidden from view. Moses bravely identified with his Hebrew brothers while living in Pharaoh's courts and later delivered them from bondage, but few remember that it was his hotheaded murder of an Egyptian that sent him into his forty-year exile. And his anger dogged the Israelites' steps all the way from Egypt to the Prom-ised Land. We also tend to forget that David passed through many "valleys of the shadow of death" between his boyhood pastures and the mountaintop palace of his later years. Each of these people who said it well whenever they spoke left a profoundly impactful body of work, created not at the end of pristine and pampered lives, but compiled throughout arduous and challenging journeys.

Perhaps a few examples closer to home will help to illustrate my point. We tend to forget that between the log cabin of Abraham Lin-coln's birth and the heroic presidency that saved our nation, he lost nearly every political race he entered and struggled with depression throughout most of his life.

Charles Spurgeon rose to incredible fame by the age of twenty-two and is still known today as "the prince of preachers," yet he often fell into periods of dark depression. The press and his peers castigated him continually for his style of preaching as "deceptive," likened his ministry to flypaper, and called his church a "chamber of horrors." History has judged him heroic, an unparalleled communicator, but leaders from all walks of Christendom attacked his preaching as dangerous.

Few recall that soon after leading Great Britain through her darkest hours of World War II, Winston Churchill—a fellow stutterer, by the way—was voted out of office shortly after Nazi Germany's defeat. He led the opposition for several years until regaining office in 1951, all the while battling his own "black dog" of depression. All of that enhances his message.

My point, of course, is this: those who "say it well" don't learn to do that overnight; they go where they are called to go, do what their life purpose demands of them, communicate authentically out of their long journey and deep devotion, and God gives significance to their words to change their worlds—our history.

Your Journey

Are you where you're supposed to be? Are you doing what you're supposed to be doing? Or have you remained too long in a place, a position, a vocation, or a set of circumstances when God is calling you to make a change? I'm not suggesting you leave a good situation just to make a change, merely to shake things up a bit. Nor do I advocate running from difficulties. I merely hope to encourage you to release your tight grip on the status quo and to remain sensitive to the telltale signs of God's leading:

- Unexplained restlessness despite good circumstances
- An opportunity to exercise trust in God in following a certain course of action
- The encouragement of wise, impartial friends to accept a challenge
- A realization that your current role or circumstance doesn't fit you and it never will
- Internal turmoil over your present course
- Lack of excitement and enthusiasm over remaining where you are

None of these subjective feelings, taken alone, indicates you should leave where you are or stop what you're doing. They merely warrant careful consideration. Like a tap on the shoulder, they should prompt you to pause and turn around to see what might need your attention. Because, if you're not where you belong and you're not doing what you should be doing, you will find it increasingly more difficult to stand before others and say what must be said... and "say it well."

CHAPTER FOUR

Digging

Preaching that costs nothing accomplishes nothing. If the study is
a lounge, the pulpit will be an impertinence.

—*John Henry Jowett*[5]

I'm not a genius; I'm a drudge.

I have seen some truly gifted communicators—people with a genius-level ability to move audiences with their words—but I am not one of them. I earned top marks in school by training my memory muscle through constant repetition, unlike some classmates who could read a chapter once, recite it back to you almost verbatim, and never lose it. Not me. Some of my fellow students absorbed Greek and Hebrew like parched sponges. Not me. I have an affinity for those languages, but I still had to spend hours memorizing vocabulary, and verb charts, and paradigms. If I am mistaken for a genius, it's because the casual observer has merely seen the results of hard work. Genuine geniuses can accomplish great things with less effort because their remarkable intellect gives them certain advantages over the rest of us. If I, on the other hand, accomplish anything worthwhile, it's because I'm dogged and disciplined; I stay at it until I get it right.

The hard work that yielded good grades in school also keeps me going in the pulpit. Whatever I may lack in oratory brilliance I make up for in diligence. If what I do can be called a "success," then there's hope for anyone who wants to "say it well." Only a few qualify as a genius. Even fewer truly possess a natural gift of speech. But anyone can become an effective public speaker if he or she wants to work hard. Any man called to pulpit ministry can become an effective preacher with concentrated effort. It takes "digging."

A truly impactful sermon—in fact, any effective speech—begins with good research. That's what prompted me to find a good seminary once I discovered my calling. I didn't go to school to learn how to preach; I went to seminary to have something to say. The professors at Dallas Seminary taught me sound doctrine, but they didn't stop there. They handed me a shovel and taught me how to dig into God's Word on my own to find answers to the problems that my congregation and I would inevitably face.

I like the term "digging" for a couple of reasons. First, when beginning to build anything worthwhile, breaking ground is the first step. Every construction project begins with a hole in the dirt. Skyscrapers rise from huge pits dug deep enough to find bedrock. Homes rest on piers sunk into the ground all the way down to blue rock or upon slabs of concrete poured in trenches dug beneath the frost line. Similarly, an impactful sermon requires a solid foundation of truth, or it will crumble under its own weight. The same can be said of an effective speech. Anything you say must be built upon truth or your words will have no lasting impact. That holds true whether you stand in the pulpit as a preacher of God's Word, or on the community platform as the voice of leadership, or in front of a sales team as a motivator, or behind a lectern as a

> An impactful sermon requires a solid foundation of truth, or it will crumble under its own weight.

teacher. The same applies to the CEO casting a vision for her company, or the politician leading his constituency, or the charity organizer rallying her donors, or the military commander preparing his troops. Anyone who stands before others to speak must stand upon truth.

Second, the term "digging" carries the connotation of labor, the kind of exhausting work that calls for a strong back and a willingness to get dirt under your fingernails. Some preachers have teams of researchers who gather, sort, and arrange information for them— everything from historical backgrounds, linguistic insights, commentary excerpts, even current-event clippings or human-interest stories for illustrations. For them, sermon preparation is merely a process of assimilating and assembling the data into a Sunday morning message. But I can't do that. I need to be down in the trench—as it were—digging all of that for myself. As I labor, I not only find truth to share, I am personally transformed by it. The truths that impact me and cause me to change are most likely the truths others need to hear as well.

Whatever your purpose for speaking—especially if you're preaching—I would urge you to do your own digging. The benefits far outweigh the effort.

All public speakers could learn a few lessons from preachers. The men who stand in pulpits regularly are a special breed among those who address gathered hearers. A public speaker may address audiences a hundred times or more in a year, yet prepare only a handful of speeches. A preacher, on the other hand, must build a compelling message (often several) from the ground up no less than once each week. Some who serve in certain churches are expected to stand and deliver *three times* each week—Sunday morning, Sunday night, and Wednesday evening—in addition to marrying,

> All public speakers could learn a few lessons from preachers.

baptizing, counseling, and leading members of the congregation! Consequently, the preacher must become a digging expert.

God, the Universe, and Various Subjects

While the demands on the preacher are relentless, he does enjoy a distinct advantage over other kinds of public speakers. It's a difference I feel whenever I speak somewhere other than the pulpit of Stonebriar Community Church. Week after week, preachers stand before a familiar audience. We have a routine and an established time for delivery. Exegetical expository preachers also have the advantage of a topic established for them by the biblical passages they preach. (More on that shortly.) But if I'm scheduled to deliver a keynote to an audience I do not know, at an event with a specific theme, I have a lot of creative thinking and digging to do.

> I typically ask the one who invites me two initial questions, which might lead to further probing.

I typically ask the one who invites me two initial questions, which might lead to further probing. First, I want to know how much time has been allotted to me and where my speech occurs in the program. What occurs before I speak and what happens afterward? This information will help me know how to introduce and conclude my message. I might deliver the same core speech at two different events but, depending upon the context, shape them differently. For example, if I'm addressing a group of Christian executives on a corporate retreat, after an afternoon of golf and a casual dinner, my introduction must acknowledge where they are emotionally and then transition them smoothly into my topic. That will look very different from a lunchtime plenary session at a trade conference, where my audience has just completed two or more breakout sessions that same morning.

Second, I ask the organizers what topics they think would interest the group or, even better, what needs the people have in common. Some are more helpful than others. I received a call from Goodwill Industries—too many years ago to remember exactly who called—asking me to address their group near downtown Dallas. I said, "Sure, I'd be glad to. How many are you?"

"Oh, roughly two hundred people from all segments of our operation."

"Good, that's helpful to know," I said. "Do you have any idea what might be a good topic?"

The person in charge casually replied, "Well, I guess you can speak on God, the universe, and various subjects."

With about thirty-five minutes to speak, my instincts told me I might have to narrow the scope of my speech just a tad, or I would slide into what my mentor and longtime friend, Howard Hendricks, calls "the slimy ooze of indefiniteness."

Every preacher and every public speaker, regardless of the situation, faces the same problem when given an allotment of time and free rein on any subject. On what do you speak and how much do you say? You don't want to make the rookie mistake of completing your forty-five minute talk in twenty minutes. And you *never* want to go past your allotted time by more than a couple of minutes. In our time-conscious culture, anything you say will be forgotten if you don't use your time wisely.

> You *never* want to go past your allotted time by more than a couple of minutes.

I heard about one plenary speaker at a pastor's conference who was given forty-five minutes to speak. One hour and ten minutes later, he concluded his final point and, with a great sigh of relief from the audience, began his conclusion. Too short a presentation is embarrassing; too long is just plain disrespectful. You offend the audience and you insult your host. Event planners know the audience, they know what the group has done throughout the day, and they know the audience's state of mind when they sit down to listen; so, planners have a good feel for how long a speech should run. Furthermore, event coordinators operate under intense time constraints put on them by the facilities staff. An extra fifteen minutes taken by you sets a domino effect in motion that causes problems for every subsequent activity—including other speakers!

Realistically, if you fail to use your allotted time wisely, no one will remember anything else.

So, choose a subject that addresses a need in your audience about which you are an expert and they are not. The meat of your presentation should then fit into *half* the time allotted to you. If you have forty-five minutes at the podium, you should be able to deliver the core information—that is, develop your key points—in roughly twenty-two minutes. That will give you eleven minutes to acknowledge and thank your host, establish a rapport with the audience, and hook them with a compelling introduction. It also leaves you eleven minutes to seal your message with a memorable, compelling conclusion.

Do the math for a twenty-minute speech, and the stakes get higher. Five minutes to greet, thank, and introduce. Ten minutes to expound. Five minutes to conclude.

My time estimates might appear disproportionate at first, but in my experience, taking adequate time for a stimulating introduction, allowing yourself and your audience time to settle in, gives the body of your presentation the best chance of being heard. And if you rush your concluding wrap-up, few will remember what you said. In this case, the old adage is true: less is more. If you only have a few minutes to speak, offer fewer points and make each one memorable.

Having defined the scope of your message—which points you can develop in half the time allotted for speaking—

In this case, the old adage is true: less is more.

you now have a good handle on the digging you must do.

Advice from the Pastor's Study

Before I get into the process of "digging," now is a good opportunity to pass along some other helpful perspectives from a preacher to all public speakers.

A sermon targets the heart of the listener to create a crisis of the will and then presses the individual for a decision, whether to place one's trust in Christ for salvation or to make a specific, substantive change to live out that earlier decision. A sermon that doesn't do that falls short of the mark. Preachers, therefore, must have specific application as their goal throughout every stage of preparation and delivery. While a speech doesn't have the same primary objective as a sermon, it nevertheless must seek to impact its audience. A speech that neglects to call for specific action or fails to inspire substantive, observable change is little more than lighthearted entertainment. While you must be interesting to keep your audience engaged, your communication must achieve a greater purpose: impacting those who gather to hear you. Never speak to a group without providing a truth to ponder, a principle to apply, or a decision to make.

Naturally, to impact an audience, you have to know something about them. You stand the best chance of presenting something meaningful when you know who has come to hear you and you let their needs guide your preparation. (I am never more nervous than when I prepare to address a group I do not know.) What information do they lack? What attitudes do they hold? Should you affirm and encourage their present behavior, or should you persuade them differently and then press for change? Is the crowd hostile or sympathetic? Are they stubborn, reluctant, willing, or eager to alter their present course? Will their culture help your communication or present obstacles to understanding?

Preachers become more effective as they grow more intimately involved with individuals in their congregations. Learn from their experience. Try to discover as much as you can about the people gathered to hear you. As you begin your research, consider these two questions:

> People don't have much patience for the obvious; they want insight.

First: *What information or insights can I share that the majority of my audience doesn't already have?* As I stated earlier, people don't have much patience for the obvious; they want insight. Ideally, your topic should align with your area of expertise, but that doesn't mean you have to be the smartest person in the room. I often address individuals whose intelligence dwarfs that of most people, including mine. Very often, they work in industries completely foreign to me. So, if I can't offer information they don't already possess, I look for a perspective they might not have.

For example, I was invited to address a group of publishers. I know very little about the inner workings of the publishing industry or the details of their business. Furthermore, I have never worked for a publishing house. So, rather than tell them something about their own field of expertise, I chose to speak on, "What an Author Really Needs from Publishers." The title alone grabbed their attention, and they, in turn, grabbed their pens and pads.

At the time of this writing, I am preparing to address a group brought together by the Christian Embassy, a close-knit team of Christians working on Capitol Hill, in the White House, at the

Pentagon, or among those in foreign diplomacy. These are politicians, flag officers, ambassadors, elected officials, and their spouses. Having addressed them many times over the years, I know most of them very well. I don't, however, know what they know. Therefore, I won't pretend to be an insider with advanced knowledge of their realm. But I know the Bible, and I know the challenges they face because they have been open and transparent over the years. So, I have prepared a series of four messages examining the life of Moses with special attention given to how God prepared him for his unique role in governmental leadership. I know ahead of time that the topic will connect well with their world.

To help make the next several chapters as practical and as helpful as possible, I'll use my notes from this series of messages. (Images of these pages, just as I have prepared them, appear in the appendix.) I will refer to them as I explain my particular methods.

Consider, also, a second question: *How do I want my audience to think differently and then respond after my sermon or speech?* The answer becomes your objective.

Ideally, you want to begin your preparation with the answers to these two questions in mind so your objective can guide the rest of your preparation. But that's not always possible. Very often, the process of research will help you identify the audience's specific need, which points to a specific objective. So, as soon as possible, write down an objective in a single compound sentence. Don't worry if it's vague at first. Throughout the process of digging, you will find yourself modifying and clarifying the objective.

> As soon as possible, write down an objective in a single compound sentence.

As you begin digging, never forget what day it is and what time it is. As a preacher, perpetually digging for the next sermon, I know precisely how long I have before Sunday morning demands *a polished message*. Not a rough draft. Not an outline. Not something I've run through a couple of times. But a whole message, complete with introduction, points, illustrations, corroboration, applications, and a conclusion. To guarantee I don't come up short on Saturday evening, I set milestones. (I'll describe my process in more detail later in this chapter.) I know by the day and time where I should be in my preparation. That means at a certain time, I must stop one phase of digging and move on to the next phase.

An effective sermon must involve both the heart and mind of the audience, and it must appeal to each appropriately. Sometimes, the people are willing to make needed changes and lack the required knowledge; in this case, feed their minds and go easy on their consciences. Other times, people have all the knowledge they need but remain unwilling to do what is right; that's when you must give passing reference to the information they know and speak with great passion to their hearts. Do each in proportion to the needs of the congregation and let your strategy guide your digging. Research is not only about gaining more or new information to convey, but choosing the *right* information to share with a view to communicate clearly and then encourage change.

When you're digging, avoid these four common mistakes:

• Don't load your sermon or speech with information *you* find thrilling. I love history, and, if I'm not careful, I can overwhelm a congregation with endless factoids that fascinate me but serve no other purpose. When I'm painting the cultural scene of the Crucifixion of Christ, they don't need to know the names and dates of all the Roman emperors from Caesar Augustus to Septimius Severus.

• Don't load your sermon or speech with research in order to prove you've done your homework or to establish yourself as an authority. Audiences have only a passing regard for great intelligence; they deeply appreciate speakers who make a personal connection. Never forget that people don't care how much you know until they know how much you care. Because information tends to get in the way of rapport building, use only as much data as necessary to be accurate and clear.

• Don't be a perfectionist. When establishing a point or making an argument, you might be tempted to tie up every loose end, anticipate every potential objection, or clarify every lingering question. If so, your sermon or speech will be tedious, bogged down in minutiae, which leaves listeners exhausted and, ironically, more confused. More facts and figures won't help.

• Don't lose yourself in the process of discovery. Learning is exciting and fun. It's one of the great benefits of preaching. But don't forget what day it is and what time it is. At some point, you have to stop learning and prepare to stand and deliver. Set a firm deadline, at which time you will begin putting your sermon together.

Digging the Foundation

Preachers have a saying: "Sunday comes every three days!" Whenever I quote it, fellow preachers invariably respond with a knowing laugh. A preacher may or may not be a gifted communicator, his week may have been quiet or hectic, he may have been spared the relentless pecking of details or he may have struggled to find more than thirty minutes of solitude, but it doesn't matter. Like a lumbering freight train, Sunday morning rolls toward him with steady, relentless inevitability. He must, therefore,

> Preachers have a saying: "Sunday comes every three days!"

choose either of two options: prepare to preach or prepare to get out of the way!

While some churches require the pastor to prepare three different messages each week—Sunday morning, Sunday evening, and a midweek service of some kind—our church takes a different approach. I share the burden of leadership with many other capable leaders and we don't hold Sunday evening and Wednesday evening services; so, I prepare one sermon each week, which I deliver twice on Sunday morning. In the past, I have preached as many as five times on a Sunday. Thankfully, those days are over!

While the relentless approach of Sunday morning can become the preacher's most pressing challenge each week, it has also become an effective schoolmaster. In roughly fifty years of pastoral ministry, I have prepared for no fewer than two thousand Sunday mornings (a conservative estimate). To survive, I developed a weekly routine for sermon preparation. Consequently, after so many preparation-preaching cycles, I can safely call myself an expert in one area: I'm a "digging expert."

Deciding what to say can present the public speaker with a difficult challenge. The first couple of speeches come fairly easily for most; we all have a few insightful lessons to teach after a few years in the school of hard knocks. If you have followed your calling and have dedicated yourself to preparing, you probably have several more good messages to share. But few people have more than a dozen solid speeches tucked in their brains. So, once those are spent, what's a preacher to do? Many spend the rest of their careers struggling to sound eloquent and authoritative without revealing they have very little more to say.

> But few people have more than a dozen solid speeches tucked in their brains.

The preacher dedicated to exegetical expositional, however, never has to wonder what he's going to say each Sunday. Preaching that is "exegetical" means the message is drawn out of the biblical text. Preaching is said to be "expository" when sermons explain the meaning, purpose, and import of a given Bible passage. And, of course, for a speech to be called a "sermon," it must create within each listener a crisis of the will that urges a specific response. The exegetical expository preacher's sermon won't revolve around a hot topic ripped from the headlines or a clever insight he gained through personal experience. Rather, he chooses a book of the Bible, divides it into manageable segments, and then preaches a sermon from each segment in order, from beginning to end. On any given Sunday, the passage itself provides the subject.

A preacher might also preach a series of messages around a particular subject, such as marriage or the family, a Bible personality, a specific doctrine or some prophetic theme. The preaching can be exegetical and expository if the sermons are based on a compilation of passages that speak to the topic at hand.

When I preach through a book of the Bible, I generally read the entire work as a whole and then break it down into manageable segments. I don't share this with anyone, because I invariably adjust the plan along the way. But this helps me get a sense of how many weeks it will require, including holidays and breaks, and it helps the rest of the staff (especially our pastor of worship and music) plan their activities.

With that in mind, here is a typical week for me.

Sunday Evening

I *love* Sundays. I never feel more fulfilled than when I'm in the pulpit, preaching a well-prepared sermon that pours from the overflow of my own personal digging and spiritual life that ultimately resonates within people in the congregation. I can't hit a home run every Sunday, but I rarely strike out anymore. And, when I walk to my car after the last service of the day, a place deep within my soul where anticipation and energy once surged becomes filled with tranquil satisfaction and gratitude to God for His grace in giving me the energy, the insights, and the ability to minister.

I never feel more fulfilled than when I'm in the pulpit.

I usually enjoy lunch with family and friends, and return home for a long afternoon nap (hopefully, in front of a football game). Later in the evening, I can't resist a peek at next Sunday's passage. I rarely do anything more than read it. Then, once it's in my head, it becomes the nucleus around which other thoughts later gather.

As I turn out the light at my bedside, I invariably think, *Six days between now and Sunday.*

Monday

I really should take all of Monday off to rest or take care of things around the house. But our church communication department needs an outline by Wednesday, so I need to have a sufficient grasp of the text and where it's leading by then. So, I'll devote some time during the day on Monday to reading the passage—initially, out loud in my study—and to drafting a very rough outline, which I'll refine later, of course. If the needs of the church staff didn't demand an outline by midweek, I wouldn't do this. It's not ideal for sermon preparation, but ours is not a perfect world. You gotta do what you gotta do.

I could, of course, adjust my method to begin research the previous week, but I find it difficult to research one sermon while completing another. If you can do that, I admire you and I highly recommend it, but I can't. After weighing the pros and cons, and after years of trial-and-error, I find that digging out one message at a time works best for me. Remember, I'm not a genius; I'm a drudge.

Initially, my digging seeks to understand the human author's purpose for writing. I want to know what prompted him to relate the narrative, write the letter, record the prophetic vision, or compose the poem. I'm not thinking about today. I'm not searching for an application. I'm trying to discover the need of the *original* audience. While the times change and the particulars of our circumstances are different, people remain the same. Therefore, discovering the needs of the ancient audience will reveal challenges confronting my contemporary audience; the principles God revealed in Scripture will apply just as perfectly today.

> I'm trying to discover the need of the *original* audience.

Tuesday

Tuesday is a big day for study. I begin with observation in the original language, initially without the aid of any references except a few favorite lexicons. I pay attention to key terms and take note of significant syntax. Some expositors parse every verb and diagram every sentence, but I don't. I reserve deep linguistic study for words and phrases that are unusual, intriguing, or otherwise important. For example, Matthew 1:16 states, "Jacob was the father of Joseph the husband of Mary, by whom Jesus was born, who is called the Messiah." I immediately noticed that the relative personal pronoun "whom" is singular and feminine in Greek, which doesn't come through clearly in English. Matthew carefully crafted that sentence to assert that Jesus was the biological son of Mary—and Mary, alone. I won't bore the congregation with unnecessary word studies and lessons on Greek syntax, but that's information I'll definitely include.

Computer software can be incredibly helpful in this stage of digging. Using thick reference volumes with tiny print to look up Greek or Hebrew terms can be exhausting for lengthy passages—not to mention tough on the ol' eyes. Then, parsing the verbs, declining the nouns, and analyzing the use of prepositions can easily consume half a day or more, even with a brief section of Scripture. The right Bible software, however, can accomplish the same task—and more—in just minutes. When using one of the best, a user simply points to an English word to see the original language term, its definition, pronunciation guide, and parsing or declination. Another click reveals all other occurrences of the Greek or Hebrew term in the Bible, or the term defined in any one of a dozen lexicons and dictionaries.

Good Bible software can also give easy access to background information on people, places, or things mentioned in the passage. I click on "Jacob" in the passage above, and I instantly see his entire family tree, a list of verses mentioning the patriarch, as well as links to entries in several different encyclopedias. If I click on a place name, I instantly see several different maps, including a present-day satellite image. How great is that?

After I have observed the passage thoroughly, I begin the work of interpretation. I want to know what the human author intended to communicate at that time and for what purpose. Over the years, I have invested money in my library, collecting a full spectrum of reference publications that allow me to understand the circumstances surrounding any given passage in the Bible. What a literary treasure it is! I want to know as much about the human author as possible: his influences, his perspective, even the circumstances and location of his writing. I'll examine the historical setting that prompted his work, including the needs of the original audience, their location, culture, influences, and circumstances. If the text includes figures of speech, metaphors, references to the Old Testament, or stories, I want to consider them from the perspective of their time and culture. Encyclopedias, dictionaries, history references, atlases, and commentaries can supply most of that information.

> Encyclopedias, dictionaries, history references, atlases, and commentaries can supply most of that information.

I also want to do the work of correlation, which examines how the passage fits within the context of the book itself, the Bible as a whole, and especially in light of other passages that speak to the same issues. Paul and John may have said different things about the same issue. Because they both wrote inerrant divine truth, I need to understand how their words correlate. Many of the Lord's experiences were described by three or more Gospel accounts; I want to see them all. Sometimes, one passage alludes to another; I study both. This adds depth as well as breadth. The discipline of checking cross-references is worth all the effort.

As I think about my audience and what I hope to accomplish with the sermon, three crucial elements begin to take shape in my mind: potential applications, a title, and an introduction. I make note of them as I go so I won't lose them, but I remain focused on studying the biblical text. Exegetical exposition calls for serious, lengthy study of the Text. Eventually, however, I feel compelled to work on those three elements, beginning with an introduction.

In the next chapter, I will discuss how to build the supporting structure of a message: title, introduction, body, and conclusion. In subsequent chapters, we'll flesh out the frame with illustrations, humor, and applications.

Wednesday

Almost without exception, the application has started taking shape sometime the day before. I haven't given much time to crafting the actual wording, but it's become increasingly clear in my mind, especially in the hours after I stopped digging. The routine experiences of life—chores, errands, dinner conversation, reading, my other duties at the church—have helped to gel the practical application of the passage. A title also has taken shape. I may have started working on the introduction on Tuesday, but I will devote most of Wednesday to crafting it very carefully. I already know where the sermon is going and I know which parts of the text I will highlight, so my opening becomes extremely important to me. It refines where I go with the message and clarifies how I'm going to move the congregation toward that destination. I usually have a full page of handwritten notes devoted to the introduction alone. Ultimately, I will memorize my opening line—no more than fifteen words—to give the sermon a strong start. I spend extra time getting that opening line just right.

I will complete the outline as it will appear in the worship folder for Sunday and send it to our communications team—the folks in charge of printing.

Thursday

I dig all day Thursday. I will spend most of it detailing the message. With the introduction written and the rough outline complete, it's now a matter of determining how much emphasis to give each point and how to explain some of the more technical aspects of the language or clarifying the theology. I want to share only the information that provides additional insight or makes the point clearer. I want to avoid anything pedantic if at all possible. Sometimes, however, you can't avoid it; you have to include a fact or a bit of technical information that's too crucial to omit. When I do, I always remember that those listening need to know why I'm highlighting something that technical.

> I want to share only the information that provides additional insight or makes the point clearer.

For example, a famously and frequently mistranslated verse appears near the end of Matthew's Gospel, correctly rendered by the NASB: "Go therefore and make disciples of all the nations, baptizing them in the name of the Father and the Son and the Holy Spirit" (Matt. 28:19). Some expositors with only a rudimentary understanding of Greek grammar have noticed that the verb for "go" in Greek is a participle, while "make" is a command. They then suggest the translation, "*While you are going*, therefore, make disciples of all the nations..."

In a sermon, I had to correct this increasingly common error by explaining a unique feature of advanced Greek grammar. The word "go" is—okay, hold on to your seat; this is exciting—"a participle of attendant circumstance."[6] Using a little humor, I then spent a *very* few minutes explaining the principle. In terms of application, this small technical point becomes important. Jesus didn't tell His followers to "make disciples" as they were going about their normal daily routines. As followers, we certainly should do that, but the Lord was emphatically intentional in this particular command. He told us first and foremost to "go," presumably somewhere other than where we are. Technical explanations such as that are always followed by a few very practical comments, where I apply certain truths related to my previous explanation.

Having written my introduction and knowing where I want to carry the audience, I then make a quick outline of the logical steps I want to take from beginning to end. Think of the introduction as a statement of where we are now and the application as the destination. I ask myself, *What information would I need to be convinced?*

and I place the answer to that in reason-

What information would I need to be convinced?

able order. I used to do this by hand as a separate step, but after so much practice, I now do this while typing out my full outline on my typewriter.

Yes, I prefer my IBM Selectric to a computer. You may laugh… but don't judge me! It was advanced for its time and the method still works for me. While I'm typing, I often talk through the message audibly so I can hear my tone, inflection, and cadence as I plan to say it on Sunday. Very often, hearing my own voice affects how I structure the message—where I build momentum, where I place illustrations, where I include planned pauses, even where I insert humor.

While I don't have a standard outline, I do follow a reasonably consistent order. (I will offer more detail later using notes from one of my sermons.) My introduction states a problem as experienced today, connects the problem to my audience, and then transitions to the Bible to find answers. I then describe the time, date, author, audience, and circumstances of the Bible passage to highlight similarities between our situation and that of the ancient audience. I highlight specific features in the Bible text that support one or more timeless principles. I call attention to other passages that provide additional clarity or insight. Before concluding, I turn timeless principles into practical, meaningful, actionable suggestions based on real-life challenges. The conclusion then challenges each individual to turn the suggestions into imperatives, depending upon his or her specific situation. (Since all of that is so crucial, I suggest you go back and read the paragraph again.)

Whereas the applications came to me earlier, I'll wait until I've crafted the message before putting the timeless principles into their final form and then listing several practical applications. I think of the applications in terms of how they relate to people's lives, starting with my own.

As I'm laying down the logical stepping-stones from beginning to end, I imagine which points need additional clarity through illustration. Again, that means I must know my audience. A room full of seminary students will have different needs from a Sunday morning congregation. A story that resonates with a group of single mothers would fall flat when addressing a men's group.

Again, that means I must know my audience.

Whereas Tuesday and Wednesday involve a lot of study time, I can tolerate interruptions fairly easily. Thursday, however, I really need uninterrupted time to put everything together and to prepare my notes. So I protect Thursdays more than any other day. By the end of Thursday, I usually have the sermon in near-complete form.

Friday

I devote Friday to other duties, but the sermon is never far from my mind. I mentally review it and let it steep. Occasionally, I'll move some things around or even type out a replacement page to refine a section. But the digging part of my work is minimal at this point.

Saturday

I make the passage and the sermon a matter of prayer much of the day. I also sit alone and read through my notes several times. I often read the passage of Scripture in a couple other versions. Sometimes, I'll come up with an even better introduction. If so, I type it up and place it in front of the old. I do keep the old introduction with my notes, however. It might be useful for another occasion.

While reading through the notes, I quietly talk out loud, which means I need solitude. I can't have anyone around, or my mind goes to him or her instead of my message. I'll pause occasionally and ask myself, "Is this clear? Does it make sense?" I put myself in the listener's place and wonder, *Will he or she get the point?* If I have doubts, I return to my study and rework that part. I have this constant drive to connect with my hearer. I never forget the folks who are uninitiated.

Sunday

I'm up early…really early…sometimes by 3:00 a.m. Time to preach! I resist the urge to make last-minute adjustments, although some are necessary. Because I don't have much opportunity to go through my notes again on Sunday morning, the second time I preach is usually better delivered than the first.

When it's all over, I file the notes in the order I preached them, keeping the illustrations with the notes. The downside is that I don't have ready access to the illustrations at another time because I don't take the time to make copies and keep them indexed. But when I preach the sermon again in another context, I have everything clipped together and I'm ready to roll.

Sunday, after lunch, I typically collapse in my recliner and sleep for several hours. The process of preaching leaves me absolutely drained. Satisfied, but completely wrung out.

Stuck in the Mud

Occasionally, in the process of digging, I get stuck. I don't know where the passage is taking me, or my research opens a can of worms, or I don't understand the human author's meaning, or I'm struggling to see how the passage relates to our experiences today—the ways to get stuck are myriad. Unfortunately, the clock keeps ticking and the pressure's on. I have a couple of strategies that may help, some more obvious than others.

First, remind yourself of your audience's needs. It all goes back to serving them. The mind has a marvelous way of making connections, especially when relaxed, and reviewing their needs in light of the information you have recently gained can help a lot. I often realize that the matter causing me trouble has no bearing on what the people need to hear. I'm not expected to answer every question about every detail. It's okay to sidestep troublesome issues as long as they don't become conspicuous on their own.

> Remind yourself of your audience's needs.

Second, examine the work of other expositors (or, in the case of a speech, other experts in your field). I use commentaries—usually a broad spectrum of theological perspectives—to see how other experts divided the Text into sections and to learn how they deal with issues of interpretation. For example, First John is notoriously difficult to outline. Unlike Paul, John didn't follow linear logic when writing this letter, so when preaching through that letter, I examined the work of many different scholars.

Third, examine parallel, cross-referenced, and related passages for insight. This often supplies information or perspectives that keep me moving forward. In the case of a speech, check the footnotes of the sources you have selected. This will broaden your scope research, which can trigger new insights.

Fourth, pray! (More on this in chapter 6.)

Fifth, take a break. Get up and leave your study for a while. I usually run an errand, think of what I'll prepare for supper (I do much of the cooking), get outside and engage in some exercise... and it's amazing! Return to the same books, the same stack of information, and the missing pieces of the puzzle fall into place almost immediately. Sometimes, the mind gets tired, but you don't feel physically fatigued. Give your mind some varied and different stimuli, and the results can be remarkable.

Broaden Your Horizons

I have made a lengthy case for preparation, the cultivation of deep knowledge in a specific discipline. I also advocate continuing education in one's realm of expertise, not only to stay current, but to keep in touch with other experts and their thoughts. Nevertheless, I have deliberately cultivated a broad range of interests in my personal reading. Of the books I read for my own pleasure, perhaps one in ten will be a Christian, nonfiction publication. I gravitate toward history and biographies, adventuresome tales, human-interest stories, accounts of survival and achievement, military information and stories, and anything sports related.

> I also advocate continuing education in one's realm of expertise.

Depth of understanding in one discipline is good, but those who "say it well" also have a wide field of vision. They are naturally curious people who crave knowledge and possess a broad familiarity in lots of different subjects. Moreover, effective communicators never lose touch with popular culture—entertainment, sports, current events. If, after the events of 9/11, a speaker didn't acknowledge the tragedy with at least some thoughtfulness, the audience would have thought, *This person is not in my world.* Having a broad range of knowledge, being well read in several areas, helps to build bridges to others who may have little awareness—or even little interest—in your realm of study.

Our goal is communication. We can't merely present facts and expect our audiences to care. We can't presume to exhort a group of listeners to accept our information and insights without first connecting with them. As communicators, we have a res-ponsibility to build a bridge from our world to theirs, cross that bridge to enter their experience, and then, through a sermon or speech, escort them into our realm of profi-ciency. We bridge our two worlds by learning what interests others and then sharing common knowledge.

Our goal is communication.

As you dig deeply, invest some energy in digging a broad founda-tion. Your audiences will not only thank you, they'll come back for more!

In the next chapter, I will explain how I structure a message based on the information gathered in research.

CHAPTER FIVE

Building

The first minutes on the pulpit are the most favorable, so do not waste them with generalities but confront the congregation straight off with the core of the matter.

—*Dietrich Bonhoeffer*[7]

Moses didn't look like Charlton Heston. In fact, by the time he stood before Pharaoh, two-thirds of his life had passed him by. Once a prince in the court of the most powerful kingdom on earth, he returned from exile a desert dweller, bearing the dust of forty years in pastoral desolation. His skin was dark and leathery, his face deeply furrowed by wind and sun, his white beard long and unkempt. He was a man with a criminal record, forced into the wilderness after falling from the heights of royal privilege. He was forgotten, obscure, broken, unfulfilled, confused, reluctant, guilty, and—by his own estimation—"slow of speech" (Exod. 4:10). Not the typical adjectives used to describe a leader. Nevertheless, this prince-turned-shepherd was the man God had selected to deliver His people, the man He prepared to stand before the world's most powerful monarch, the man who, in the declining years of his life, the Lord pressed into service against stubborn resistance.

This eighty-year-old sheepherder, back from the far side of nowhere, didn't try to impress Pharaoh or his court. I doubt he spoke with the defiant, basso voice of a Hollywood actor when he addressed the king. (Did I mention that he was a stutterer?) In fact, he most likely didn't speak all that much, choosing instead to relay his message through his brother, Aaron. Yet, he didn't cower or tremble. His time in the desert and his encounter with God had taught him to fear the Creator, not His creatures . . . to draw confidence from the power of the Almighty and not cower before the bravado of men. So, he obeyed the Lord and delivered the message he had been given to carry. Without pretense or affectation, Moses presented Pharaoh with words of divine truth: *Release the Israelites or face grave consequences from the one true God.*

The rest of his story is—as they say—history. Eventually, Pharaoh heeded the word of God. Moses led the Hebrew people out of Egypt and into the land God had promised Abraham and his descendants. Along the way, he established their cultural identity and wrote their constitution, as it were. His place in history as an exceptional government and spiritual leader (among other things, of course) is secure. Jews today call this founding father of Israel their greatest prophet.

Jews today call this founding father of Israel their greatest prophet.

When I received the invitation from the Christian Embassy to speak to Pentagon flag officers, members of Congress, and ambassadors, I felt certain Moses would make an excellent model for people serving in military or government positions. Moses began with a promising future his first forty years, but his personal flaws brought his career crashing down. He spent the next forty years in obscurity, tending sheep in Midian on the back side of the Sinai desert, undoubtedly feeling shelved. During those decades, God shaped his character. And when the time was right, Moses "the failure" became Moses "the deliverer." Who in Washington can't identify with that? When I presented this suggestion to the person organizing the Christian Embassy retreat, he enthusiastically affirmed my subject.

The program affords me four opportunities to speak: one brief introductory message on Friday evening after the attendees arrive—no more than twenty minutes—and then three forty-five-minute sessions. So, I will use the introductory message to set the broad context and preview the upcoming sessions. As the chapter you are now reading takes shape, I am preparing the four messages using notes I first prepared long ago (1975). The basic structure will remain the same—that's why I chose them—because the core principles fit the audience's needs perfectly. Consequently, how I exegeted the scriptural texts will work nicely as well.

After fifty years of digging, I have a good stockpile of Bible research and sermon material from which to draw, but I never really preach the identical message twice. Some people can do that, but I can't. It's been more than thirty-six years since I first preached the original sermons. My children were still in school, I had only been serving a California church four years, and—as if you hadn't noticed—our nation was a very different place. So, I can't deliver these messages the same way today. Nevertheless, having the original notes keeps me from having to start from scratch.

I still go through the same digging process when I use an old sermon, but now I'm digging through soft soil. It goes much faster. I ask the same two questions, but I don't have to think as long about the answers. I ask:

I still go through the same digging process when I use an old sermon, but now I'm digging through soft soil.

"What information or insights can I share that the majority of my audience doesn't already have?"

and

"How do I want my audience to think differently and then respond after my sermon or speech?"

As I began digging into the life of Moses—more than thirty-six years ago and again this week—I reexamined his times, culture, personality, circumstances, and experiences. Along the way, I jotted and doodled my thoughts by hand on a tablet, wadding up a dozen or more sheets in the process. I noted that Moses' 120-year lifespan can be divided into three 40-year segments. As I pondered the phases of his life and grazed through Exodus, I doodled and sketched, eventually creating a rough chart that gave my audience an overview of Moses' life.

Panorama of Moses' Life

The First Forty Years	The Second Forty Years	The Third Forty Years
Thinking he was somebody	Learning he was a nobody	Discovering what God can do with a nobody
Egypt	Desert	Hebrew People
1. Nursed at home, adopted	1. A father, shepherd, servant	1. Deliverance
2. Schooled, skilled	2. Alone, broken	2. The Law
3. Self-willed, impatient	3. Humble, obscure	3. The Tabernacle
4. Exiled from Egypt	4. Reluctant, obedient, useful to God	4. Wanderings
Exodus 1:1–2:15 Acts 7:20–29a	Exodus 2:16–7:6 Acts 7:29b–34	Exodus 7:7–40:38 Deuteronomy 34:5–12

Out of this exercise came a few ideas for titles. I often start with titles because they tend to capture the heart of a problem shared by both audiences, ancient and modern. As I continued to read the Scriptures, I considered the common problems shared by Moses and people in positions of power. Three titles emerged, which could be refined as I continue preparing.

Session 1: "God's Will, My Way"
Session 2: "Lessons Learned through Failure"
Session 3: "The Desert School of Self-Discovery"

Even before I began digging in preparation for the Christian Embassy retreat, I intended to focus on Moses' life *before* he achieved everything the world calls "success." My studies confirmed that choice and, by the end of my three main messages, I decided on an objective. I want the audience to see that Moses' real success was achieved in the *middle* forty years of his life, the so-called obscure years when he undoubtedly felt like a failure. The final forty years of his life merely reflected God's triumph over Moses' heart while attending the obscure University of Midian.

All of that led to my title for the series: *How God Prepares Us for the Future*. When I called later to confirm the title, the organizer said, "You couldn't have chosen a title more relevant to what's on everyone's minds than that one."

In this particular case, I don't have to build from the ground up. I have, as it were, a fine structure already in place. If the older sermon is a building, I will gut its interior and strip it down to metal and concrete, then build it back out using new, updated material. To continue the

> If the older sermon is a building, I will gut its interior and strip it down to metal and concrete, then build it back out using new, updated material.

metaphor, think of the basic structure of a message as the concrete foundation and the steel framework consisting of four fundamental components: title, introduction, body, and conclusion. Those elements tend to be timeless, so I simply need to add new illustrations (chapter 7) and targeted application (chapter 9) to suit the specific audience.

For now, let's concentrate on the first three fundamental components: title, introduction, and body.

Title

The title for a sermon or speech, just like for a book, can be crucial to its success. If people have a chance to see the title beforehand, it will either attract or repel them. Here are some examples of titles guaranteed to keep the audience small:

> "An Analysis of the Function of Greek Anarthrous Participles in Oblique Cases"
>
> "Abductive Logic in Theological Method: Its Role and Character"
>
> "Evolutionary Justification for Belief in Moral Realism"

These are actual titles for technical presentations intended for a meeting of theological scholars. I have spent enough time in the world of academia to understand the meanings of these terms, and the titles probably describe the content of the presentations very well, but they don't tell me *why* I should attend. Only those with a specific interest will attend, even though the information may be very useful to a wider audience. Unfortunately, these titles reflect the style of most theological conferences, which one colleague described as "a contest to create the longest title with the least number of words." With some creative adjustments, these present-ers might have created the opportunity to share information many people didn't know they needed.

Believe it or not, deeply technical presentations need not be bor-ing to be scholarly. Take this title, for example:

"Does God Have False Beliefs on Open Theism?"

I'm intrigued. What does he mean by God having "false beliefs?" Most likely, it's an ironic commentary on the fallacies of "Open Theism." The title is just provocative enough to make me want to hear his answers. That's because a good title—often, but not always—alludes to a problem people find difficult to overcome. The very fact that you're speaking implies that your message will offer solutions.

> That's because a good title—often, but not always—alludes to a problem people find difficult to overcome.

While we want to attract potential audiences with a good title, the content of the sermon has to deliver what was promised. Many years ago, while Cynthia and I attended a little church outside Houston, the pastor promised, "Two weeks from today, I'm going to speak on what the Bible says about T.V." Around that time, television sets had become cheap enough for almost anyone to afford, so virtually every home had one. The tech-nology was still new, so many began to wonder, *Should we allow television to enter our homes and, if so, what are the spiritual implications?* The nervous rustling in the congregation suggested it was a troubling question.

The next week, the pastor again announced, "Next Sunday evening, I'm going to address the question of what the Bible has to say about T.V. I'm giving serious thought to the subject and I think there are some things you need to hear." Our interest in his message intensified.

That Sunday morning, he again urged the congregation to hear what the Bible says about T.V., and that evening the little church was *packed*. Standing room only. They brought in extra chairs. Some had to sit in the choir loft. Others stood around the perimeter of the sanctuary. After the preliminaries and a great evening of singing, the pastor stood at the pulpit and the crowd fell silent.

"Tonight, I'm going to speak on what the Bible says about T.V." Long pause. "Total victory." He then brought a message on living the victorious Christian life. But before he hit the transition from the introduction to the main body of his message, people started filing out. His clever yet deceptive idea had insulted those who had given him the gift of their time. Many never returned.

Don't play games with your audience. They resent being misled, so deliver what you promise in the title.

> Don't play games with your audience.

A good title also sets the tone for the sermon. The title should, in about seven words or less, prepare the listener for what he or she is going to hear. Is the message lighthearted? Gravely serious? Do you plan to target the congregation's conscience, or will you offer practical, encouraging instruction? The title should reflect the mood of the sermon and anticipate the response you hope to inspire.

For example, I preached on Samson's struggles with self-control. I planned to convey some serious warnings, but chose to keep the mood from becoming too heavy. So, I titled it "Samson: A He-Man with a She-Weakness." (You know you have a good title when others want to use it.) My use of humor in the title helped the warnings feel less threatening, which is a good approach if you don't know your audience very well or if they are unfamiliar with you.

On another occasion, I wanted to discuss David's sin with Bathsheba, highlighting similar points, but driven home with a decidedly more grave approach. Humor would not have set the right tone.

I titled it "Autopsy of a Moral Fall." I almost went with "Postmortem of a Moral Fall," but I felt the connotation of finality and hopelessness was too strong. "Autopsy" carries the nuance of scientific examination, which was my approach. Any term involving "mortem" bears the heavy gloom of death. I wanted to offer warnings without suggesting there's no hope for those who have suffered a particularly shameful fall. God's grace offers life after sin.

Haddon Robinson, on the other hand, used it very effectively for his sermon, "Judas Iscariot: Postmortem of a Suicide." Perfect. The warning is clear. Judas is a hopeless case. He protected his sin by leading a double life, and rather than seek forgiveness from God, he took his own life. The implied warning is clear: "Don't go down the path Judas traveled."

When I preached a sermon series on death, I called it *The Path of the Pale Horse,* an allusion to John's apocalyptic image in Revelation. In fact, one of my very first publications was a mimeographed booklet taken from that study on death.

In choosing a title, be careful not to overpromise and underdeliver. There have been times my title was so strong it overshadowed the message. That prompted me to go back, overhaul the introduction, refine my points, select relevant illustrations, craft a stronger closing... and choose a better title! Sometimes, a great title can help you improve the message. Whatever happens, don't let the title be the best part of your message!

> Whatever happens, don't let the title be the best part of your message!

Introduction

Once I have the basic idea for a sermon or speech, I begin to think about how I want to launch the introduction. Many would counsel you to outline the body of your talk and then decide how to introduce the information, but I can't do that. With all of the information gathered from my digging swirling around in my head, it helps me to think in sequence: title, introduction, body, conclusion. I can begin writing my introduction first because I have a good idea of where I'm going, even though I may have to—and often do—go back to make adjustments.

The week before leaving for the retreat in Washington, I preached on Mark 10:32–45, which describes the Lord's final journey to Jerusalem. While the disciples enjoyed another routine trip to the temple, Jesus thought of His destiny, which carried Him inexorably toward the suffering that awaited Him there. The day after I had completed my initial digging for that message, I began to think about the introduction and "just happened" to read an article about Niagara Falls, where at the time thirty million gallons poured over the precipice each minute. Somewhere just upstream of that sheer drop is a sign indicating the point of no return. If you fall into the river beyond that point, you're going over the edge. This image tied in perfectly with that moment in Jesus' life. Somewhere in my introduction, I said, "He would walk into Jerusalem, but He wouldn't walk back out; His disciples would carry Him out." Obviously, I don't mean that literally, but it makes the point sufficiently clear. I wanted the congregation to feel the pull of Jesus' destiny drawing Him toward Jerusalem. It was a destiny He willingly chose, but it pulled Him nonetheless.

I have to be satisfied with my introduction, or I cannot move on to the rest of the message, as hard as I might try. I stay at it until I have something that prompts me to say internally, "That's it…I *like* that."

Then, once I have a good angle established by the introduction, I go back and craft a strong opening sentence that's short, if possible—ideally, less than fifteen words—and, most importantly, memorable. Once I have it down, I memorize it. For the brief introductory message that first evening, I'll begin, "God knows what He's doing." I will then quote the late Alan Redpath: "When God wants to do an impossible task, He takes an impossible man and crushes him."

I'll deliberately pause to let that statement sink in for a few seconds before continuing,

> *Dr. Redpath made that statement in chapel my first year at Dallas Seminary in 1959. I don't remember what he said after that, but those words have haunted my memory ever since. That's because I have found them to be true in my own life. And most of you, if you're honest enough to admit it, have found them to be true of yours. In fact, you may be—at this very moment—crushed. The dreams you have today may not be the dreams you began with. Reality may have dashed the dreams of your youth…*

For the message, "God's Will, My Way," I will open with "One of the greatest battles Christians face is doing God's will *God's way.*" I will amplify that statement: "Our problem is not doing God's will, but doing God's will God's way." I will then draw some examples from common experience to validate the statement and to pull the audience in. If my examples resonate well, I will see several in the audience literally lean forward. My goal is to see an expression on various faces that says, "You're describing me perfectly. Now tell me a better way to go."

For the message, "Lessons Learned through Failure," I will begin, "There are three common mistakes we make on our journey from earth to heaven." I'll state them next:

Once I have it down, I memorize it.

Running before we are sent.
Retreating after we have failed.
Resisting when we are called.

Again, I'll let that sink in for a few seconds. Hopefully, those statements will resonate so deeply the audience will nod in wistful agreement. Many will want to write it down, so it's often helpful to repeat such statements before beginning to unpack them.

Having stated the contemporary problem, I'm ready to transition the audience into the body of the message, the main points of which provide answers to difficult questions and solutions to vexing problems. Each point is either supported by authoritative knowledge or proven through sound reasoning. In the case of exegetical expository preaching, the Bible provides the supporting facts while carefully worded theology connects them to life.

Body

Most of my research can be described as very detailed observation. I have studied the biblical passage to discern the author's original intent for the ancient audience—his purpose for writing and the problem he attempted to correct—all the while thinking about how their circumstances relate to those of my contemporary audience. So, the digging I do really pays off here. The body of my message essentially retraces my steps in research, showing how the problem plaguing us today also afflicted the original audience. I want individuals in my audience to see their own struggles reflected in the

Text and to identify with the historical individuals in a poignantly personal way.

Making this connection is crucial. When your audience feels the pathos of the passage and relates to the humanity of the people involved, they will stay with you for the duration of the message. At the conclusion, if you have done this well, they will pay you the ultimate compliment of "making the Bible come alive" or "making the Scriptures relevant." Neither affirmation is correct, of course. The Bible *IS* alive. The Scriptures have *always* been, and always will be, relevant. What these newly energized listeners mean—and what you should hear—is, "You helped me *see* the relevance of this ancient Book."

> I want individuals in my audience to see their own struggles reflected in the Text and to identify with the historical individuals in a poignantly personal way.

One Sunday, at the end of a service, a mother approached me with her two daughters. The twenty-year-old hadn't been in church for years; the fourteen-year-old had shown little interest in the Bible. After the sermon, however, both told their mother, "We're in this church to stay, and we need to get our own Bibles." When they told me that, I thanked them and said, "So, the message made sense, then?"

"Made sense?" they laughed. "It was right where we live! I felt like you were telling my story."

At that point, I could have walked on a cloud. How encouraging! That's exactly what I hope to hear. My digging had paid off. My presentation hit the mark. My effort became the means by which God drew those two people to Himself. Frankly, that's what I *live* for! I have few greater joys than knowing I helped someone realize how helpful and how insightful God's Word really is!

My purpose in the body of the message is not to teach history, but to teach about life and the application of Scripture to living. If, in the process, people learn about geography, history, theology, or Greek grammar, great! But that's not my overriding purpose for including those details. I try not to exhaust the Text; otherwise, I risk exhausting the audience. If I include information about Idumea, Samaria, Capernaum, or Jericho, it's to make the context clearer. I dwell on grammar only to clarify the author's meaning. But I guard against becoming too tedious. Everything I say must serve the purpose of connecting life today to the passage at hand.

> I try not to exhaust the Text; otherwise, I risk exhausting the audience.

For the sake of time and clarity, I have to omit much of what I learn while digging. That can be painful because I want everyone to benefit from all that I discovered. But if I'm not careful, I can include unimportant or incidental information, force fitting nonessentials into the message. So, rather than unpack every term in every verse, giving the history and culture behind every person, place, or thing, I ask myself, "Does this congregation need this specific information to understand the author's meaning or to personally connect with the passage?" Answers will change depending upon the occasion. Facts that connect with a government worker might be irrelevant to a business executive. Details that enhance a keynote speech at a seminar wouldn't be appropriate for a funeral.

The unveiling of grammatical, historical, cultural, and theological information contained in a passage of Scriptures is what I call exegetical exposition, which has three primary objectives. First, *exegetical exposition removes barriers to understanding.* I look for terms or quirky idioms that need explanation. For example, to support his policy that people rendering service to the

> I look for terms or quirky idioms that need explanation.

church should be paid, Paul cites a principle from the Old Testament: "You shall not muzzle the ox while he is threshing" (1 Tim. 5:18, Deut. 25:4). Unless you're preaching somewhere in America's "breadbasket," very few in your audience have threshed grain, and I'm reasonably certain none of them used an ox to do it. So, this needs explanation for today's culture.

Another example: Jesus asks His disciples, "Are you able to drink the cup that I drink, or to be baptized with the baptism with which I am baptized?" (Mark 10:38). Cup? Baptism? What does He mean? The disciples didn't fully understand the Lord's questions, until after His resurrection. Exegetical exposition helps the audience understand the figurative use of "cup" and "baptism," and why the disciples remained clueless until later. While I'm typing out my notes, I'll include the words "cup" and "baptism" along with a couple of lines summarizing the explanation, or I'll indicate an illustration I've clipped to the pages of my notes (yes, I definitely preach using notes!).

Second, *exegetical exposition increases clarity.* John's Gospel records Jesus saying, in His last moments on the Cross, "It is finished" (John 19:30). The precise meaning doesn't change much in the way of doctrine, but how much better when we explain the cultural relevance of that phrase. John the apostle chose to quote Jesus using the Greek word *tetelestai*, an accounting term found on canceled loan documents, relieving a debtor of future payment. When the last payment had been made, the paper was stamped *tetelestai*, meaning "paid in full." If the lender wished to forgive the debt, he could stamp the document *tetelestai*, meaning "fulfilled" or "completed." With just a short explanation, the listener can see the Lords' declaration in high-definition color. Furthermore, it perfectly leads to an explanation of salvation as a gift of grace.

Third, *exegetical exposition helps the audience personally connect with the passage.* Without a little help, very few people identify with Moses. He's such a legendary figure of history it's easy to forget he was just a man. We have to pull the heroes of the Bible off their pedestals so others can learn from, and identify with, their failures and successes. Other times, we have to reveal the humanity of a villain to show that we're all just a hair's breadth from becoming just like him. Good exposition shows us what we can learn even from a man like Pharaoh.

As I prepare, I always keep the uninitiated in mind. I don't have to do much explanation for the serious student of the Scriptures. I don't preach to seminary professors, although some regularly attend our church. They might benefit from the application, but I don't have to explain the Lord's use of "cup" and "baptism" in this context. They already get it. The uninitiated, on the other hand, need more and more help as our society becomes increasingly more ignorant of the Bible. We can no longer afford to assume people know their Bibles.

> We can no longer afford to assume people know their Bibles.

Early in my ministry, people used to complain that I spent time explaining the obvious, but I *never* hear that today. Not long after my commentary on the Gospel of John was published, a reader stated in a review, "I had read the gospel of John before, using a study bible (NIV) but I never really knew who 'John' was, apparently. I always thought he was John the Baptist (goes to show what I know) so I was very confused at first then the author spoke of John following John the Baptist around."

Of course, the reader confused the two Johns. Why shouldn't he? Anyone not familiar with the Bible would follow the logic that there was only one John. I will admit that I was almost twenty years old before I discovered that John the Baptist wasn't a Southern Baptist! After all, my Southern Baptist teachers traced their tradition back to him and they did nothing to clarify my misunderstanding. Because of all that, I've formed the habit of calling him John the baptizer.

I once had a very bright man—a highly educated, top-performing professional—come up to me after a service to thank me for explaining that in John 3:16, the 3 indicates the chapter and 16 refers to the verse in the book called "John." "All my life," he said, "I've wondered what those numbers meant." He's not stupid; he's simply acknowledging his first-time discovery. Rather than laugh at him, I commended him. The Bible is a mystery to most people. It's often scary because they've heard all sorts of things, many untrue or distorted, and they feel unqualified even to read the Scriptures. They've heard that it's a best seller; they just don't know why. And they will remain in darkness until you and I exercise the privilege of explaining the Bible to them...and what a privilege it is!

As I deal with technical issues, I structure the body of the message with life in mind. I look for ways to highlight similarities between the ancient audience and the people sitting before me. That's where I really hit my stride. In the message "God's Will, My Way," I want to help the Washington insiders to see themselves reflected in Moses' early years. I will use the narrative flow of the biblical text to summarize his life from birth to age forty. He was adopted by Pharaoh's daughter and groomed for power. At some point, he apparently became aware of his destiny as the deliverer of Israel, but took matters into his own hands by killing an Egyptian and hiding him in the sand. To escape Pharaoh's wrath, he fled across the Sinai desert to take refuge among itinerant shepherds. All of a sudden, he found himself highly qualified to be completely useless.

In my notes, I highlight specific details, such as Josephus' comment that Pharaoh's daughter, after finding the infant Moses floating in the Nile, designed Moses for the throne, as the Pharaoh had no son (*Antiquities* II 9:7). I also use historical references to show that Moses had received the best education of the times. In addition to learning math, astronomy, medicine, philosophy, and art, he was trained in the strategies of war. I show from Stephen's speech in Acts 7 that Moses became a man of power and influence. His star had risen quickly and many came to see him as a man to admire and follow.

Exegetical exposition must have a connection with today's world. Otherwise, you're building up a storehouse of knowledge without helping the audience see why it's important or how to put that knowledge to work. While I will use Exodus for my presentations in Washington, we're not going to stay in Egypt all weekend long. We're going to learn enough about Egypt to discover that it wasn't very far removed from their own experiences, studying political science at Columbia University, or military strategy at West Point, or international law at Stanford. If I don't make this connection...ho-hum!

> Exegetical exposition must have a connection with today's world.

I hope everyone in that room leans forward as I describe the rise of Moses. I hope each individual thinks, *Wow, that's me. I graduated top of my hometown high school class, and I rose through the ranks of my Ivy League college, and I have a promising career among the most powerful people in the world.* I want them to see their lives reflected in Moses' early years because, in just a few moments, I'm going to describe his downfall and reveal what brought him to it. I want them to see themselves in Moses' sandals. I want them to breathe Egyptian air and to see the great Pyramids on the landscape of their minds.

As I draw the audience into the biblical passage, as the Bible story becomes their story, I will start to draw some timeless principles. Principles are not applications. Principles are statements of truth that apply to every person, in every culture, throughout all time. For

> Principles are not applications.

example, "Stealing is wrong." You can say that to a child in a toy store, or to a bank employee, or to a career car thief in a courtroom. You can travel back four thousand years and this truth will be just as true then as today.

As I draw this message to a close, I will land on this verse: "When Pharaoh heard of this matter, he tried to kill Moses. But Moses fled from the presence of Pharaoh and settled in the land of Midian, and he sat down by a well" (Exod. 2:15). Then, I'll offer two principles drawn from my observation of the passage in the body of this message:

1. When self-life has run its course, we settle in a desert.
2. When the self-life sits down, and gives up, the well of new life is near.

I will examine each principle to show how they operate today. I might give a few present-day examples of people like Moses, who started out thinking they were "somebody," pursuing their own glory, only to end up broken, obscure, disillusioned, and confused... in exactly the place God wants them. I'll take it a step further, asking them to probe their own experience. I'll ask young, up-and-coming leaders to examine their current path. I'll ask retired military officers to consider what God might do with their remaining years. (Moses was eighty! He was entering the last third of his life before becoming Israel's leading statesman.) I'll ask those wounded by a recent failure to reconsider the future God has planned for them. I'll remind everyone that Moses considered his exile proof positive that God had no more use for him... yet history has made him a hero.

Very often, I will use a portion of the principles in the introduction. Like a signpost, it teases the audience's curiosity while giving them a clue as to where we're going. I find that giving the audience a peek at the principles at the beginning also helps them see my points reflected in the Text as I later develop them. That way, by the end, they have proven the veracity of the principles for themselves. By the time I state the principles, the audience has already accepted them. I merely give succinct and memorable form to them.

Once I feel the audience has embraced the principles, I transition to the conclusion, in which I offer specific application to the principles and then challenge the audience to take action immediately. (I will discuss this in detail in chapter 9.)

> By the time I state the principles, the audience has already accepted them.

Teaching through Preaching

Another great feature of exegetical exposition is the opportunity to teach people how to study the Bible on their own. Homiletical exposition merely communicates the fruit of your work in the study. There are times for homiletical exposition. When your audience has no access to a Bible while they're listening, or when the audience is hostile to the Bible, or in circumstances that call for pastoral care, such as funerals, weddings, ordinations, and receptions. But when you have the opportunity to preach exegetically, do it! Don't leave your exegesis on the pieces of paper you throw away. Incorporate your digging process into your notes. People want to know where you found your answers and how you arrived at them. Moreover, they want to know how to find their own answers in the Scriptures. Show them...by example...as you preach. Explain, explain, explain. They will love it as long as you remain enthusiastic and keep it interesting.

> People want to know where you found your answers and how you arrived at them.

Encourage listeners to look at their own Bibles and follow along as you read. Call their attention to the details you discovered in your study. Don't hide your enthusiasm. When preaching from Exodus 3, you might say, "Notice the repetition of the expression, 'God of your fathers.' See verse 6? There it is in the singular, referring to Abraham. Look at verse 13, there it is again. A little further down in verse 15, there it is again. And yet again in verse 16. You think the Lord might be trying to make a point? Whenever you see something repeated, pay close attention! If it appears three times, really take note. Four times? That's a neon sign pointing to something crucial." Most folks I hang around with find those explanations very helpful. They truly love being taught!

"The Lord wanted Moses and the people of Israel to know that He had been their God long before they knew He existed, long before He gave them laws to obey, long before they even existed as a nation."

As I lead the audience to discover timeless truths in the pages of God's Word, I get to see discovery dawn in their faces. It's like a light goes on behind their eyes, and I *love* it when that happens! That can happen only with exegetical exposition. When you preach exegetically, you not only teach people how to study the Bible for themselves, you also remind them that God, speaking through the Scriptures, is their authority, *not you*. You have studied the Word, so that gives you authority to explain and clarify the passage, but the moral authority remains with the Lord. He—alone—is God. They need to know that, and the process of exegesis keeps you real. Some preachers want to leave the audience thinking, *Oh, wow, he's so good, I want to come back for more of this.* The best Bible expositors I know have a much different goal in mind. They want to send their audiences back into the world thinking, *This passage of the Bible is so intriguing, I'm going to do some digging myself.* Exegetical exposition at its best creates a hunger in others to know the mind of God,

Exegetical exposition at its best creates a hunger in others to know the mind of God.

and it gives them confidence to read and study His Word for themselves.

If you preach, be that kind of preacher. If you incorporate the Bible into your speeches, exposit the passage exegetically. Your audiences will thank you over and over again.

Advice for the Non-Preacher

While I am a preacher and my messages are lifted from the Bible, I want this book to be helpful to anyone wanting to "say it well." If you have the opportunity to speak to an audience, many of the principles of preaching still apply, even if your message isn't biblical. Once you have identified a problem experienced by your audience, and your digging has surfaced information or perspectives that address their need, the structure of your speech follows the same rationale as a sermon.

Craft a title that somehow reflects the audience's need and/or promises a solution. For example, the title of the series I will present at the Christian Embassy retreat, *How God Prepares Us for the Future*, touches on a problem all of them now face. In the week leading up to this particular retreat, lawmakers are deadlocked over the national budget—and increasing national debt—with a deadline looming just days away. If they don't come to an agreement, they risk shutting down government services. The future and its uncertainty are very much on their minds. Some are retired or in their final years of service, and many others struggle with uncertainty and hopelessness, wondering if they should continue serving in government.

Your introduction is your opportunity to connect the audience to the problem you hope to solve with the information in your speech. Make it personal. Remind them of the pain that an unsolved problem causes. If they have never experienced the problem, help them see it through another person's eyes. When you have drawn them into the problem, transition to the main points of your speech that offer solutions.

The body of your speech offers information that addresses the need, supported by verifiable facts, sound reasoning, and touches of humor. You might also think of your points as the stepping-stones of a path leading from where they are, intellectually, to the logical conclusion you hope to prove. Hopefully, by the end, the audience will have followed your journey to see the problem and solution as you do.

Having presented the information, offer specific actions individuals can take either to solve the problem or to join others in making a difference. Make the actions easy to accomplish. For example, if you're selling a product, make the product available on the spot. If that's not possible, provide order forms, or computer terminals, or response cards—whatever you can provide to make follow-through simple for the audience.

Make the actions easy to accomplish.

If you're implementing a company policy, offer a means for the audience to commit to the policy or take first steps toward implementation right away, preferably before leaving. Explanation leads to action. Those who are motivated by your presentation are ready to get involved. Help them do that.

Then, motivate the audience to action with a strong conclusion. Urge a decision so that your speech—the solutions you have suggested—can become reality.

In the end, whether preaching a sermon, selling a product, proposing new technology, defining different policies, or presenting innovative techniques, we want words transformed into action.

When Moses stood before Pharaoh, he wanted the words, "let the sons of Israel go out of [your] land" (Exod. 6:11) to become reality. He spoke in order to begin a procession of Israelites leaving slavery in Egypt. We speak to bring about other kinds of change. Problems solved and progress made. That's what makes a speech success-ful. That's what makes a sermon memorable. That's really what it means to "say it well."

CHAPTER SIX

Praying

> *[We must not] conceive of prayer as though it were an overcoming of God's reluctance, when it is, in fact, a laying hold of his highest willingness.*
>
> —*Richard Chenevix Trench* [8]

When all else fails, pray."

Not only bad advice, it's bad theology. However, it is all too often the theology we practice. We pray when all our efforts have come to nothing. We pray when all other alternatives have yielded no results, when failure appears inevitable. We pray when despair has smothered every smoldering ember of hope. Finally... after nothing else works, we pray. We pray not for mere supernatural intervention, but a deus ex machina reversal of fortune. And if we're honest, we most often resort to prayer to avoid reaping the harvest of seeds we have sown.

For speakers, the most common seeds are procrastination, dawdling, neglect, misplaced priorities, and sheer laziness. Their harvest: an approaching speaking engagement with nothing to say. For sure, preachers are no exception. We, too, struggle to overcome procrastination. We will even mollify our chaffed consciences with feeble reassurances that the needs of the congregation keep us from our studies. For some weeks, the excuse is more valid than others. Trust me; I know. I've baptized, married, and buried all in the same week. I've had crises under my own roof make sermon preparation virtually impossible. In fifty years of pulpit ministry, I have seen virtually every conceivable interruption to preparation known to preachers. Still, Sunday keeps coming. When the time comes for the pastor to step behind the pulpit, no one cares how hard a week he's had. That's not to say people lack compassion; they merely accept the same truth the preacher, himself, cannot ignore: preaching is like the main course at a banquet; when poorly prepared, the hungry are unsatisfied and disappointed.

> Preaching is like the main course at a banquet.

Not all preachers have major struggles with procrastination, however. Frankly, I rarely put off anything. I'm naturally given to duty and responsibility (it's called being driven!), so I am seldom tempted to avoid the discipline of digging each week. Instead, I—like many preachers—struggled to overcome another problem, a debilitating condition of the heart known as self-reliance. When I first began to shoulder the responsibility of preaching every Sunday, I was an eager young pastor up in Waltham, Massachusetts, full of pent-up energy and idealism. I bore no illusions about the difficulties of preaching every week, but I determined to meet the rigors of pastoral ministry with the same roll-up-your-sleeves work ethic I learned from my father and honed to a razor-sharp edge as a combat-ready marine.

As I understood prayer at that time, talking to God punctuated the end of human effort, either to bless it or to accomplish what could not be done otherwise. I thought (in this order), *I do my part while God does His part, and the job gets done.* I, therefore, prayed as either a matter of duty or for rescue when my own efforts proved inadequate. Fortunately, the Lord diverted my course, kept me from crashing, and, in the passing of many years, forever changed my understanding of prayer…along with my whole approach to life, preaching, ministry, and even marriage.

Independence

I was the youngest of three children born to parents whose lives had been shaped mainly by work. Hard, honest labor. They met and married during a difficult time in the United States, on the heels of the Great Depression. As giant walls of dust rolled over Texas, blown east from the Dust Bowl, fear of unemployment haunted every hardworking person in America. In 1934, one out of every four people couldn't find work, crops withered, banks failed, and families in every neighborhood risked foreclosure and homelessness. That's when I came along. Actually, I was a "mistake." I know this because my parents told me.

My father escaped unemployment, and, as the nation recovered, he thrived in the insurance business—in no small way due to his strong work ethic and positive mental attitude. Then, while he was driving to enjoy a few pre-Christmas days of vacation at my grandfather's bay cottage near Palacios, Texas, a startling announcement came over the radio in our new 1941 Ford. The Japanese had bombed Pearl Harbor; the United States had declared war on Japan; and on top of all that, it was announced that we would also enter the fight against Hitler in the carnage of Europe. My father immediately turned the car around and headed for home. "This is no time for a vacation," he said quietly as my mother began to weep. A short time afterward, he resigned his job selling insurance, and we moved from my sleepy little hometown of El Campo to Houston, where he began work in a defense factory in support of the war effort. Too old for military service, this was my dad's way of serving his country. He said it was the least he could do. He supplemented the lost income by working double shifts.

I learned from my father that hard work is an honor. I learned to love education because of my mother. She maintained high ex-

> I learned from my father that hard work is an honor.

pectations in our household, which spurred my older brother, Orville, to make the most of his near-genius intellect. He supplemented his straight A performance with personal science projects, which usually involved the kitchen refrigerator. I remember his warning my dad, "Be careful which milk bottle you use. I've labeled these, which have agar-agar for raising my drosophila melanogasters."

"Your dropsy whats?"

"Fruit flies, Dad. I'm raising Mediterranean fruit flies for an experiment. Don't open those special bottles."

As I said, my father worked double shifts. He usually returned home late at night hungry for a bowl of cereal before bed. And— you guessed it—weary and sleepy, he blindly reached for the wrong milk bottle and popped it open, instantly releasing a sudden puff of tiny coffee-colored specks. Within minutes, my brother was alerted to the disaster.

"My drosophila melanogasters!" he shrieked. With the milk bottle held close to his chest, he gingerly pinched fruit flies by their wings and then trapped them under the napkin lid. The rest of us joined the midnight fly roundup, looking like a clan of frenzied hunter-gatherers searching for invisible gnats. "Look for the males," Orville barked as he continued snatching up the tiny tan dots with a net.

"The males?" my sister, Luci, asked in disbelief. I knew what was running through her mind. Like me, she imagined turning them over like they were puppies. What a night!

We eventually recovered from the great drosophila melanogaster disaster and Dad learned to scrutinize the contents of the refrigerator before eating. Orville eventually earned a scholarship to Rice University, then known as the Rice Institute, an outstanding college dedicated to "the advancement of literature, science, and art." My brother made an ideal candidate. He was well read, he nurtured a keenly scientific mind, and he played the piano like a virtuoso. He also enjoyed the distinction of being my mother's favorite.

Luci, my older sister, was a joyful adventurous spirit from the day of her birth. Her grades never failed to impress and her talent as an artist emerged early. I don't know which she did best, writing, painting, or singing, but she was outstanding at all of them. She later sang for many years with The Dallas Opera and she's written more than a dozen books. But Luci's most striking feature has always been her desire to live fully and fearlessly. To this day, that is how she pursues life. In the 1950s, men dominated the corporate scene, but Luci the adventurer became a cartographer for Mobil Oil and then an executive. She left after thirty years to help us in various ways at Insight for Living, and now she speaks to more than half a million women each year with Women of Faith.

> But Luci's most striking feature has always been her desire to live fully and fearlessly.

Luci's breadth of interests and her ability to be good at all of them endeared her to our father. She was clearly my dad's favorite.

I don't say this to gain pity or to mash sour grapes, but to explain my mind-set going into ministry. My mother adored my brother, my father favored my sister...and, remember, I was a "mistake." Like my siblings, I pursued a number of interests. I often joke about my grades, but I did well enough to become a member of the National Honor Society. I overcame my stuttering on the debate team and the drama department, eventually earning the lead role in our senior production. I played in the school band, learning most of the woodwind instruments, and I even became the drum major in our local high school. So it wasn't that I didn't do anything worthy of my parents' attentions, yet for reasons I do not know for certain, they rarely, if ever, attended a single performance and barely acknowledged my achievements. Rather than let that embitter me, I learned to place no expectations on others and to seek my approval from God rather than people. This mind-set created within me a strong sense of independence and a powerful drive to succeed—all on my own.

> I learned to place no expectations on others and to seek my approval from God rather than people.

This independent, industrious attitude is very American. It got my parents' generation through the Depression and fueled a remarkable double victory in World War II. In the 1950s, the entrepreneurial confidence encouraged my generation to pick ourselves up, create our own future, take full responsibility for our lives, put a good idea to work, and make something of ourselves. Following my tour of duty in the Marine Corps, I arrived at Dallas Theological Seminary in 1959. I found myself among kindred spirits practicing a virile kind of Christianity and bursting at the seams to evangelize the world. And after more than four years of personal mentoring and practical training under Dr. Pentecost, I didn't lack for confidence that my work ethic would transform any pastorate willing to give me a chance. But two New England winters quickly cooled my belief in self—that and a cold splash of reality in my face.

I found myself in a jam. The church in Waltham had called me for all the right reasons, and I went to minister there with all the right motives, but it wasn't working. I wrote earlier that I wasn't a fit—being a Texan among New England Yankees was the least of my struggles—but that certainly contributed to my inner struggles. They were happy with the preaching and they responded positively to my leadership in other areas, so I can't say I failed, per se. Yet neither could you call my efforts a smashing success. Fulfilling my responsibilities felt like trying to push a rope, but my work ethic demanded I stay at it. I prayed for the ability to press on, not unlike summoning the willpower to keep jogging those four or five miles when, during the first half hour, your body resists every stride.

That's when my prayers started to change, imperceptibly at first. I began to awaken to a reality that my being in Waltham wasn't what I envisioned, but it was where God wanted me—at least for that time, and for how much longer, I didn't know. My prayers didn't make the work easier, or even more successful (whatever that word means). Instead, they created within me an assurance that God was in control and that my job boiled down to being faithful to my duties. My praying turned drudgery into a kind of rhythm that kept me going when my goal-oriented self-motivation ran thin.

> God was in control and...my job boiled down to being faithful to my duties.

Around that same time, our marriage had its difficulties. Cynthia challenged me with a sobering request. "I would appreciate it," she said one evening after supper, "if you would stop calling us '*partners.*' We are married, and I love you, but what we have between us is *not* a partnership."

At first, it angered me. In fact, I argued with her about it. But as I reflected on how I had been accomplishing ministry, I had to admit that I had cultivated a lone ranger style. I interacted with others, but I didn't engage them in the work. I related with the people I served, but I didn't involve them. I took upon myself all the burdens of the church, all the responsibilities of ministry, thinking that everyone expected me to do as I had always done all my life: succeed on my own. As I shouldered all the burdens of life—in the church and at home—I thought I was doing everyone a favor. Instead, I was withholding from them the opportunity to contribute, the dignity of responsibility, and the joy of accomplishment. By bearing all responsibility, leaving none for any others to carry, I also neglected the opportunity to connect with them. People bond through shared struggles, so by "sparing them additional hardship," I said, in effect, "I don't need you." Rather than feeling grateful, my friends, parishioners—and, by then, even my wife—felt rejected, like they didn't matter.

> By bearing all responsibility, leaving none for any others to carry, I also eliminated the opportunity to connect with them.

What does this have to do with prayer? Think about it. I was treating God the same way. I genuinely believed that ministry operated on the basic principle, *"I do my part while God does His part, and the job gets done."* And my prayers said as much. Meanwhile, ministry in Waltham was flowing easily...but I felt increasingly more frustrated.

The work of God on a soul is indeed mysterious. The Lord allowed me to use my self-reliance and then He intervened to give me something better. My individualism helped me overcome many difficulties in the past. My self-reliance fueled my drive in high school, and pushed me to adjust to the rigorous demands and grow stronger in the Marine Corps. After all that, it enabled me to excel in seminary. But the time had come for that to change. My gift of internal resilience became a liability as I became a spiritual leader because the self-reliance that had served me so well has no place in ministry. (Read that sentence again...slowly.) As I came to terms with that realization, my prayer life began to change. I no longer considered prayer one of the many "duties" of ministry, but a magnificent relief. I learned that prayer provides unlimited access to the power God longs to give those who serve Him.

I once punctuated my human efforts with a prayer, saying in so many words, "Okay, Lord, I've done all I can; You take it from here." Like He served as the final leg in a relay, receiving the baton in a race

I started! Give me a break! The entire race is God's. All the burdens are the Lord's. The ultimate responsibility is His. And that includes my sermon next Sunday.

The entire race is God's. All the burdens are the Lord's. The ultimate responsibility is His.

In the beginning, I preached competently, but not authentically. In following my calling, I had discovered my identity, and in preparation I had learned to accept myself, but I had not yet learned to be myself in the pulpit. I became a raggedy man, patchwork preacher, stitching together the best qualities of the men I respected most: the keen scholarship of Dr. Pentecost, the exuberant excitement of Dr. Hendricks, the linguistic acumen of Dr. Waltke, the commanding theological strength of Dr. Walvoord. Ray Stedman's easy authenticity, however, continued to elude me. Then, I began to see that ministry is God's job, and that we are invited to join Him in what He's doing. With the burden of "success" finally released and removed from my shoulders, my approach to preaching changed dramatically...beginning with how I prayed.

Dependence Day

I now understand that Sunday's sermon isn't really my responsibility. I'm the one who must prepare, and I have been scheduled to stand before the congregation to speak, so, if I don't do what I must, Sunday will be an awkward experience for everyone. Yet the sermon isn't my responsibility; in the final analysis, it's God's. He *wants* a great message for His people. It's not like I have to convince Him to help me. He's not withholding His help until I pray long enough

He's not withholding His help until I pray long enough or fervently enough to satisfy His vanity.

or fervently enough to satisfy His vanity. He wants His Word explained, proclaimed, understood, and applied *more than I do!* After all it is His Word that reveals His will, which is to be done for His glory.

My responsibility, therefore, is to become the means of God's doing what He already wants to do. I am merely His co-laborer. He called me to do this, not because He desperately needs me, and not because He cannot proclaim His own Word or do so through others, but because it pleases Him to use me—my voice, my personality, my style, my whatever. Prayer, then, isn't a punctuation at the end of my effort; prayer is my first introduction to what *He* wants to do on any given occasion—Sunday or otherwise. Rather than pray as a last resort, after all else has failed to produce a worthwhile sermon, I now pray first and often, asking God to let me in on His plan.

While this Sunday's sermon is God's responsibility, He has done something remarkable. He's granted me the privilege of contributing to His work by being His voice box, His face, hands, feet, and personality. He even allows me to shape many details of His plan and gives me a genuine stake in the accomplishment of our joint venture. Consequently, I will sometimes struggle. I will endure hardship as I shoulder some of the burdens He has shared with me. I'll adapt my week to accommodate interruptions and fight to keep my focus in the midst of distractions. I will grapple with mysteries beyond my scope and search diligently to find helpful illustrations. He has shared His responsibilities with me, not because He's limited, but to establish and strengthen a connection...with me! What a difference this kind of thinking makes!

> He has shared His responsibilities with me, not because He's limited, but to establish and strengthen a connection...with me!

My prayer begins with an acknowledgment that God wants to do something good through the message I will prepare.

I pray for His supernatural illumination of the passage or topic as I begin digging, and I "pray without ceasing" (1 Thess. 5:17) through the hours of my sermon preparation.

Martin Luther typically gave the best hours of the day to praying, often three hours at a time. To be candid, I don't think I have ever prayed for three consecutive hours. Let's be honest; all of us can pray more, and the time spent in prayer is never wasted. But "praying without ceasing" doesn't mean you and I must spend all day in our prayer closet. "Pray without ceasing" means to pray off and on...off and on...with the frequency of a hacking cough. I devote some time to focused prayer, but then I get busy digging. Prayer then becomes a running conversation with God as I interact with His Word. The consistent theme of my praying is that He help me to understand the Text when I study, to structure it well when I outline, to evaluate it well when I review the material, and then to say it well when I stand and deliver.

Praying helps me in several specific ways.

Praying keeps my focus on God's approval rather than the applause of people.

When preparing a sermon or a speech, pride has a way of slipping into the room

Praying keeps my focus on God's approval rather than the applause of people.

with you. It'll cozy up beside you, it'll get inside your head and probe your deepest insecurities, and then set an impossible standard, usually based on the approval or applause of people. Let me say this straight: *that* can be paralyzing. Praying keeps me focused on the true measure of success: faithful communication of truth for the good of the hearers and the glory of God. Praying calms me down. Praying sets a guard around me to block out worry over what others may think about what I say. Praying diminishes the importance of human approval as it intensifies the value of what

God wants listeners to hear. It diminishes all concerns over others' responses.

Praying keeps me from shooting from the hip when I know a passage very well.

Merriam-Webster's Collegiate Dictionary defines complacency as "self-satisfaction esp. when accompanied by unawareness of actual dangers or deficiencies."[9] Some passages of Scripture can become so familiar we think we have a better grasp of their meaning and import than we do. While the Bible does not change, I see the Scriptures through very different eyes than when I was a wet-behind-the-ears seminarian. My understanding of God has grown much deeper since then, so I don't run the risk of spouting off insights that are no longer insightful. Praying restrains that urge.

Praying keeps me in submission to what God wants to say. Praying reminds me of the importance of relying on the One who originally spoke through the written Word, if I am to be His vocal instrument. Praying encourages me to evaluate past insights, and to build upon them, but to seek the mind of God continually as I dig and as I deliver. Amazingly, praying keeps each delivery fresh, even when I preach the same sermon back-to-back each Sunday (three of them each Easter).

Prayer slows my pace in the face of deadline so that I don't become so enmeshed in details that I lose the big picture.

As a preacher, you think, *Sunday's coming soon.* Or as a speaker, the thought comes, *The event approaches. I don't have forever to prepare.* That deadline demands progress, but you can't allow even that to become your master. Praying throughout the process allows me to back away from the collage of details and, as I discuss the information with the Lord, I gain an appreciation for the big picture. There is a natural sense in which meditating should accomplish the same thing, but it doesn't for me. The Lord can certainly influence a person who's meditating, but, generally speaking, when you meditate, it's all you. Your thoughts, your reasoning, your internal dialogue. Prayer invites the Lord to influence the internal conversation and to achieve supernaturally what you and I cannot do on our own. Prayer becomes the means of mind transformation (Rom. 12:1–2), and that's where insights are born.

> Prayer becomes the means of mind transformation, and that's where insights are born.

That's not to suggest that prayer is a substitute for study. On the contrary, study fuels more effective prayer. Therefore, you should plan on including plenty of time for prayer as a part of your study.

Praying reminds me that I don't have to be omniscient to faithfully proclaim God's Word.

Because so many people look to me for answers week to week, it's easy to let their expectations define who I should be. Even if I study and proclaim the Scriptures for seventy-five years, there will be mysteries I cannot hope to unravel, theological conundrums I will never resolve, questions and issues that I will have to reconsider as I learn more. Praying becomes a faithful reminder that I am not a fountain of knowledge. There's nobody out there with a checklist, making sure I've dotted every *i* and crossed every *t* in my sermon.

On those occasions when I encounter a thorny passage, or something difficult to explain, praying gives me permission to admit, "I don't know." Candidly, in all my years of preaching, I have never been criticized for admitting my inability to explain a particularly complex mystery. In fact, many have expressed relief to know that an experienced pastor sometimes struggles to understand the Bible. While I don't believe it's wise to parade every level of ignorance, on occasion it is healthy to remind the congregation that you're not

> On occasion, it is healthy to remind the congregation that you're not omniscient.

omniscient. That helps to keep the pulpit authentic and the pastor transparent. Moreover, it lets the congregation know that complete knowledge is not our goal; coming to terms with what we already know is our first priority.

Prayer helps you discern how to translate your vulnerability and transparency to the pulpit so that it's constructive.

Many hundreds of years ago, God wrote His Word complete and we have a catalog of exegetical exposition prepared by hundreds of great minds amassed over two millennia. Yet, still, there is a need for preaching. That's because God ordained it so. When we gather in local communities for the purpose of worship and instruction, we do not praise God through song and then merely read the Scriptures aloud. Nor do we open the vault of Christian wisdom for a choice sermon from yesteryear to memorize and recite from the pulpit. In fact, if preaching were all about exegeting a passage, and deriving principles, and proposing applications, we could program a computer to complete those tasks, on time and without error each and every week. But preaching is more than the transfer of information and more than compelling oratory. When Paul wrote about the gift of preaching, he didn't think of the gift as an ability given to a person; preaching is the gift of a person granted to the church (Eph. 4:11–12). From the beginning, God intended His Word to be sheathed in living, breathing, human tissue and, in church, proclaimed by an imperfect person who earnestly desires to live out the message he carries.

There's something comforting about an imperfect vessel bearing God's Word. It's somehow reassuring to know that Moses, moved by impatience and anger, struck the rock (Num. 20:8–11). David's poems move us because, through his weakness, he gave words to our pain. Solomon's aphorisms ring true because his mistakes yielded wisdom. In the same way, the preaching function is nothing apart from the preacher, whose vulnerability and transparency makes the Living Word of God accessible to those who hear him. Therefore, authenticity is the quintessential characteristic of the preacher—or, at least, it should be—and prayer is what melds Scripture and the preacher's authenticity together to form a sermon. Remove Scripture, and the sermon becomes the preacher's mea culpa. Remove authenticity, and the sermon dries up like a sunbaked desert. But the two together allow parishioners to see God at work in a flesh-and-blood life.

> Authenticity is the quintessential characteristic of the preacher.

It's no surprise that people in need of help rarely stop by the church to ask for a DVD; they want a person who has suffered as they have, understands their struggles experientially, and has helpful, hopeful, realistic words of instruction. Praying gives me the courage to let the cracks in my life show; praying keeps me real to the core.

If preaching is like cooking, then prayer turns the recipe into a meal.

Preaching is the artful blend of several ingredients: history, linguistics, theology, illustration, humor, clarity, enthusiasm, timing, emotion, application, and insight. Praying, from the first moments of digging through the final syllable of delivery, transforms the individual components into something profoundly more—not merely blended, but catalyzed into a savory, satisfying feast that nourishes the soul.

When I'm preparing the sermon, I can tell when it's coming together right, and if I don't have that inner assurance, I keep working and I keep praying until I experience a breakthrough. When something in my spirit says, "I've got it," the sermon almost writes itself. I love it when that happens

> I keep working and I keep praying until I experience a breakthrough.

during digging; it often occurs much later. There will be times when I have to renege on a social engagement because I still don't "have it"…and Sunday's fast approaching. I'm like a chef trying to figure out what's missing from a bland, tasteless dish. And it drives me mad until I find that one missing ingredient that will unlock the flavor. I can't enjoy going anywhere and I can't have any fun once I'm there until I find it. So, I'll pray, "Okay, Lord. I'm at Your mercy. I've done all the work I can do. I trust that You will bring everything together or guide me to the missing piece to make this message effective."

Sometimes, I will wake up in the middle of the night with the insight I was missing. I'll experience the breakthrough: *Oh,* that's *what's missing.* And I'll get up and go straight to my study—I don't give any thought to what time it is—and retype a page of notes to include the certain "something" that was missing. When I experience the breakthrough and hear my internal voice say, "I *like* that," I'm relieved, knowing I am finally ready for Sunday morning. My prayers take on the tone of a priest offering a sacrifice. I lay the sermon on the altar of my mind and I intercede for the people who will soon hear it, praying specifically for the difficulties I imagine they have and asking the Lord to use the message as the means of touching others with my words.

Interdependence

Hearing Cynthia's heartfelt rebuke that cold, gray evening in Waltham, Massachusetts, wasn't easy. Sometimes the truth hurts even as it sets you free. Over the next several months, I began to share responsibilities and burdens with others. I surrendered my self-reliance and received the warm support of those who love me and genuinely desire to serve the Lord. I also enjoyed a much-needed role reversal in my service to God. Best of all, things slowly began to change in our marriage. It took years... but I finally learned some of the secrets of building a relationship with the one I love and live with.

Ministry is a kind of voluntary interdependence in which the Lord chooses an individual, equips him or her for service, and then accomplishes an objective through his or her efforts. The Lord is omnipotent, so He doesn't need the help of anyone. Nevertheless, He chooses to work in, and through, human servants. He deliberately calls us to join Him in His work. Without compromising His own sovereign control, He nonetheless gives us a genuine stake in the success or failure of the mission. While we bear the responsibility for faithful obedience and for giving it our best, the objectives are the Lord's, and He is responsible for seeing them through. It's His reputation that is all-important, not mine. Put simply, our job is to be faithful; the Lord will define success and see to its fulfillment.

> Put simply, our job is to be faithful; the Lord will define success and see to its fulfillment.

It's a marvelous arrangement! He expects me to take the mission seriously, to be diligent and faithful, to be a conscientious contributor to His objective, but in none of this am I to feel a do-or-die pressure to avoid failure. Consequently, my prayers are not those of a terrified, desperate man. They are the requests of a field marshal seeking orders from a commander in chief destined for victory.

The same can be said of you, especially if you are called to preach. Regardless, if you are "in Christ," if you have received God's gift of eternal life through His Son, you have unrestricted access to the throne of the universe. Your all-powerful Creator knows you, He has equipped you to fulfill your calling, He has planned your future and is accomplishing a divine purpose in your activities. The question is "What does He want to accomplish in you and through you?"

Praying throughout the process will answer that question, although the answer won't come in the form of a sentence, either audibly or whispered within. And, for sure, you won't read it in a cloud formation or see it in some late-night vision. The answer most often appears in retrospect. After you have studied to understand... after you have grappled with issues... after you have struggled to overcome difficulties... after you have prepared the best you know how... sometimes, after you have given it the best of your ability and have walked away feeling like a failure—that's when God gives you a glimpse of the crucial role you played in His plan. A note from a grateful individual will speak volumes. The earnest reassurances of colleagues will be affirming. Tangible surprises will appear unexpectedly. At such serendipitous moments, you'll suddenly know you're on the right track. That will give you the courage to engage in the struggle again. At those special moments, you'll realize you are truly in partnership with the Lord.

The end of my time in New England coincided with the conclusion of my lesson on God reliance and marked a major turning point in my ministry... and my marriage. Many years later, I overheard Cynthia in a conversation in which she called the two of us "partners." It rolled off her lips as naturally as saying my name. I smiled to myself and silently thanked God for how far we had come.

It never would have happened without prayer.

CHAPTER SEVEN

Illustrating

Let every bookworm, when in any fragrant, scarce, old tome he discovers a sentence, a story, an illustration, that does his heart good, hasten to give it.

—Hartley Coleridge[10]

It was a beautiful late-summer evening several years ago when Cynthia and I stood on the main deck of a large ship leaving the New York harbor. The lights of Manhattan passed by the port side and faded behind us as we headed for the highly elevated Verrazano Narrows Bridge and the open sea. Fellow passengers lined the railings, snapping pictures and panning the skyline with video cameras, doing their best to take it all in. My focus, however, lay ahead on the starboard side, just past Ellis Island. I craned my neck to catch a glimpse of our nation's most iconic monument, the magnificent Statue of Liberty.

As the ship slid quietly through the dark waters of the upper bay and passengers chattered excitedly about the voyage ahead, I stared in silence at the Lady. Since 1886, she has maintained her stately vigil over what millions of immigrants saw as the gateway to freedom. Her left arm cradles a tablet bearing the date of our Declaration of Independence. Her right arm extends high into the sky, her torch lighting the way to a new life. Her loose robe falls in graceful folds to the top of the pedestal on which she stands. At her feet, broken shackles, representing the overthrow of tyranny.

My eyes drifted over toward Ellis Island, where boatloads of bewildered, frightened, and lonely immigrants once stood in long lines leading through a labyrinth of questions and forms, procedures and examinations. There they stood with children at their feet, thousands of miles from everything that had once defined home, struggling to understand a strange language, hoping to find refuge in "the land of opportunity." I imagined what they must have thought as they stared across two thousand feet of water at our symbol of freedom and hope. Only then, viewing the statue from a similar vantage point aboard a passing ship, did it occur to me that these Americans-in-waiting couldn't see anything of the monument except her molded copper skin. But, as anyone who has been to Liberty Island can tell you, there's much more to the great Lady than her lovely green patina façade.

> My eyes drifted over toward Ellis Island, where boatloads of bewildered, frightened, and lonely immigrants once stood in long lines.

A bronze plaque on the pedestal under her feet bears a sonnet by Emma Lazarus, ending with:

Give me your tired, your poor,
Your huddled masses yearning to breathe free,
The wretched refuse of your teeming shore.
Send these, the homeless, the tempest-tossed to me:
I lift my lamp beside the golden door.

The Lady stands silently on a massive pedestal made from 27,000 tons of concrete and granite extending fifty-three feet below grade. Go inside the statue, and you will see 125 tons of iron and rivets designed by Gustave Eiffel to support the entire structure. The foundation, pedestal, and iron framework are indispensable. The statue wouldn't stand three minutes without them. But we don't treasure the Statue of Liberty for its sturdy base or its iron skeleton. The message of liberty is

> But we don't treasure the Statue of Liberty for its sturdy base or its iron skeleton.

borne by the intricate shapes of her sculpted metal skin. Remove those hammered sheets of copper and what do you have?

A message is like that. Every sermon, every speech must have a solid foundation supporting a sturdy internal frame...but those elements do not convey the speaker's message. He or she needs to put skin on the structure, an artful presentation so seamless, so inspiring, so clear, and so compelling that no one really cares to

know what's underneath. In fact, the audience should simply depart better equipped and fully committed to take action without being overly conscious of why they feel that way.

Frederic Bartholdi used hammered copper plates to express his vision; preachers and public speakers use illustrations, the most malleable and versatile material known to all who communicate. Those who say it well seamlessly clad their presentations from head to toe using carefully chosen and perfectly tailored illustrations so that the outline is barely noticeable. Your notes may follow a neatly delineated point/sub-point format, but your message should present to the audience a graceful, unified sculpture in words. I like to open a sermon with a strong illustration, draw from it periodically as I establish my points, and then bring it back to seal the ending. It's not often you can find an illustration that rich, but when you do, you've found a treasure. It makes the whole message that much clearer.

While I make copious use of illustrations in every message, I want to be careful not to leave the wrong impression. My word picture of the Statue of Liberty notwithstanding, the illustrations are not the message; they merely *convey* the message. We have to be careful not to let our illustrations take over. I knew one very imaginative speaker who did such a great job weaving metaphors and painting word pictures that audiences seldom knew what he was talking about. They remembered the illustrations perfectly, but they never quite got his point.

> The illustrations are not the message; they merely *convey* the message.

In your digging and building, you determined how you want your audience to think and behave differently, and you established how you're going to move them, logically, from their current way of thinking to a new perspective. That's what I'm calling the structure of your message. Now we'll use illustrations to make your structure both attractive and approachable. But before I show you how, let me explain what an illustration is and what makes an illustration work.

A One-Thousand-Word Paragraph

An illustration uses something familiar to the audience as a means of explaining something unfamiliar. But an illustration is more than mere analogy or metaphor; an illustration has two, equally important objectives. The first is *clarity*. A good illustration clarifies what seems mysterious or obscure to the listener.

I recently received an e-mail from the mother of an eleven-year-old boy...via Facebook. (Yes, I'm on Facebook. I have no idea what that means or even how Facebook works. Fortunately, I have a great staff that sorts through the messages and puts them in a form I can deal with.) Anyway, he said, "I like listening to *Pastor Church* because he's fun to listen to and I understand him."

That preteen doesn't know my name, but he gave me the greatest compliment I could have received from a kid his age. My message was clear to him, most likely because I used the right illustrations. When teenagers approach me after a service to talk about the message they just heard, I usually ask, "Did it make sense?" Almost without exception, they'll say, "Oh, yeah. I liked the story about..." They remember the illustration and (thankfully) they see how it connects to a biblical truth. The illustrations brought clarity.

The second objective of illustration is *motivation*. A good illustration not only helps to clarify the mysterious or obscure, *it also helps the listener appreciate the relevance of a particular point*. Warren Wiersbe wrote this about the Lord's use of parables, a particularly effective kind of illustration:

> A good illustration not only helps to clarify the mysterious or obscure, *it also helps the listener appreciate the relevance of a particular point.*

A parable starts off as a picture that is familiar to listeners. But as you carefully consider the picture, it becomes a mirror in which you see yourself, and many people do not like to see themselves. This explains why some of our Lord's listeners became angry when they heard His parables, and even tried to kill Him. But if we see ourselves as needy sinners and ask for help, then the mirror becomes a window through which we see God and His grace.[11]

Similarly, an illustration starts out like a picture, bringing clarity to a truth. It allows the listener to "see" what's being said. Then an illustration turns into a mirror, allowing the listener to gain "insight" into how this new truth affects him or her. Finally, the illustration becomes a window, and therefore provides "vision," transforming the new truth into mental images that prompt the listener to envision the world.

In a practical sense, an illustration paints a picture in the imagination using the listener's own experiences. Never forget, however, you're creating this work of art in the listener's mind, so you're not limited to colors and shapes. You can also paint with sound, flavor, aroma, texture, and even emotion. In fact, the more senses you can involve in creating an illustration, the more powerfully clear you can make your point and—most importantly—demonstrate the relevance of this new truth.

> The more senses you can involve in creating an illustration, the more powerfully clear you can make your point.

This Sunday, I'm preaching on Mark 9:38–50, which describes the reaction of Jesus' disciples when they encounter someone outside their circle conducting ministry in Jesus' name. The Lord's warnings carry grave implications for all who call themselves followers. I want to apply one of those warnings to the specific problem of *jealousy*. It's an important message, but I have a problem. We're approaching the end of March, so I'm going to have more than one person thinking about the upcoming deadline for income tax returns. As I step behind the pulpit, several will be thinking, *April 15 is right around the corner and I don't have enough to cover the amount owed, so I probably need to get a loan...* I need to snap them out of their distraction. I need to grab their attention with something that says, *You can't afford to miss what's going to be said in the next forty minutes.*

I plan to begin Sunday's message with "Life is often like a jungle." I'll say it with a deep sense of foreboding and let it sink in before continuing. When I have used a line like that in the past, I've seen people lean to one side to look around the person in front of them, suddenly giving me their complete attention.

I'll then follow that opening line with this illustration:

I need to grab their attention with something that says, *You can't afford to miss what's going to be said in the next forty minutes.*

For years, I have kept close at hand a newspaper clipping about a man who fought a snake. He was hunting for deer in a remote wildlife area of Northern California when he climbed onto a ledge and whoomp!, *a snake lunged at him, barely missing his neck. He instinctively grabbed the serpent several inches behind the head to keep from being bitten as the snake wrapped itself around his neck and shook its rattle furiously. When he tried to pull the reptile off, he discovered the fangs were caught in his wool turtleneck sweater . . . and he began to feel the venom dripping down the skin of his neck.*

He fell backward and slid headfirst down the steep slope through brush and lava rocks, his rifle and binoculars bouncing beside him. He ended up wedged between some rocks with his feet caught uphill from his head. Barely able to move, he got his right hand on his rifle and used it to disengage the fangs from his sweater, but the snake had enough leverage to strike again. The serpent lunged at him, over and over and over. He kept his face turned so the rattler couldn't get a good angle with its fangs, but he could feel the snake bumping its nose just below his eye.

At this point, I'm fairly certain *no one* will be thinking about income tax forms! The majority of the congregation may have never seen a snake outside a cage, but at this moment, all of them are fighting for their lives against a venomous enemy wrapped around their necks. And that's exactly how I want them to feel. I will make the point that jealousy is like that poisonous snake.

By using this illustration in the introduction, I will not only make the point that jealousy is hard to cast off, I hope to convince everyone that getting rid of jealousy is sometimes an urgent matter of life or death.

A Good Illustration Is Real

How would you respond if I told you I made up the whole story? How would you feel about me, the points I made, and the entire sermon if I admitted that the hunter doesn't exist and his life-or-death struggle never took place?

As it happens, the story is true.

Are you relieved?

It's amazing how the truth of an illustration carries such weight. Because a real man engaged in a real fight for his life, the audience feels his urgency. Their skin crawls. They experience the life-or-death struggle more keenly. Their stomachs churn. That's because they can empathize with a real person unlike some hypothetical character in a made-up story. If I later admitted, "Actually, that never happened," the illustration would shrivel to nothing. And any insights I might have connected to that illustration will have disintegrated along with it.

If you have to use a story or a situation that isn't true, say so up front.

If you have to use a story or a situation that isn't true, say so up front. Otherwise, the audience will feel they have been deceived…because, in fact, *they were.*

Do your research. The digital age has given each of us—even electric typewriter guys like me—unprecedented access to information, offering quick and easy access to the truth behind a story. I'll give you a few examples of how good research impacted my use of some very popular stories I had used for years. Each example illustrates the power of truth and the value of going the extra mile to find it.

When in doubt, disclose.

One of my favorite illustrations helps to answer the question "Why does God use people to accomplish His work when He can do everything without the help of anyone?" After each of the twentieth-century world wars, the great classical pianist Ignacy Jan Pederewski held benefit concerts to raise money and awareness for the plight of his native Poland. One evening, the virtuoso stood in the wings, deep in thought, as the music hall filled to capacity. The gathering crowd included a mother hoping to encourage her young son's progress at the piano. As the audience milled about, talking about politics, the two great wars, and the evening of music they would enjoy, she failed to notice that her son had slipped from her side and made his way to the piano onstage. Having mounted the bench, he began playing, note by single note "Twinkle, Twinkle Little Star." The simple tune could be heard throughout the hall, prompting laughter from some and shouts of righteous indignation from others. "Get that kid away from the piano!" one man shouted.

The commotion drew Paderewski from his mental preparations to see the youngster still playing. He slipped quietly across the stage and bent down behind the boy and whispered in his ear, "Don't stop; keep playing." With his left hand the pianist filled in the bass, and he encircled the child with his right to play a running soprano obbligato. A sudden hush fell over the crowd as the little boy's simple melody blended perfectly with the master's glorious accompaniment, their impromptu duet holding the audience in rapt wonder.

What a perfect picture of the Lord graciously using our meager efforts, surrounded and uplifted by His power, to create something beautiful! Unfortunately, I can find *no* evidence the incident ever took place. No newspaper clippings from the period. No credible eyewitness accounts. Nothing. Yet, I can't find any reason to suggest it didn't happen, either. Consequently, I'm not excited about using it. If I do, I will probably preface the story with a qualification: "There's a great story about the classical pianist, Ignacy Jan Paderewski, which may or may not be true. Regardless, it helps us appreciate the Lord's desire to accomplish His work through us."

While the illustration may lose some of its emotional impact, initially, I don't worry that my audience will be disillusioned or discouraged later when they learn about the story's loose connection with reality.

Get the details straight.

An illustration can be true, yet quickly dissolve into a work of fiction if the details of the story aren't correct. Don't be satisfied with the way it's told in someone's book or a compilation of illustrations and quotes, and—for goodness sake—be careful with the Internet. Each person telling the story adds a little detail or shifts the context ever so slightly to make a point, and, before you know it, the true story is far beyond the realm of truth!

Be careful with the Internet.

I have seen various incarnations of a story about a young man whose prominent port-wine stain birthmark covered the side of his face. When asked how he could be so confident with such a prominent feature many would consider "disfiguring," he replied, "My dad taught me, as far back as I can remember, that this part of my face was where an angel must have kissed me before I was ever born. He said to me, 'Son, this marking was for Dad, so that I might know that you are mine. You have been marked out by God just to remind me that you're my son.'

"All through my young days, as I grew up, I was reminded by my dad, 'You are the most important, special fellow on earth.'

"To tell you the truth," he said, "I got to where I felt sorry for people who *didn't* have birthmarks across the sides of their faces!"

This story appears in various forms, involving a variety of people, some even telling it in the first person. It's a birthmark in one, a birth defect in another, a scar from birth complications in yet another. They all get the basic story right, but the variants might lead one to believe it was one of those nice stories that never really happened. Fortunately, I know for certain that it *is* true. The man was a fellow student I knew at Dallas Seminary...I was the one who asked how he could be so confident.

Check your facts. It will take some extra time, but trace the story back to its source, and then weigh the source carefully. Try to find the original newspaper article, magazine story, interview, or even direct conversation with the people involved.

Check your facts.

Discover the deeper truth.

The second illustration recalls the flight of Russian cosmonaut Yuri Gagarin, who climbed into a rocket and left the Earth's atmosphere to become the first man in space. Upon his return to Earth, he was quoted as saying, "I looked and looked but I didn't see God." One Sunday, W. A. Criswell, the pastor of the First Baptist Church of Dallas, remarked, "If he had stepped out of that space suit, he would have seen God!"

That's funny! It makes a great point. In fact, I wanted to use this story to underscore a critical point in my commentary, *Insights on Luke*. But as I dug into the research, I encountered a sobering interview with Gagarin's longtime friend Colonel Valentin Petrov. According to this 2006 interview, the words were not actually spoken by the cosmonaut, but attributed to him after a statement by Nikita Khrushchev in a meeting of the Central Committee of the Communist Party in Moscow. While promoting the state's official atheist policy, the premier said (according to Petrov), "Why should you clutch at God? Here is Gagarin who flew to space but saw no God there."[12] At the time, the Central Committee wanted the quote attributed to Gagarin, and he was in no position to contradict them! So the quote stuck.

None of this changes the impact of Dr. Criswell's quip. The pastor, like the rest of the world, took the quote at face value and his response exposes a host of flaws in atheistic thinking. But my digging led me to a deeper, richer story. According to Gagarin's friend, the first cosmonaut was a humble, soft-spoken, reluctant hero and a man he knew as a believer (at least in the Russian Orthodox understanding of belief). The government blamed Petrov for "drawing Gagarin into religion," but both men shared the same perspective all along, actively encouraging Orthodoxy among their younger students in the Air Force Academy, even taking them to visit monasteries. While the world saw him as a pugnacious atheist, he was, in fact, continually in trouble with his Communist leaders for his personal and deeply held religious beliefs.

> But my digging led me to a deeper, richer story.

I'm not sure how or when I may use this extensive story, but it holds a lot of promise.

A Great Illustration Is Personal

If a good illustration is true, then a great illustration is personal. I mean by "personal" something you experienced or witnessed first-hand. Believe it or not, your audience wants to know about you as a living, breathing individual, not just what you have to say. Your speaking from firsthand experience allows them to connect with you personally, almost as naturally as meeting you one-on-one. For example, if you were to begin your presentation with "Let me tell you about my week...," you will find them leaning toward you with interest. (Of course, you want to follow that with something both relevant and interesting...and true!)

> Your audience wants to know about you as a living, breathing individual, not just what you have to say.

Personal illustrations work for the same reasons true illustrations do. People empathize better with a real person than a fictional character, and they can empathize better with you than anyone. You're *there*. They can see you. And if you tell the story from the heart, they will feel your emotions as you relate what you experienced. Here's an example:

In the latter years of his life, Moses probably felt surprised, and even a little confused, when others called him great. When I addressed my Christian Embassy friends in Washington, I searched for some way to illustrate that kind of humility. Fortunately, the week before I left, I witnessed a perfect example.

On Sunday morning, Stonebriar Community Church highlighted our special needs ministry in both morning services. In the first service, a little boy with mental disabilities sang "Majesty," a simple tune well known to almost everyone in our congregation. Most likely, his disabilities will keep him from leading a life most would call normal, but he reminded everyone that we all stand equally needy before our Savior. While the quality was nowhere near Pavarotti's, there wasn't a dry eye in the house. As the last note left his lips and dissolved into the hush that had fallen over the sanctuary, our congregation stood to their feet in thunderous applause.

> While the quality was nowhere near Pavarotti's, there wasn't a dry eye in the house.

The boy stared blankly at the standing ovation. When his teacher took his hand to lead him off the platform, he asked, "Why are they standing up?"

His unassuming, innocent response to applause is a poignant picture of humility. I am convinced that, by the end of his days, that's how Moses must have responded to those who heaped honors upon him. He, too, must have wondered, "Why are they applauding?"

I give you permission to use that illustration, but I'll warn you ahead of time that it won't be nearly as effective for you as it was for me. Not because I can do something you can't, but because I witnessed it with my own eyes. I heard the applause. Tears filled my eyes. I can describe my own internal response when I saw the boy's confusion. I felt the impact of that remarkable moment and my audience will absorb my emotions as I tell it. The same will be true when you share an illustration from your personal experience.

By the way, transparency is generally a very good quality in a speaker, as long as you use some discretion. You don't have to tell them everything. (In fact, please don't!) It's unwise to use the pulpit or the lectern as a psychologist's couch. And you want to avoid any illustration from your own experience that might distract the audience from understanding your point more clearly and feeling its relevance more deeply. You don't want to erode your audience's confidence in your ability to speak to an issue. I once expressed how upset a situation had made me and I described my reaction with such fervency, it appeared I hadn't gotten over it. Instead of connecting with my congregation, I worried them. I had hoped to let my audience know that the circumstance hurt me just like it would anyone. But, after the service, instead of hearing affirmation, I had people wanting to give me advice!

If you have blown it in some way and the matter hasn't been resolved, it's best not to tell the world. Unresolved problems and ongoing conflicts don't make good illustrations because they take the audience out of learning mode and put them in problem-solving mode. I repeat, the goal is to bring clarity to the topic, not introduce issues that might become a distraction. If, on the other hand, you didn't do something right and you made an effort to correct your error, then you might feel free to share it. Let them see failure followed by a determination to do what is right. Who can't relate to that?

> The goal is to bring clarity to the topic, not introduce issues that might become a distraction.

It's also helpful to let your audiences know about past failure when sufficient time has passed. If I were to tell you, "There was a time ten years into our marriage I wasn't sure we were going to make it," I doubt you'd lose sleep tonight. That was forty-plus years ago! An audience of struggling married couples would probably find comfort in my admission. It lets them know that *all* marriages experience crises, and, having shared my own struggle with marital conflicts, they're ready to hear what I have to say about making marriage last.

On the other hand, imagine the effect of revealing serious marital difficulty too soon. Imagine your reaction if I were your pastor and I said, "This time last year, I had serious doubts that our marriage was going to make it." See the difference? I've just thrown an anchor in your mind. You'd probably want to start a collection for marriage counseling for the Swindolls instead of listening to my advice on building harmony in your marriage.

Be transparent, but keep the focus on clarity and relevance.

If you use someone you know—and especially someone known by the audience—be sure to get his or her permission ahead of time.

If you use someone you know—and especially someone known by the audience—be sure to get his or her permission ahead of time. I even do this with my own family, including my children. Almost without exception, the person graciously agrees. However, if there is reluctance, I honor it by not going there.

Cultivating a Preacher's Eye

Whether you're a teacher, politician, company executive, community leader, attorney in the courtroom, or professional public speaker, I suggest you learn to see the world through the eyes of a preacher. Because we who speak to virtually the same group of people each time must build a new sermon from scratch every week, we're constantly on the lookout for good illustrations. There's hardly a morning that goes by when I don't say to myself, *I need something to help establish this point or communicate this perspective clearer.* In fact, I often make mental notes when I encounter something that might *someday* make a good illustration.

It helps to cultivate a broad range of interests outside your realm of expertise and interest. For me, that's Bible, theology, Christian living, and church. So, I read a lot of books and other material that have nothing to do with Christianity. I enjoy history, which provides some of the best illustrative material. I love sports—mostly football and basketball—and (perhaps like you) I'm glued to the television during most of

It helps to cultivate a broad range of interests outside your realm of expertise and interest.

the Olympic events. Athletic competition brings out the best and worst in humanity, both on the field and off, so the world of sports is a treasure trove of illustrations. I'm also fascinated by nature and animals, which keeps me in good supply as well. I'm often drawn to humorous events or situations with unexpected endings. Stories make great illustrations.

Over the years, I have learned to see the world from the perspective of an impartial observer. I watch people and their reactions to various circumstances. Almost without thinking, I take note of details I might otherwise have missed, and I'm constantly seeing metaphors at work in life during mundane happenings. I think that keeps my memory exercised so that it has become a repository of illustrations from which to draw at the right moment. I am forever observing people, watching reactions, absorbing the unusual.

I used to keep a filing system for clippings and other random illustration material. I meticulously labeled file folders:

Aa, Ae, Ai, Ao, Au
Ba, Be, Bi, Bo, Bu
Ca, Ce, Ci, Co, Cu

And so on. Then, if I found something that illustrated "jealousy," I would file it under "Je." An illustration for "divorce" would go in "Di." After several years, however, I stopped. I found that I was putting more time into keeping the system and hunting for scraps of paper than the effort was worth. Now, I highlight and bookmark passages in the books I read, but I rarely keep clippings anymore. Admittedly, I now rely heavily upon my memory. I'm grateful that God gifted me with the ability to remember.

When I use an illustration, I clip it to my sermon notes and then archive everything together. Once I've used an illustration in a sermon once, it's usually easy to

> When I use an illustration, I clip it to my sermon notes and then archive everything together.

find it again. I call to mind the passage or the context in which I used it, and return to those notes.

How and When to Use Illustrations

Illustrate to introduce your message. Earlier in this chapter, I demonstrated how I plan to introduce this Sunday's sermon. I will use the vivid, true story of a hunter's fight for his life against a venomous enemy. That will accomplish three important objectives. First, I will help my audience set aside distractions and focus on what I have to say for the rest of my message. Second, I will impress upon them the seriousness of the biblical truth I will present. Third, I will establish a thematic framework for the entire message, which leads to the next use of illustration.

Illustrate to make something memorable. The snake is only one danger in the jungle I plan to explore on Sunday morning. I will describe the quicksand of deadlines and demands. I will point to the alligator-filled swamps of overcommitment and underachievement. I will expose the prowling lion of criticism and the crouching leopard of others' expectations.

I won't overwork the jungle imagery, which could quickly backfire and cause the Lord's warnings to sound trite. But I will use analogies to help the congregation remember the dangers, and hopefully how to avoid them. Criticism is such an abstract concept, I think the image of a prowling lion not only characterizes the danger fairly well, it gives the listener something concrete and vivid to remember.

> But I will use analogies to help the congregation remember the dangers, and hopefully how to avoid them.

Illustrate to clarify the mysterious or the obscure. The words "theology" and "doctrine" tend to turn people off. Unfairly,

I think, thanks to preachers and teachers who use their education to make themselves look smarter than they are. Regardless, people generally feel out of their depth when you start using terms like "omniscience," "substitutionary atonement," "kenosis," "eschatology," or "incarnation." A down-to-earth illustration will help bring those ethereal concepts into real life so everyone can understand them.

> A down-to-earth illustration will help bring those ethereal concepts into real life so everyone can understand them.

The late A. W. Tozer was a master at illustrating complex theological ideas so effectively even young people could understand. For example, when explaining how the limited autonomy of humanity fit within the sovereign plan of God—*see what I mean?*—Tozer offered this simple illustration:

Suppose a ship leaves New York City bound for Liverpool, England, with a thousand passengers on board. They're going to take a nice, easy journey and enjoy the trip. Someone on board—usually the captain—is an authority who carries papers that say, "You are to bring this ship into the harbor in Liverpool."

After they leave New York and wave to the people on shore, the next stop is Liverpool. That's it! They're out on the ocean. Soon they lose sight of the Statue of Liberty, but they haven't come yet in sight of the English coast. They are out floating around on the ocean. What do they do? Is everyone bound in chains, with the captain walking around with a stick to keep them in line? No. Over here is a shuffleboard court, over there is a tennis court and a swimming pool. Over here you can look at pictures; over there you can listen to music.

The passengers are perfectly free to roam around as they please on the deck of the ship. But they're not free to change the course of that ship. It's going to Liverpool no matter what they do. They can jump off if they want to, but if they stay on board, they're going to Liverpool—nobody can change that. And yet, they're perfectly free within the confines of that ship.[13]

Some might take exception to his illustration, but his point of view is clear enough. I happen to like his illustration very much. I often pair it with a little joke, just to keep the mood light.

A pair of men, an Arminian and a Calvinist, climb the stairs at the front of a church. Both stumble and fall hard against the concrete. The Arminian says, "I wonder how that happened." The Calvinist says, "Man, I'm glad that's over with!"

Following that, I'm ready to unpack the illustrations and apply them to a very complex, sometimes very confusing issue for people. They might not resolve the theological conundrum—after twenty centuries, no one really has—but they will at least understand the issue better.

Illustrate to show relevance. As I stated earlier, clarity is only the first task of illustration; impressing upon the audience the relevance of a point is the other. Jesus used the image of a sower broadcasting seed—something everyone in first-century Israel either had done personally or had seen in person—to illustrate various reactions of the heart to the gospel message (Matt. 13:3–23). He not only clarified the issues, He impressed upon His hearers the importance of choosing what kind of soil they would be. He didn't have to say, "Oh, by the way, each of you is represented by one of these four

> Clarity is only the first task of illustration.

types of soil." That was obvious. He merely inserted the warning, "He who has ears, let him hear" (Matt. 13:9). The Lord's original audience, just like readers today, felt the gravity of His warning.

Illustrate to elucidate history. The apostle Paul urged Timothy, the pastor of the church in Ephesus, to pay a fair wage to people serving the congregation. He justified his command with a curious statement: "YOU SHALL NOT MUZZLE THE OX WHILE HE IS THRESHING," a direct quotation of Deuteronomy 25:4. Timothy and his parishioners would have understood the Old Testament illustration because farmers still used oxen to power their farm equipment. Furthermore, most people living in that time had either harvested grain themselves or had witnessed threshing every spring.

Many people today don't even know what it means to "thresh" or how to use an ox to complete the chore, much less why it's not good to muzzle the animal. Even if you explain the process, Paul's word picture won't have the same effect today as it did in his first-century, agrarian culture. We need a present-day, commonly experienced illustration that connects, making the same point. We might offer something like "Don't defraud the person who manages your investments," or "Don't be stingy with the one who works for you," or "Don't let your tank run dry then expect to drive twenty more miles."

Illustrate to kindle the emotions. I often close with an illustration that's calculated to connect the intellectual content of the message with the listener's emotions. This is not to coerce a decision or manipulate people in any way, but to communicate with the whole person. I may have been successful convincing an audience that doing something may be the morally right decision and even a personally beneficial thing to do,

> Close with an illustration that's calculated to connect the intellectual content of the message with the listener's emotions.

but if I ignore their emotions, I have failed to engage their nonrational motivations, such as fear, compassion, relief, love, or loyalty.

In one message, I spoke about the spiritual dangers of difficult circumstances and how we must guard ourselves against bitterness. Sometimes a sovereign God allows evil to prevail in the short term in order to achieve a long-term victory on our behalf. As I developed my third application point, I noted how we can even allow petty nuisances to take away our joy and ruin our reputations as Christians. I then closed with this illustration, which is transcribed from the actual message.

We were in the home of Mary Graham and Ney Bailey. Mary is the president of Women of Faith Ministries and my sister ministers with them and... and while we were together laughing and having fun and singing and whatever, Mary told us a story. And it made such an impact and it tied in so perfectly with my point here, I asked her if she would give me the particulars.

She said, "We were in Sacramento as a Women of Faith group, the Arco Arena back in 1999. Our ticket agent had inadvertently over-sold the arena by 1,500 seats. As a result, we had to reseat 3,000 women to make room for double the number of chairs on the main floor. We did that in 24 hours by changing out the seats for smaller, plastic ones. And by reconfiguring the floor seats as they do sort of at a boxing match, right up to the platform. Many of them literally had to lean their heads back to see the speakers. We phoned everyone ahead of time to alert them. (Imagine that, 3,000 calls.) And then we took the time to re-ticket and reseat the women on Friday night.

"In the opening we apologized profusely. It wasn't long into the program, however, before folks began to register complaints. They just didn't like their seat. Since Joni was to

*be our first speaker (referring to Joni Eareckson Tada, who
if you don't know has been paralyzed since the late '60s from
her dive into the Chesapeake Bay and her story is a magnificent story of victory beyond the paralysis. She's a quad-
riplegic and will be 'till she dies.), I asked her if she'd mind
addressing the issue again, if she was comfortable doing that.
To express another apology for us or perhaps to just pray is
all I had in mind. She agreed.*

*"We wheeled Joni up on the platform and her opening
words were, 'I understand some of you are not sitting in the
chairs you expected to be sitting in tonight. Well, neither am
I and I've been in mine for more than 30 years.' And then she
said softly, 'I have at least 1,000 friends who would give anything to be sitting in the chair you are in if only for tonight.' "*
Mary adds, "Nobody complained after that."

Some illustrations are so powerful or so poignant, you really don't
need to say anything afterward. In fact, you could diminish its effect if
you say much or anything at all. In this case, I tied the illustration to my
final point in four short sentences and then prayed. It perfectly fused
my three application points and sealed the message with an unspoken
and unforgettable admonition: *Don't be like the bickering, complain-
ing people in Joni's audience; remember how good you have it.*

I can't imagine preaching without using illustrations. Those who
don't illustrate are saying, in essence, "I don't care if you don't
understand; that's your problem." That may sound overly harsh,
but I actually heard a seminary professor say to students, "You're
speaking to a lot of people who don't think very deeply; that's their
problem." Of course, that made the hair on the back of my neck
stand up. That was many years ago. Today, I would be tempted
to push him aside, take over the class, and say, "No, actually, as

a proclaimer of truth, you must make the audience's shortcomings *your* problem. It's your job to help them understand God's truth and think deeply."

Every time you stand before others to say anything, never forget that they have given you a priceless, irretrievable gift: their time. They could have given that time to a loved one. They could have invested that time in self-improvement or a business venture or in some much-needed leisure. They could have spent that time any way they wanted, but they voluntarily gave it to you. You can't be responsible to make people listen, but you must do everything possible to overcome the innumerable barriers between your message and their hearts. After all, we don't speak merely to be heard; we speak so that the truth we tell might become a catalyst for change.

> Every time you stand before others to say anything, never forget that they have given you a priceless, irretrievable gift: their time.

That's a tall order for any public speaker. It's a matter of eternal consequences for the preacher. The change I seek from my position behind the pulpit has everlasting significance for the souls of the people gathered on Sunday morning, so I will use every resource at my disposal to reach them. Those who say it well erect a solid structure of truth and then put skin on it using illustrations that escort that truth into others' lives.

CHAPTER EIGHT

Laughing

You should always go to other people's funerals, otherwise they won't come to yours.

—Yogi Berra[14]

Sometimes the Bible gives me the best laugh I have all week.

Take, for example, the story of Balaam. He had been chosen by God to be His mouthpiece—a rare distinction in all of human history—but Balaam didn't take his job seriously. When a pagan army assembled to block Israel from entering the Promised Land, their warrior king sent a bribe to the prophet, promising great wealth if he would ride to the battle front and pronounce a curse upon the Hebrews. He wisely refused, sending the messengers back without him. When the king promised him anything he asked— anything!—the prophet-for-profit couldn't resist. The next morning, he saddled his donkey and started off to the battlefront. Along the way, the Lord stopped him. The narrative then reads like a Jim Carrey farce.

As Balaam and two servants were riding along, Balaam's donkey saw the angel of the LORD standing in the road with a drawn sword in his hand. The donkey bolted off the road into a field, but Balaam beat it and turned it back onto the road. Then the angel of the LORD stood at a place where the road narrowed between two vineyard walls. When the donkey saw the angel of the LORD, it tried to squeeze by and crushed Balaam's foot against the wall. So Balaam beat the donkey again. Then the angel of the LORD moved farther down the road and stood in a place too narrow for the donkey to get by at all. This time when the donkey saw the angel, it lay down under Balaam. In a fit of rage Balaam beat the animal again with his staff.

Then the LORD gave the donkey the ability to speak. "What have I done to you that deserves your beating me three times?" it asked Balaam. (Num. 22:22–28, NLT)

I don't know about you, but if a donkey asks me a question, I'm not sticking around for a conversation. But not Balaam.

"You have made me look like a fool!" Balaam shouted. "If I had a sword with me, I would kill you!"

"But I am the same donkey you have ridden all your life," the donkey answered. "Have I ever done anything like this before?"

"No," Balaam admitted. (Num. 22:29–30, NLT)

Outwitted by a donkey. Now, that's funny! You'll never convince me that God doesn't have a sense of humor.

Here's another favorite of mine: David was on the run from Saul, who wanted to kill him. He eventually wound up in Gath, the hometown of the giant he had killed. When captured and brought before the king of the Philistines, David pretended to be crazy in order to escape imprisonment

> You'll never convince me that God doesn't have a sense of humor.

and possible torture. In the timeless words of a true politician, the king exclaimed, "Must you bring me a madman? We already have enough of them around here!" (1 Sam. 21:14–15, NLT). I think that's hilarious!

One more. This time from the New Testament. Paul had gained a reputation for healing the sick and for casting out demons. Not to be outdone, a few nonbelieving men decided they would try their hand at exorcism, perhaps for a modest fee. One particular group traveled from town to town until they found a demon to fight.

They tried to use the name of the Lord Jesus in their incantation, saying, "I command you in the name of Jesus, whom Paul preaches, to come out!" Seven sons of Sceva, a leading priest, were doing this. But one time when they tried it, the evil spirit replied, "I know Jesus, and I know Paul, but who are you?" (Acts 19:13–15, NLT)

That's funny.

Then the man with the evil spirit leaped on them, overpowered them, and attacked them with such violence that they fled from the house, naked and battered. (Acts 19:16, NLT)

And that's downright hilarious! "Naked and battered." Why would you not laugh at that?

Years ago, before I learned to be myself when preaching, I laughed out loud while studying the passage in the privacy of my study only to skim over the humor on Sunday to highlight the gravity of spiritual warfare. Then I realized I wasn't doing the passage any justice. Luke, under the inspiration of the Holy Spirit, included this scene for a reason, not the least of which is to make us laugh. So, I did the unthinkable the next time. I gave myself permission to laugh out loud on Sunday morning in front of God and everybody. Amazingly, nobody picked up stones to stone me. On the contrary, they laughed along with me.

Today, laughter in church isn't a radical thought, but in the 1970s, when I first learned the value of authenticity, very few risked more than a chuckle when preaching. I can't remember when I first let out a big laugh from the pulpit; it just came naturally as my confidence in being genuine grew. At some point, however, I thought nothing of enjoying a good belly laugh, and, not surprisingly, the congregation roared. By then, my sermons were broadcast on the radio through the ministry of Insight for Living, which prompted a few colleagues to warn that criticism would soon follow. Instead, I started receiving letters that read "Don't ever stop laughing, Chuck. Yours is the only laughter that comes into our home."

It is a dark world in which we live, so a touch of humor in the church is conspicuous by its absence—at least to me. Many well-meaning preachers, perhaps moved by the seriousness of their role, see no need for humor in the church and deliberately suppress laughter. That's something I've never quite understood. Laughter should come easily to a place characterized by joy. While we shouldn't try to manufacture humor, neither should we overlook things that are naturally funny.

> While we shouldn't try to manufacture humor, neither should we overlook things that are naturally funny.

Before I go much further, however, I want to put humor into context. A preacher who eventually failed and left the ministry once advised me, "Always leave 'em laughing." I knew immediately that he had given me terrible advice. Great entertainers know how to leave their audiences laughing, but I wasn't called by God to entertain. I'm not a comedian; my job is not to be clever and put on a show. I was called to help those who are willing to give me the gift of their time a greater understanding of the Scriptures and practical guidance on how to put God's timeless principles into action. Everything I do in my role as a preacher must serve those two primary goals. I want to leave them thinking. I want to leave them convicted. I want to leave them motivated. I want to leave them free from shame and excited about walking in grace. But I don't want to "leave 'em laughing." To conclude a message with something funny is to leave the impression that everything I just said shouldn't be taken seriously.

As long as I keep my priorities straight, I have found humor to be a seriously effective tool in communication. Those who "say it well" know how to make the most of laughter and use it effectively.

Connecting through Laughing

Laughter is a universal language; consequently, humor is a very effective way to establish a rapport with an unfamiliar audience. That's why I almost always open with something humorous when addressing an audience I do not know. And when I do, many will shift in their seats to assume a more comfortable posture, and the whole room seems to take a collective deep breath and settle down. It's like we've now connected. It's amazing.

> Humor is a very effective way to establish a rapport with an unfamiliar audience.

As I stated earlier, I'm rarely nervous before speaking. However, addressing a group I don't know, or about whom I know little, makes my stomach do a few subtle flips. If I can find a good way to make a connection right away, my nerves settle and I am better able to concentrate on "saying it well." So, when I was invited by a Dallas Seminary colleague to speak at a church in Peoria, Illinois—a very distinguished Presbyterian congregation—I felt a little anxious.

Other than my friend's son, who served on the church's pastoral staff, I didn't know a soul in Peoria. While I felt confident about the message I had prepared, which perfectly suited the occasion, I didn't know how to break the ice. And on the morning of my talk, I was still churning. I wasn't sure how to connect with a church full of strangers.

Still praying for inspiration, I went downstairs to the hotel restaurant, where I ordered an omelet, fried potatoes, and coffee. I asked the waitress for some ketchup for the potatoes, which she brought right away. And, as I always do, I gave the bottle a vigorous shake. Unfortunately, the waitress, trying to be helpful, had loosened the top for me, and...

Yep. Ketchup everywhere. Up my shirt. Across my tie...even into the vest pocket of my sports coat. And an especially generous pool washed around in my shirt pocket. I looked like I had been stabbed. It was 8:15; they were to pick me up at 9:30. I left my breakfast uneaten and hurried back to my room where I would try to do some damage control. I remember looking in the mirror and thinking, *Where do I start?* Then, I thought, *What else am I going to wear?* I had packed light for a quick stay, so I had only *that* shirt, *that* tie, and *that* coat. (I have since learned to carry a backup outfit.)

I stripped to my waist and started washing my shirt and tie in the sink. (By the way, I have since learned to use *cold* water, or the red merely turns a bright pink.) The tie was a hopeless case, so it's now somewhere in the Peoria landfill. But it was all I had, so I retied it, stain and all. I was able to scoop out the coat pocket and get the majority of the ketchup off the front, so I was good to go there. By 9:30, I greeted my ride in a pink-and-white shirt, reddish-brown tie, and a sports coat. If the driver noticed anything, he didn't say. I greeted the pastor, and if he noticed anything, he didn't say.

On the short drive to the church, I asked my driver about his church and he said, "Oh, about three-quarters of the congregation listens to you on the radio and they're very excited that you're here." That, of course, made me even more nervous. What a great first impression I was about to make!

My opening statement: "I will never forget Peoria, Illinois, for the rest of my life." And they burst into applause. As the ovation died down, I continued, "And it all ties in with a full bottle of ketchup." Silence. By the time I concluded the story, and held open my jacket to show the giant pink stain, we had an immediate connection. They laughed and I laughed. We shared a moment of real-life humanity—everybody has their own ketchup story—and I was able to talk with them like friends.

Fortunately, by that time in my life as a preacher, I had learned the value of humor. As soon as I got past the initial shock, my nerves settled into a warm confidence. My breakfast disaster was a godsend. I had an opening that I never could have engineered. Several months later, I received a letter from the pastor telling me they were still talking about that message. The blend of vulnerability and humor established an instant connection that allowed what I had to say to slip past their defenses and find a warm welcome in their hearts. They no longer saw me as the man behind the voice on the radio; I was just a klutz like everybody else.

If you're able to laugh at yourself, you will find lots of opportunities to connect with audiences. I have found that audiences are rarely hostile. In normal preaching or speaking situations, everyone in the audience wants you to do well; in fact, they're pulling for you. For that reason, mistakes can become an opportunity to lower your guard, make yourself vulnerable, let them see your imperfections, all of which draws them closer to you. For example, when you foul up in the middle

> If you're able to laugh at yourself, you will find lots of opportunities to connect with audiences.

of a message, acknowledge it! That includes words you mispronounce.

When I preached on the Hebrew conquest of Canaan, I described how Joshua and the people of Israel "*circumcised* the walls of Jericho." Why I had chosen to use the word "circumscribed" I don't know. At first, I didn't realize what I had said, but the congregation kept laughing. Finally, I got it. Oh, my!

Another time, I described the oppressive rule of the Caesars as "living under the roke of yome." More than once, I have directed the congregation to the wrong passage. Then, having read several verses—with great energy and conviction—I had to pause and say, "This is a wonderful passage of Scripture...but it has *nothing* to do with what I meant to read today." The touch of humor helps everyone glide past my mistake.

Let awkward situations become an opportunity for humor. You can't hide it. You can't take it back. All you can do is run with it.

> Let awkward situations become an opportunity for humor.

Laughing at yourself, and allowing the audience to laugh with you, acknowledges their goodwill. It's like sharing an inside joke with the entire group. Far from undermining respect, their admiration and acceptance will increase many times over. And when their respect for you grows, they will allow you greater access to the tender areas of their lives. They give you permission to talk about sensitive issues more freely.

The power of humor to build rapport is so profound I often look for ways to laugh before diving into a sensitive subject. And when I find something suitable, I treasure it like gold. Take, for example, child rearing. If I had to reduce the role of parenting down to two words, they would be "worry" and "guilt." As a result, parents are touchy when you start giving advice on how to be a good mom or dad. They're either cynical or defensive. So, a little humor helps to ease the tension. When preparing the sermon series *You and Your Child*, I told this true story, which begins with a letter I received from a woman after a conference at Moody Bible Institute. She wrote,

> *Dear Chuck,*
>
> *Humor has done a lot to help me in my spiritual life. How could I have raised 12 children, starting at age 32, and not have a sense of humor? After your talk last night, I was having fellowship with friends I met here. I told them I got married at age 31. I didn't worry about getting married. I did leave my future to God's will. But every night I hung a pair of men's pants on the bed and knelt down and prayed this prayer: "Father in heaven, hear my prayer. And grant it if You can. I've hung a pair of trousers here. Please fill them with a man."*

I loved the letter, so I read it to my congregation the following week. It so happened that we had, among others in the worship service, half a family. The mother was home with a sick daughter, so only the father and older son came to church that morning. I knew the family well, and I watched as the father cracked up laughing, but the boy looked rather serious. Several weeks later, I received a letter from the young man's mother:

> *Dear Chuck,*
>
> *I'm wondering if I have something to worry about. I've noticed that our son, when he goes to bed at night, has a bikini hanging over the foot of his bed!*

I had fun writing her back: "You have nothing to worry about. Just pray that the bikini will be filled with a man...I mean, with a *woman* before long."

With a little storytelling drama, people laugh at stories like that until they cry. As the laughter crests and begins to fade, while their defenses are down, that's the perfect time to transition to the message with something like "Parenting is one of the toughest jobs on earth because you never know what to expect." I might follow that with a statement of the subject, which accomplishes several things.

First, the story gives them permission to laugh at the struggles every parent inevitably faces. In the South, we often say, "You have to laugh to keep from cryin'." Humor allows everyone to take a step back, take a deep breath, gain a more balanced perspective, and then give it another go.

> Humor allows everyone to take a step back, take a deep breath, gain a more balanced perspective, and then give it another go.

Second, laughing helps beleaguered parents take themselves a little less seriously. To cope with worry and guilt, people build strong defenses that can prevent healthy self-examination. After a good laugh, I'll see complete strangers give one another a knowing nod that says, "Yeah, I admit it; I'm in over my head and I need help."

Third, a good laugh gives the preacher or speaker the opportunity to climb down from the pedestal, to identify with the audience as a friend, and then offer helpful advice as a fellow struggler rather than an exalted "expert." Difficult messages are easier to hear when the listeners' pride has been removed as a barrier.

While this specific example involves parenting, well-chosen humor can accomplish the same good when approaching any sensitive or difficult topic.

When to Avoid Humor

Humor is risky. Since I risk a lot, I sometimes get bitten. Over the years, that's helped me identify three common danger zones. Use humor carefully and rarely...or, better yet, avoid it altogether in these three situations.

Solemn Events. Some occasions and venues naturally lend themselves to humor, such as banquets, receptions, award ceremonies, commencement exercises—any occasion in which celebration is central. Conversely, you are wise to avoid humor on any occasion involving sadness or loss. I have seen more than one well-meaning pastor try to lighten the hearts of a grieving family at a funeral, only to prompt nervous, awkward laughter. If

> You are wise to avoid humor on any occasion involving sadness or loss.

there's going to be humor, let the family use it. Even if you know the deceased extremely well, and you have a funny story about your personal experience with him or her, humor rarely if ever fits with your role. You're there as a comforter, shepherd, guide, and friend. Your attempts at humor will appear either flippant or callous. I'll be honest with you: I have *never* looked back at a funeral and wished I had used humor.

Similarly, avoid inserting humor into solemn occasions, such as communion services, ordinations, dedications—any event the audience takes seriously or any matter you want them to take seriously. Generally speaking, the more formal and dignified the event, the less room there is for humor.

Painful Issues. I stated earlier that humor can make sensitive or difficult subjects easier to address, but I must caution you: *humor and pain do not mix well.* The more painful the subject, the greater risk you take in trying to insert humor. And some subjects are just too painful to be even remotely amusing: suicide, murder, terminal diseases, war, natural disasters, or any sexual sin, such as adultery, rape, incest, and pornography. The pain caused by these issues runs so deep and the impact is so life altering, no one in his or her right mind could laugh.

Of course, there are less painful subjects in which humor is not necessarily out of the question, but very risky. I steer clear of humor when talking about obesity, psychological issues, or physical disabilities. Again, the pain runs deep for people either suffering personally or dealing with someone they know who is suffering. If you're trying to make a connection with an audience, you don't want to risk alienating any one of them through misplaced humor.

I can't stress this enough. You might be thinking, *Come on, Chuck, we get it. Give us a little credit for some common sense.* But bear with me. "Common sense" is a very subjective quality, and it becomes a less reliable guide the larger your audiences become. I had a lot more leeway for mistakes when addressing a small congregation in New England. The risk of causing harm with misplaced humor was almost insignificant. The risk grew, however, when speaking to several hundred in Irving. Even more so in Fullerton. And on the radio? The risk of offence is immeasurable. As the numbers in my audiences grew, I learned—often painfully—just how poor a guide "common sense" can be.

I say that, not to make you paranoid, but to encourage you to make humor a matter of discipline. Avoid spontaneous humor, which can be misunderstood easily. It's amazing how quickly an offhand comment, taken the wrong way, can completely derail your presentation. Suddenly, you're digging yourself out of a hole rather than delivering the message you spent hours preparing. Avoid unnecessary risk. Plan what humor you will introduce, plan when you will insert it, plan how you will word it, and think about how different segments of your audience will receive it.

> Make humor a matter of discipline.

Unfamiliar Territory. A comedian once told me, "Cross-cultural humor doesn't work; it'll flop every time . . . except for mother-in-law jokes. Those, everybody gets." And I've found his advice to be mostly right. Humor depends upon familiarity and shared experience. That's why stand-up comedians use "observational humor" to get laughs. Jerry Seinfeld became a master at finding comedy in everyday experiences his audiences shared in common. For example, "Do the people who work in the little shops in the airport have any idea what the prices are everywhere else in the world? 'Yeah, fourteen dollars for a tuna sandwich; we think that's fair.'" That's funny to anyone who's had to grab a quick meal between flights. But, what about someone who's never been on an airplane?

The more unfamiliar your surroundings, the less likely your humor will be effective. An audience that knows you and trusts you will let you get away with a lot. If you're a guest somewhere, however, humor can cause offence without your knowing it. Either steer clear of laughter, or find the greatest area of commonality and stay in that zone.

Getting Personal

Humor is like a razor-sharp kitchen knife; you have to handle it with care. Used correctly, humor can cut tension in a room like nothing else, but it can slice into a person just as easily. So, be very careful when making another person or group of people the butt of a joke. Generally speaking, if you make fun of anyone, let it be yourself. You can rarely go wrong taking the brunt of humor yourself.

> If you make fun of anyone, let it be yourself.

With that in mind, however, you can make someone else the object of laughter under certain circumstances. For example, I made fun of two venerated professors in a chapel service at Dallas Seminary, and no one was offended. I preached on the calling of Moses, stressing that the man was eighty at the time. I highlighted his forty years receiving a world-class education in Egypt and his forty years of obscurity among the woolies in Midian. The man God spoke to was eighty! I then said, "Only two people in this room can understand what that would be like: Stan Toussaint and Dwight Pentecost."

The student body cracked up, and the two professors laughed the loudest. And I continued, "Can you believe it? *Sixteen years ago*, Dr. Pentecost was eighty!" That brought the house down. I concluded my message,

Some of you sitting here have a future that will be so surprisingly great, right now you'd never believe it. I know the feeling. Fifty years ago, I sat in those chairs thinking I was the last guy who should be here, and I never would have believed what God had in store. So, fifty years from now, when God has blessed your ministry, call me. And if I'm not alive, call Toussaint and Pentecost, 'cause they'll still be around!

The chapel roared with laughter. And no one laughed harder than those two heroes of mine.

I never could have done that with Dr. John Walvoord or Dr. S. Lewis Johnson, for a few reasons. First, neither man had a vigorous sense of humor. I don't mean they were humorless or that they didn't enjoy a good laugh as much as the next guy, but they simply weren't wired for fun comments. It didn't suit their personalities. Second, I didn't share that kind of rapport with those men in private, so I would never do that in public. For decades, I have enjoyed a respectful, yet very informal rapport with Drs. Toussaint and Pentecost, which gave me permission to presume upon their goodwill. Third, I didn't know Drs. Walvoord or Johnson nearly as well as the other two men. Our closeness allowed me to take lighthearted liberties with our friendship. And finally, the majority of those present *knew* how much I love and respect those two men. All of those factors gave me permission to take that risk.

Interestingly, that was the day we welcomed prospective students to tour the campus and to take part in all our activities. While everyone was laughing, many of the visitors looked at Dr. Pentecost and Dr. Toussaint to gauge their reaction before joining in.

You can also laugh at someone's expense with prior approval. I, unfortunately, learned this the hard way. On the spur of the moment, in the middle of a sermon, a perfect illustration involving Cynthia popped into my mind. I didn't think it was a problem; it wasn't flattering, but it didn't make her a villain. Besides, I felt sure everyone would merely see her as human and then empathize with her. But she didn't feel that way. When we returned home, she said, "I would appreciate it if you wouldn't take advantage of me like that." She was wounded by my humor, and I was at fault for saying what I did. Lesson learned! I quickly apologized.

> You can also laugh at someone's expense with prior approval.

I made the same mistake, using a funny story about one of our children, who was a young teenager at the time. Later my daughter said, "I didn't know you were going to say that today, Daddy. I felt like they were laughing at *me*." I tried to explain that the congregation was laughing at the *situation*, not her specifically, but it didn't help. I was missing the point. I owed my daughter an apology, which I took care of that very day.

In both instances, the element of surprise caused my wife and daughter to feel mistreated. If I had received their permission prior to my remark, neither would have felt embarrassed. I vowed never again to use an unflattering illustration without the person's permission. Amazingly, I rarely have someone refuse. In fact, more often than not, the person is delighted to know his or her bad experience will help others avoid the same mistake. The same story, told with their approval (and very carefully worded), doesn't leave them feeling disrespected. And to put the audience at ease, I usually say, "I have so-and-so's permission to use this illustration..." That not only relieves any sense of awkwardness, it makes a hero out of the person in the story.

Know Thyself

Warren Weirsbe once told me this about a preacher I often quote: "I'm glad you never knew him; you wouldn't quote him as often. He was a much better writer than a speaker. He had virtually no sense of humor, which may explain why he never held a church of any great size. His severity limited his ability to lead." Until Warren told me that, I was not aware of the man's lack of humor.

Without humor, a preacher or speaker comes off as severe and unapproachable. You want to be taken seriously; you don't want to be seen as severe. Humor eases that tension. You want to be clear, not overbearing. Humor makes difficult truths easier to accept. You want to laugh, but never at people or their pain, not unless *everyone* can laugh together. Humor gives us permission to be vulnerable with dignity. It keeps us from taking ourselves too seriously.

> Humor gives us permission to be vulnerable with dignity.

Having said all of that, let me caution against trying to become someone you're not. Some of the very best communicators did not have a great sense of humor. I think it's worthwhile to lighten up and, perhaps, consider how you might introduce a little humor into your presentations. But if you're not naturally funny, please...don't force it. I don't want this chapter to suggest that preaching or speaking cannot succeed without humor. I merely hope to demonstrate the many benefits of humor if it's a natural part of your personality. If I accomplish anything in this chapter, I hope you will feel greater permission to be humorous if that's who you are, and to offer some practical guidance on how and when humor can help you "say it well."

When I told Cynthia about this chapter on laughing, she reflected on our first meeting. That was back in the mid-1950s when I was one of the leaders in "youth revivals." It was often my job to come up with funny skits. These had absolutely *no* spiritual point, absolutely *nothing* to teach. They were just plain fun. And one of her favorites was "The World's Most Famous Spitter." Jimmy Draper stood on one side of the room and went, "Phtup" while I ran like an outfielder on the other side with a bucket, which I thumped on the bottom at just the right moment. Those kids cracked up with laughter . . . and that allowed us into their world.

Remembering those crazy skits, Cynthia said, "I fell in love with your laughter before I fell in love with you."

If you laugh easily, if you enjoy a good sense of humor, let me encourage you to take it with you into the pulpit and on to the speaker's platform. Humor will help you "say it well." When handled with care, humor will also endear you to your audiences, who will then give you greater access to their hearts.

CHAPTER NINE

Applying

A good sermon is an engineering operation by which a chasm is bridged so that the spiritual goods on one side—the "unsearchable riches of Christ"—are actually transported into personal lives upon the other.

—Harry Emerson Fosdick[15]

If people thank me for anything, more often than not, it is for suggesting specific, practical application of the Scriptures. Frankly, that surprises me. And it makes me a little sad. Why would a preacher or a public speaker spend all that time digging, building, praying, and illustrating only to quit before telling his or her audience how to put what they have heard into action? Unfortunately, many pastors offer fine explanations and colorful illustrations of the Scriptures only to stop short of answering the question on everybody's mind: "So what?" Audiences want to know how to turn theory into practice.

> Audiences want to know how to turn theory into practice.

I remember sitting under the teaching of a very fine Bible expositor who frequently ended his messages with the exhortation, "Now, may the Lord apply this to our hearts and lives…let's bow in prayer." And

I thought, *If the Lord guided you to help us with the* interpretation, *doesn't it seem reasonable that He would have you guide us in the* application?

I have to admit, I was born with a pragmatic streak that I'm sure made me a challenging student to my elementary, middle school, and high school teachers. My DNA compels me to seek a practical use for everything—that includes knowledge, which I do not retain unless I see how it will serve a purpose. Because I have this compulsive need to know how information relates to life, I naturally think others want to know the same. Consequently, I automatically start asking the question, "So what?" very early in the digging process. My research often refines the application, which in turn, guides my study. Usually, at least a rough approximation of the application is settled early in the week.

Because application comes so naturally to me, trying to explain the thought process would be like my trying to explain how to breathe. I don't think about it; my body just does it for me. So, thinking through the process in order to explain it will be a challenge. But it'll be good for me. Who knows? I might even learn something new from myself!

Principles for Living

Naturally, I'm coming at this as a preacher. If you're a different kind of speaker, bear with me. All effective presentations lead to the "So what?" question. Even if you're reading a technical paper at a scientific symposium, your audience will want to know what can be done with your information. Their desire offers you the opportunity to prompt their action. Therefore, lift what might be relevant to your kind of speech from my detailed description of preparing a sermon.

In the process of digging, we analyzed the section of Scripture to discover its meaning. Contrary to the teaching of some, there can be only *one* interpretation. It doesn't mean different things to different people. The discipline of interpretation is not subjective; if you read the passage and do not arrive at the meaning originally intended by the human author, you are wrong, plain and simple. You have misinterpreted his writing. People

> The discipline of interpretation is not subjective.

often say, "Every time I read a passage, I get something new out of it," but they aren't describing interpretation; they are referring to *application*. They have discovered new principles from the passage and begin to see new ways to apply them. That's because a section of Scripture can yield several timeless principles leading to many practical applications.

Think of it this way: The Bible is like aspirin. The chemical name is "acetylsalicylic acid," a compound that remains unchanged regardless of the reason you take it, and it has the same effect on the body every single time. Nothing about the compound or its effect changes. However, you can take it for a number of reasons. It's great for getting rid of headaches. You can take it to ease arthritis pain. Or reduce inflammation. Or break a fever. Or thin your blood, which will discourage blood clots, thereby reducing the risk of stroke or heart attack. It's commonly called a wonder drug, used in greater quantities, and for more reasons, than any other medication. Likewise, a biblical passage has one, and only one, interpretation. That interpretation can yield several timeless principles, which lead to a broad range of applications depending upon the audience.

The process of digging should answer the question "What did the passage mean to the original audience?" You should be able to express the basic idea in a couple

> You should be able to express the basic idea in a couple of sentences.

of sentences. Furthermore, the original human author wrote instructions to the original audience expecting them to apply it to their circumstances. Those specific instructions contain within them one or more timeless principles—truths that apply to all people throughout all time regardless of culture.

For example, let me return to my example from chapter 5. Moses wrote to the Hebrews entering the land of Canaan, "You shall not muzzle the ox while he is threshing" (Deut. 25:4). The instructions were easy for them to interpret: "While you're using an ox to power your grain-threshing operation, leave the muzzle off its mouth so it can eat while it's working." Beneath that simple interpretation, however, lies a timeless principle: "Don't deny something (or someone) any needed sustenance while it's helping you accomplish your objectives." That's a rule of conduct that anyone can apply whether or not he has an ox.

Like the interpretation, you should be able to express each timeless principle in a sentence—two at the most. "Application" then is the process of giving specific instructions to your contemporary audience based on the timeless principle. Paul the apostle took the interpretation of Deuteronomy 25:4 and derived a timeless principle, which he expressed as, "The laborer is worthy of his wages." He then applied this timeless principle to his day and time, instructing churches to compensate those who diligently serve their needs as pastors, elders, and teachers (1 Cor. 9:9; 1 Tim. 5:18).

My friend and colleague, Michael Patton, put together a helpful chart to depict this process.

To review: *Interpretation* answers the question "What did the passage mean to the original audience?" The answer should be expressed in a sentence or two, which some call the "Exegetical Statement." From this meaning, we derive one or more timeless principles, which some call the "Theological Statement." *Application* then examines the circumstances surrounding the present-day

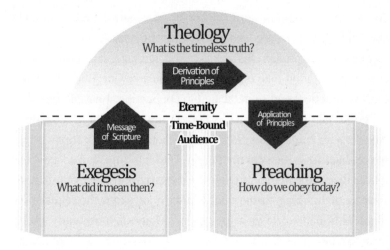

audience—their needs, their challenges, their moral dilemmas—
and offers specific instructions accordingly. An application is the
biblical instruction modified to fit the
contemporary culture. Very few people
still thresh grain and no one in developed
countries use oxen to do it. So, we apply
the interpretation and timeless principle
in ways that fit our circumstances:

> So, we apply the
> interpretation and timeless
> principle in ways that fit
> our circumstances.

- Pay employees a competitive wage.
- Render to a mechanic the usual and customary fee for repairs.
- Tip a waiter no less than the standard 15 percent—no, make
  that 18 percent—for service.
- Return a fair commission to the real estate agent who sold
  your house.

The challenge for the preacher is to determine how to apply the
interpretation so his congregation receives the greatest benefit. To

do that, three realms must converge: theological understanding, personal life experience, and knowledge of the audience.

Theological understanding. While a passage can have several applications, good theological method must be our guide. Because I am so practical and so dedicated to application, I have to be careful not to get there too quickly, both in my study and in the pulpit. Not very far into the digging process, potential applications occur to me, but rather than cut my digging and building short, I exercise a little discipline in order to give the passage thorough examination. Instead of jumping to the end, I simply jot down the application ideas on a pad for later development. Many of those early ideas, however, do not make the final cut. Those that do must be refined as a result of further study.

On Sunday, I have to restrain myself from going straight to the application. Three responsibilities keep me disciplined. First, I have a responsibility to be an exegetical expositor, to faithfully teach the passage so the congregation learns how to study the Bible by example and they gain valuable Bible knowledge.

Second, I have a responsibility to be transparent about how I arrive at the timeless principles and applications I will present. The congregation needs to know that I am not the authority; the Bible is our authority. Moreover, my explaining the passage in view of the application keeps me accountable. Exegetical exposition invites each individual to check my math, as it were, to prove to himself or herself that the applications are sound.

> The congregation needs to know that I am not the authority; the Bible is our authority.

Third, I have a responsibility to let the Word of God do its work in the hearts of the congregation. Make no mistake, that takes time. When you teach Scripture well, the principles unfold themselves, almost spontaneously, and with them a question begging to be answered: "What now? I have this knowledge straight from the mind of God; how do I put it into action?" A sermon needs to retrace the steps you took while digging and building so the congregation can arrive at your conclusions with you as their guide. Most don't have the skills to do the theological work on their own; let them benefit from your advance work.

Sadly, some preachers consider theological understanding optional. They begin with an application, search for a suitable proof text, and then work backward to spin a plausible interpretation. Clearly, that's not what we're after. Others do a good job interpreting the verses and deriving timeless principles, only to suggest applications that have little or no connection to the passage. Obviously, applications should form naturally as a result of digging and building. For applications to meet real-life needs, good theological method must intersect the preacher's personal life experience.

> Applications should form naturally as a result of digging and building.

Personal Life Experience. Preaching is very much a priestly role. A preacher bridges the gap between the world of the Bible and the world of the congregation using his own life experience. He cannot be all things to all people, but his own life experience can help him appreciate the struggles his audience must face. For example, when I address the Christian Embassy, I cannot pretend to know what it's like to be a flag officer in the Pentagon or a member of Congress. However, I am a former marine, which gives me personal knowledge of military life and culture. I have not experienced life as an officer, but I have seen them up close and I know how the military works. So, I can expand on that knowledge enough to connect with an admiral or a general. I am also familiar with the pressures of public life—the unique challenges of notoriety and how it affects people—which helps me enter the world of the politician just enough to make a few relevant observations.

In God's design for my life and where he has placed me in ministry, my past experiences form a bridge from theology to twenty-first-century life. Because I started out as a mechanical engineering apprentice, I can appreciate the accomplishments and challenges of a technical professional. Because I worked in a machine shop, I can relate to blue-collar workers. Because I struggled with a speech impediment, I can encourage others to overcome limitations. My experience in theater and music allow me to talk intelligently with professional entertainers and musicians. The same is true for you.

> You will find that God has given you the ability to connect with segments of our society that might be closed off to others.

As you review all your past experiences, you will find that God has given you the ability to connect with segments of our society that might be closed off to others. Use your personal history and a little imagination as you think about your audience and their needs. Of course, that's assuming you know your audience.

Knowledge of the Audience. At home, where I serve a middle-class congregation in Frisco, Texas, I want to remain engaged with the trials and afflictions they endure. Some pastors tend to isolate themselves, unwittingly creating for themselves a cloistered lifestyle. By that, I mean a pattern of life that revolves around the church and Christianity to a degree they rarely come into contact with people who think or behave differently. When they're not in church, they associate with Christian friends, they read Christian books, they listen to Christian music on Christian radio, and they take up Christian hobbies. They are, in essence, monks without walls. While this exclusively Christian world can be comforting, and even helpful in maintaining personal integrity, it's too easy to lose touch with life on the outside. Where bosses tell raunchy jokes and expect employees to laugh. Where refusing to throw coworkers under the bus shows poor initiative. Where more thought is given to a tattoo than whether to marry. Where guys on a business trip think an evening at the strip joint qualifies as team building.

I've had seminary professors—very smart and very gifted as writers—joke that their books don't sell very well. Occasionally, I have told them, "That's because you write to each other as experts and there aren't that many of you. Every once in a while, break ranks! Deliberately write something for people outside your theological world. Write to the truck driver, the waitress, the software engineer, or the small business owner." The longer you stay out of the

> Every once in a while, break ranks!

mainstream of life, the narrower your field of vision remains. The result? You have less to say that's relevant and interesting to "real-world folks."

To keep in touch with the world of those we hope to reach, we must leave our personal monasteries and learn how to live and walk among those to whom we want to communicate. Read literature from the current best seller list. Be aware of what your audience watches. Pursue interests outside your realm of expertise. Don't let your vocation make your world smaller; branch out. Then, take that knowledge of your audience and let it shape your message...especially its application.

Ready, Aim, Apply

By the time I have completed my digging—observing the passage, examining the original language, considering the history, culture, and issues surrounding the original writing, and then deriving timeless principles—my three realms (theological understanding, personal life experience, and knowledge of the audience) converge to yield specific applications. Those applications then become my target when building the message (title, introduction, and body). Beginning with the end in mind helps me keep the message lean and focused.

When I'm ready to nail down specific applications, I glance back at the pad with my early ideas for anything that might be usable. Then, I push everything aside, lean back in my chair, close my eyes, and use my imagination to put myself in other people's shoes. I try to see life through their eyes as I consider several different categories. First, I think about what my audience might *need*.

I think about what my audience might *need*.

When I was invited to go overseas to minister to missionaries, I took some time to recall what it felt like to be on Okinawa, cut off from everything familiar and everyone meaningful to me. Earlier, I had asked a friend what need he thought I should address and he responded with one word: encouragement. I recalled how discouraged I became, especially around holidays, and how difficult it was to have no one to lean on. I let my mind linger in the world of the missionary as I knew it, reflected on past conversations with missionaries, and thought about what might encourage me if I were in their shoes.

When I returned home, I wanted to give my friend a medal. He was absolutely right. The missionaries were feeling lonely, obscure, unthanked, cut off, and weary. My words of encouragement instantly connected. They were like splashes of cool water on parched tongues and dry souls.

What challenges, trials, or difficulties will my audience face, and how can I equip them to succeed?

I also think in terms of *challenges*. I ask myself, "What challenges, trials, or difficulties will my audience face, and how can I equip them to succeed?" When asked to speak to a group of Ryder Truck leaders, I recalled what it was like to be out of town, alone in a hotel, feeling lonely and tired, hundreds of miles from accountability—a perfect setup for a moral tumble. I remember having to be proactive in guarding my purity and the practical steps I took to remain above reproach. So, when the group convened...in Las Vegas...I spoke on integrity. The applications in my message addressed some sensitive areas, but because I spoke as a sympathetic fellow struggler, they received my practical suggestions without becoming defensive.

I wonder what *reproof* might be appropriate, although I tend to go easy with my tone. I don't want to condescend or sound like I'm scolding. I did a lot of that when I was younger, but I've since learned to phrase reproofs as warnings and that the right choice of pronouns can make all the difference. I would say, for example, "All of us need to be warned about..." and then state the danger or call out the sinful behavior. That way, I don't presume everyone in the audience is guilty, yet those who are blameworthy get the point. Also, by including myself in the reproof, I avoid talking down to my audience and coming across as St. Francis of Assisi.

I also find it helpful to use my own experience as an illustration of what not to do and how to turn a bad situation around. When I spoke on jealousy, I told the story of my own battle with that disease of the heart while dating my wife to be. I was amazed by how many people expressed both relief and appreciation for my candor. My overcoming jealousy gave them hope for their own struggle, and my practical suggestions gave them a way to engage the Lord in overcoming the problem.

As I think through the needs, challenges, and reproofs appropriate to my audience, I imagine how the timeless principles derived from the passage might address them. And then I spell out the applications as specific as possible. In the process, I tailor my notes to build toward those principles and applications. I make sure illustrations don't sidetrack the audience or divert them from a

> I make sure illustrations don't sidetrack the audience or divert them from a head-on collision with their need to implement the Lord's instructions.

head-on collision with their need to implement the Lord's instructions. I shape my message like a funnel to capture as much of the congregation as possible and then guide them all to the same destination: a personal encounter with the mind of God.

Sometimes I list off applications like action items on a "to do" list. I stay away from alliteration, rhyming, and other kinds of wordplay; they don't really help people remember the application points. Frankly, I find that stuff contrived and tedious. People remember the applications they find relevant. If you offer something practical and helpful, something that equips people in their attempt to overcome a difficulty, solve a problem, or improve their relationship with the Lord, trust me, they will remember it. I do, however, boil the application points down to their essence in short statements, which I explain in greater detail. And I try to maintain a consistent rhythm with each statement. For example, after examining Jesus' first encounter with religious opposition (Luke 4:14–30), I *wouldn't* suggest the following application points:

- Do not let opposition take you off guard.
- Persevere.
- Remain focused.

While I don't phrase application points to be memorable, I want to state them in a way that will be clear. I certainly don't desire to make them *difficult* to remember. So, I would rephrase the previous points to follow a consistent cadence.

- Do not be surprised.
- Do not give up.
- Do not get sidetracked.

Landing the Plain Truth

My mentor, Dr. Howard Hendricks, loves to use the analogy of a pilot landing a plane when talking about concluding a message. Some speeches arrive at the destination only to circle the runway tentatively until the speaker runs out of fuel and the speech crashes on the tarmac. Other speakers blaze into the airport, full throttle, and try to execute a three-point landing at Mach 3. No gradual approach. No warning. Just a white-knuckle, neck-snapping, chest-grabbing halt. Good pilots, on the other hand, begin their landing miles away from the runway, having planned their "approach." If you fly commercial airlines often, you know when you're "beginning the descent." The engines change pitch and you feel a change in velocity.

Your audience should sense when you're beginning your approach. A well-planned transition will signal the change. Using my example above, taken from my message on Luke 4:14–30, here is how I made the transition:

> Your audience should sense when you're beginning your approach.

What do you do when the tide turns against you? Are you there? Are you there right now? Have you been on one side of people's favor but now you're on the other, because of something that you did that was not wrong but they disliked? Have your friends turned against you? Family members? The

company? A roommate? A partner in life? Let me give you
a couple or three warnings when the tide turns against you.
They're not complicated. You may know them up here in your
head, you need to remember them now. If not now, soon.

With that clear shift from exposition to application, I usually see
people shift in their seats to change posture. If they've been sagging
a little, they perk up. If they haven't been taking notes, they will
often pull a piece of paper out of a purse or a pocket and prepare to
jot down the upcoming points. Some literally move to the edge of
their seats or lean forward. That's when I know I have allowed the
exegetical exposition to do its work; their hearts crave to know "So
what?" Their body language urges me to offer some answers.

I sometimes list off the application points in rapid-fire succes-
sion, then return to unpack each one. Usually, however, I explain
each point before moving on to the next. As I briefly explain each
point, I follow a fairly consistent pattern. First, I explain what I
mean. "Do not be surprised" is merely a gloss; it has no meaning or
relevance on its own. In this case, it's stated in the context of facing
ungodly opposition. So, I explain:

Do not be surprised. Usually we are. Usually our response is
"I can't believe he said that. I can't believe they're treating
me like this. I can't believe they understood me to be saying
such-and-such." We're surprised. It may be from your own
family. It may be from a long-term friendship. It may be from
those who praised you only days earlier, but they now have
your face on their dartboard. They no longer like you. Don't
be surprised.

Second, I point back to specific examples from the Scriptures to
support the point.

Look back at verse fourteen. "And Jesus returned to Galilee in the power of the Spirit, and news about Him spread through all the surrounding district. And He began teaching in their synagogues and was praised by all."

Third, I connect the example from the passage to our experiences today.

It happened to Jesus; it will happen to us. Don't even be surprised if in the midst of adulation and acceptance that your feet are cut out from under you and you become the object of their rage. It's to be expected when you're doing what's right.

This is just one more way for me to demonstrate the connection between the Scriptures and life as it really is. He's protected His Word all these centuries, and now we have a book like no other in our own tongue. And when people see the relevance of the Bible, God glories in your ministry, and, candidly, they can't get enough. The people who don't thank me for specific, practical application of the Scriptures, most often thank me for showing them the relevance of the Scriptures. That makes my whole week! That's when I know I was in the zone, which is gratifying.

Applications That Stick

People don't invest their time with a speaker or preacher to hear the obvious; they need insight. They have problems to solve, needs to meet, challenges to overcome, relationships to repair, and a spiritual war to fight. They gravitate toward those who will equip them to handle life-related issues, those who can speak peer to peer about real-life difficulties and practical, proven solutions. Two incidents told me I was on the right track with my applications.

Several years ago, I was informed by the Insight for Living staff that a man had come from out of state to confront me. He was upset by the radio broadcast because my applications were so relevant to him, personally, he was convinced I had targeted him specifically. In fact, he felt the applications so keenly, he convinced himself I had ordered surveillance equipment to be installed in his home to gather relevant data. After all, how else could I have known to be so specific? Of course, he was psychotic, in desperate need of medical and psychological treatment. But, in a strange way, I felt affirmed!

Most reactions aren't that extreme, although, I often hear people say, "I felt like you were talking directly to me." They usually don't mean it literally. Usually. I did have a man approach me after a sermon who appeared visibly shaken. Not crazy; just shaken. He waited until everyone else had gone before talking to me. He looked around and then said, "Uh, my wife...she talked with you, right?"

I said, "I'm sorry. I don't even know your name." And I shook his hand.

"My name isn't important. My wife...uh...I know she called you earlier."

I replied, "No. I haven't received any calls about anyone."

He wouldn't hear it. "The last few minutes of your sermon...that was about me, wasn't it?"

I said, "Well, you tell me! If you're wondering if I had you targeted, you can rest easy. I usually let people listen in on what I need to hear."

> People don't invest their time with a speaker or preacher to hear the obvious; they need insight.

> Well, you tell me! If you're wondering if I had you targeted, you can rest easy.

He grinned, then looked perplexed. "She didn't call you or write you or anything?" he pleaded.

"No," I assured him. "Never heard from anyone, including your wife."

"Well." He sighed. "You did everything but name my name! What you said describes exactly where we've been this last month and a half; you perfectly described our downward spiral. You're telling me you haven't talked to a friend who knows us or had any knowledge of our situation?" He remained unconvinced.

"No, I can assure you, I didn't have you specifically in mind. Until this moment, I didn't know your name. I couldn't pick your wife out of a lineup. And I don't even know what part of the message you're referring to or what you've been through. I'm assuming you don't know Christ as Savior."

"I don't know much about that stuff," he admitted. "I've come because I'm at my wits end and I don't know what else to do."

"Thank you for your honesty. We who are Christians believe that the Holy Spirit, who is God, moves among us. He helps me interpret the Scriptures, and, without my conscious knowledge, He guides me into specific application of these truths. He also knows people like you."

The man almost turned white.

"If anybody gave me any insight," I continued, "it was the Holy Spirit."

He glanced up then back at me, staring blankly for a few moments, and said, "I don't know how that works."

"I don't know either. I just know I don't have any special powers. This is God's working on your behalf. Don't let this opportunity pass." He walked away relieved but still perplexed.

He later came to faith in Christ. The couple regularly attends our church, all because the application had three indispensable qualities. The man found the application *insightful*; so spot-on relevant he thought I had been tipped off. He responded because the application perceived his situation accurately; I truthfully described his current life and identified with his perspective. Consequently, it gave my suggested response credibility.

When an application is insightful, the audience thinks, "If he understands my problem so well, perhaps I should follow through on his application."

The man also found the application *penetrating*. He felt understood, which is a common need among people in pain. They might admire from a distance a speaker with great intelligence, but they'll listen closely to someone who understands them—their flaws and their failures—without looking down on them. I'm not a brilliant scholar and I can't hold an audience transfixed with my eloquence, but (as a longtime friend once put it) I do know how to "get in their knickers." I live in a real world and I don't mince words when I call things the way they are. I've learned over many years that people want that kind of raw, frank honesty, much like a cancer patient wants a doctor to tell him or her everything—where the disease is, how bad it is, what the treatment options are, what the chances are, and when the treatments can start.

> They might admire from a distance a speaker with great intelligence, but they'll listen closely to someone who understands them.

The man responded to the application because it was *bold*. I talked about a problem that people don't mention at parties and family gatherings, and they certainly don't admit they have this struggle. (I'm not revealing the issue here because it's not important.) I said out loud what people know to be true but dare not talk about. It's that which makes a message ring true. When I do this, people in the congregation often nod without realizing it, offering their silent affirmation, "Yes, I hate to admit it, but that's true." It's a powerful moment because it offers relief from the isolation shame produces and they find hope in the practical application of Scripture.

When I was invited to address the students of Wheaton College, I was given three opportunities to speak during their chapel services. I titled the series *Invaluable Spiritual Disciplines.* I closed the series by addressing the discipline of handling failure. Some speakers come and refer to Wheaton College as the "Christian Harvard" because, in their minds, it's the pinnacle of Christian liberal arts schools. At Wheaton, like at the Ivy League schools, failure is simply not an option. "Driven" barely describes the intensity you find on that campus. So, as you might imagine, it was a bold move to talk about failure with the assumption that it would apply to anyone among the twenty-five hundred students in the room, because failure is a phantom terror that stalks everyone and yet is rarely acknowledged by any student at Wheaton College.

> So, as you might imagine, it was a bold move to talk about failure with the assumption that it would apply to anyone among the 2,500 students in the room.

I opened with the statement, "The subject I want to talk about is failure, the number one fear among most of you who fill this room today." In the middle of the message, I said, "Most of us have been raised to do our best—nothing wrong with that—to reach high goals—nothing wrong with that...And, though you are young, you find yourself a part of this student body, and there is a sense of unspoken pride in being here. Let's face it. So how can you possibly admit to a sense of inadequacy? How could you share with anybody your fear of failure? The thought of not making it through this school?" And I ended my message with a single application point: *Give yourselves a break!*

After describing some of my own failures—some fairly dismal— I closed with the following:

*The best lessons I've learned, I've learned through inadequacy and failure. Disappointment, and heartbreak, and forgiveness. By the grace of God, I've come to the place where I no longer fear failure. And I've come to the place where I will be always grateful for God's grace to forgive when I don't measure up to my unrealistic standard. Please, men and women—*please*—understand:*

Only God is adequate; you're not.

Only God is perfect; you're not.

Only Christ can set goals that high and reach them; you can't.

You do your best. But I can promise you, in the future there will be days you will be sitting across from someone you love and you'll be saying things that you need to say to build back a bridge that your pride has broken down...The good news is, God in His grace uses each one of us "warts and all."

I returned to Wheaton two years later to attend my granddaughter's graduation and the students were still talking about "that message you gave on failure." I addressed a problem everybody experienced but nobody talked about. And I delved deeply into the issue in enough detail to communicate clearly that I understood the students' secret fear. Having done that, my simple application found a ready home in their hearts. The chaplain is still thanking me for addressing what had not been addressed in all the years he's been serving there as chaplain.

> The chaplain is still thanking me for addressing what had not been addressed in all the years he's been serving there as chaplain.

Don't Save the Best for Last

Generally speaking, applications come at the end of a message. Usually, you want to lay the logical groundwork and build toward application...but not always. Sometimes I will drop an application into the middle of the exposition so that it looks like an extemporaneous aside when, in fact, it's planned. For example, in the exposition section of a message titled, "Getting Through the Tough Stuff of Confrontation," I inserted the following:

No extra charge for this little exhortation. In your choice of friends, be certain that you have a few who care less for your comfort than they do for your character. Most of us want to make our friends comfortable. Few are good enough friends to overlook the comfort for the good of the character. And if you have some who care more for your character than your comfort, you are rich indeed, you are many times blessed.

I think of a CPA. He cares more for my character than for my comfort. [audience laughter] Ah, now you got it. I have a physician who is like that. He cares more for my character than for my comfort. He doesn't say when he gets to an x-ray that looks questionable, "Oh, we won't worry about this one. This is a bad picture. Let's talk good news today. [Audience laughter] Let's go have lunch together." No, he snaps that x-ray up on that screen and he says, "Now, look at this, Chuck. That does not look good. We gotta do something about that." And so it is with a wife. And so it is with a parent. And so it must be with a friend.

If I were to coin a term for this, it might be "application ad rem." (*Ad rem* is Latin for "to the point.") And there are several

If I were to coin a term for this, it might be "application ad rem."

good reasons to break from the normal pattern and introduce applications along the way.

"Application ad rem" gives the audience a breather when the subject is heavy. When you're deep into a difficult topic, such as suicide, divorce, or sexual immorality, humor wouldn't be appropriate and an illustration won't provide the right kind of relief from the building tension. Stepping back for a few moments to apply a principle can provide just the right kind of respite before moving on. It's like providing a landing on a long flight of stairs. I'll often see the audience take a deep breath as I offer an application, then relax a little as we head into the next section of the exposition.

Sometimes, I will structure the entire message to introduce each application along the way rather than wait until the end. Here's how the outlines would compare:

Typical Outline	Application Ad Rem Outline
Introduction	Introduction
Exposition	Exposition
Point 1	Point 1
Point 2	Application 1
Point 3	Point 2
Applications	Application 2
Conclusion	Point 3
	Application 3
	Conclusion

This is helpful when you're in a passage that's peppered with lots of practical instructions. The books of James and 1 and 2 Peter, and the conclusion of Paul's letters are good examples. The Beatitude sections of the Lord's discourses are another. Holding the applications to the end would be awkward for the preacher and confusing for the congregation.

The Application Ad Rem Outline is also helpful if you need to build one application on top of another. For example, Jesus taught a process of reconciliation involving successive steps in Matthew 18:15–17. A "teach-apply, teach-apply" structure will make the process clearer by the end.

"Application ad rem" is useful when a verse prompts helpful advice your audience needs to hear, but it's not the main point of the passage or your message. When expositing Genesis 32:24–32, in which Jacob wrestles with the Lord, I might point out verse 30: "So Jacob named the place Peniel, for he said, 'I have seen God face to face, yet my life has been preserved.' " As a quick aside, I would say, "When God meets with you at a special place and for a special reason, it's sometimes helpful to name that place. Maybe even create a small monument. Then, frequently go back to that place in your mind, especially when life gets complicated and confusing."

That's not the main point of the passage, and I wouldn't want that bit of advice to detract from my primary application at the end. So, I will drop it in the exposition, introduced with a "By the way…"

As I grew more comfortable in the role of preacher, I began to allow "application ad rem" to occur extemporaneously as I'm preaching, as it occurred to me in the moment. I used to be afraid of that, but I have learned to trust my instincts and to allow for the possibility that it's a prompting from God, quite possibly for the exclusive benefit of someone in the room. Be careful with that, however. Don't let it

> I have learned to trust my instincts and to allow for the possibility that it's a prompting from God.

turn into a sermonette, or pull you offtrack. Make your point quickly and return to your outline or you'll exasperate your audience.

The Weight of the World

Application can be the most difficult part of the message, both to plan and to deliver. You're taking a huge risk because you're presuming to know what the audience needs. (Perhaps that's why some omit it all together.) You can bring your best theology, you can apply your own experience and imagination, and you can study your audience, but you can't know for sure you're hitting the mark.

Many years ago, I was asked by the chaplain of a professional football team to address the men. It was a Super Bowl team and these were some of the highest-profile names in the business at the time. I really felt intimidated, but I agreed. After I finished, I didn't feel like I had done a very good job, and, as the men dispersed, I started looking for a graceful exit when the quarterback approached me and said, "What was *that* all about?"

I said, tentatively, "Are you kidding, or are you serious?"

"I just didn't know where you were going with all of that." He shook his head and stalked off.

Man, that was tough to hear! I don't know if there's anything that troubles me more than to hear someone say, "I have no idea where you were going with that message or how that applied to where I am." The goal of preaching—and application, especially—is to lift the black-and-white printing of God's Word from the page and help the listener consume it, digest it, metabolize it, and become animated by it. If I fail to uphold my part in that process, I have wasted not only my time, but the time of every person gathered to listen.

That can be an awful burden, one too great for any mere human to bear. So, let me encourage you to do your best—dig deeply, build soundly, illustrate clearly, and apply insightfully—but keep two important facts in mind as you stand and deliver.

First, audience response is not always the best measure of

success. Entertainers thrill and delight audiences, and they receive accolades for their wit, humor, delivery, and panache. But entertainers don't change lives. Conversely, a truly impactful sermon or speech often yields few compliments and significant dividends in terms of spiritual growth.

> A truly impactful sermon or speech often yields few compliments and significant dividends in terms of spiritual growth.

After the quarterback's comment left me feeling like a failure, I mentioned our conversation to the chaplain; I wanted his feedback on where I went wrong. He said, with a sad, wistful smile, "Yeah, that's 'so-and-so.' He knew exactly where you were going. You were going where he didn't want you to go." I breathed a sigh of relief.

Sometimes the impact we have is deeper and more profound than we realize.

The second fact we, as preachers and speakers, must never forget: we are called to "say it well," which includes the responsibility of application, but we are not the Holy Spirit. We can reach the ears of our listeners, but only He can reach their hearts. Apply the truth as best you know how, and then … let God be God.

CHAPTER TEN

Ending

Having come to the end, stop. Do not cruise about looking for a spot to land, like some weary swimmer... splashing about until he can find a shelving beach... Finish what you have to say and end at the same time.

—William E. Sangster[16]

Of all the elements that comprise a sermon or a speech, none is more important than the conclusion. The last few moments you spend with an audience can, literally, make or break the whole message. In fact, when novice preachers or inexperienced speakers fail, it's typically on this one count. They usually prepare a gripping introduction, offer clearly defined points, provide vivid illustrations, and practical applications only to "wing" the conclusion, perhaps with the expectation that a good beginning and solid middle will send them on a trajectory to a great ending. But you can't fling a message toward the audience like a baseball, hoping it flies close enough to catch. On the contrary, if there's anything you *don't* leave to chance, it's the last thought you leave ringing in their ears.

> You can't fling a message toward the audience like a baseball, hoping it flies close enough to catch.

A solid conclusion accomplishes a

threefold purpose. First, to add a final "why" to the question of "how" answered by the application. Ideally, good exegetical exposition will prepare the audience's heart to say, "So what? Show us *how* to put this information into action." While the application feeds the mind, an effective conclusion appeals to the will; it prompts the audience to action. That's the primary difference between teaching and preaching. Both provide helpful information and both suggest ways to apply that new information to life, but as a matter of purpose and emphasis, preaching is all about urging action. Therefore the spirit of a sermon is motivational throughout, and devotes a greater portion of time to stimulating audience response.

Regardless, no other kind of speech should end without an appeal to have the audience act upon the message they just heard.

Second, a good conclusion satisfies the audience's desire for a feeling of closure. It says, "We're coming to the end of our discussion and will soon part ways." A message without a conclusion feels like someone turning and walking away in the middle of an interesting conversation. A hasty, unplanned final conclusion is rude, leaving the audience feeling abruptly dismissed, like they aren't important to you.

> A message without a conclusion feels like someone turning and walking away in the middle of an interesting conversation.

Third, an effective conclusion ties up any loose ends, unifies the principles and applications under a common theme, and summarizes the message. Ideally, your ending words should help the audience restate the essence of your talk in a sentence or two. If they haven't captured it beforehand, they'll need to grasp it in the conclusion.

Great conclusions don't just happen. To end well, you must plan well. As Yogi Berra once said, "If you don't know where you're going, you might not get there."[17]

The Flight Plan

By the end of the digging process, I expect to have a clear under-standing of my destination. The specific applications still need to be fleshed out as I complete the building process, but I should know how I want the audience to think differently and a general idea of how they should respond. This desired response governs every-thing as I sit before my trusty IBM Selectric: the opening statement, the introduction, the main body, the illustrations, the applications, and—just as important—how I transition from one element to the next. (More on transitions in a moment.) Like a pilot working out a flight plan, this process of building the message lets me envision how I will lead the audience from point A (their initial thinking) to point B (the desired response). Sometimes, on rare occasions, an introduction immediately spawns a great conclusion, and the mes-sage almost writes itself. I wish it always worked out that way! More often than not, I depend upon the process of planning the details of each successive element—starting with the introduction and work-ing my way through to the applications—that leads me toward my final destination: a good conclusion.

As of this writing, I am planning a series of talks for a very spe-cial event the summer of 2011. Cynthia and I will be leading a large number of Insight for Living listeners on a cruise in the Adriatic, Aegean, and Mediterranean Seas. The theme was "Meeting our Heroes in Ancient Places," and, during our travels, we will visit several important sites in biblical and church history. We'll learn about Emperor Diocletian's persecution of Christians as we visit his palace in Split, Croatia. In Athens, we'll see where Paul preached to the greatest philosophical minds of his day, and in Ephesus where he mentored Timothy. In Istanbul (formerly, Constantinople), we'll learn about Athanasius and the Nicene Creed that became the definitive statement of our Trinitarian belief. While at sea, we'll also revisit the life of David and other biblical heroes.

Most people might consider that enough. After all, everyone will gain a lot of knowledge and insight along the way. But that's not nearly good enough for me—Mr. Practical. I'm not happy filling heads with knowledge. I always want to send our guests home with something to do. My purpose always has been, and always will be, to see the Scriptures turned into action. Because we're observing heroic traits in our heroes, the application is obvious: *go and do likewise*. In the last message, I'll summarize all of the qualities and traits that made our heroes great and I'll challenge the audience to return home and become someone's hero, to emulate the characteristics we observed on our travels. "If you model those traits before a handful of people, you will endear yourself to them for the rest of their lives, and you will have encouraged them to become more than they otherwise would have been."

> I always want to send our guests home with something to do.

While I was happy with the application, I knew it wouldn't be enough by itself. I saw two problems keeping my audience from actually following through. First, we tend to think of heroes as larger than life and, therefore, excuse ourselves from responsibility. After all, those people are heroes while we're just regular people. Second, let's face it, a "go and do likewise" application is a little obvious. Obvious is boring. Obvious is mundane. Obvious is too easy to ignore. So, I needed a conclusion to transform the obvious into an imperative. As I worked through the messages for the cruise, I was also working on this book. And that gave me a great idea.

> Obvious is boring.

At the very end, I'll conclude with a short history of my heroes, men who profoundly impacted my life: Richard Nieme, Bob

Newkirk, Ray Stedman, Dwight Pentecost, and Howie Hendricks, to name only a few. I think my transparency and emotion—because it is so personal—will connect with our fellow travelers. I will then invite the audience to recall their own personal heroes. Hopefully, that will bring all of our heroes down from all their pedestals. And, by remembering how their personal heroes impacted their lives, I believe they'll see the potential of becoming a hero to someone else. I'll leave them with the challenge: "You have people back home who already admire you and consider you their hero—believe it or not. I challenge you: go home and be a hero to those people."

That's my goal. That's my destination as a communicator. Now that I have my conclusion worked out in detail, I will reexamine every element of every message to prepare the audience for that final moment. I might change out some illustrations or refine my points. For certain, as I deliver each message, I'll have my eye on the destination. Consequently, I feel strongly that we'll conclude well because I have planned well. The concluding message wraps up all of my talks on heroes and provides a needed bow on top. We will disembark from the ship not only looking back with gratitude, but looking forward with anticipation.

> I feel strongly that we'll conclude well because I have planned well.

Transitions

A well-planned conclusion doesn't feel tacked on . . . because it isn't! It fits with the flow of the message. To make that happen, you begin transitioning to the conclusion virtually from the introduction. Each element of the message must be considered an incremental move toward the final thought. Moreover, the transitions between elements need to be smooth.

For example, you might open with a strong statement followed by a spellbinding introductory illustration, a story that holds the audience in a state of suspended animation. The story about the hunter attacked by the snake in chapter 7 had that effect. Unfortunately, you can't maintain that high level of tension forever; you have to bring the audience back down as you deliver your first point. So, think about how you will lower them slowly so that remnants of the "spell" cast by the story will linger as you move forward. When a speaker loses his or her audience, more often than not, it's in the transitions.

A good transition has two crucial factors to manage: logic and energy. Logic has to do with tying one element of a speech to another in a way the audience can see their relationship. You can see it done every night on the evening news as the anchor moves from one story to the next with a verbal "segue." A humorous example might look like this:

> "Firefighters say the warehouse blaze burned hotter than usual because of all the plastic storage bins. (Pause) And speaking of hot, it was a scorcher out there today. Don, what's the rest of the forecast this week? Any cold fronts on the horizon?"

That's not necessarily a wise segue, but it illustrates the idea. If I'm moving from the snake story to the first point, I need to keep the snake imagery alive, at least until I'm well into my explanation of the point.

> *"...with the snake coiled tightly around his shoulder and arm, the rattle shaking furiously, and its teeth caught in the wool of his turtleneck sweater, the man could feel drops of venom dripping down his neck. (Pause) This may be difficult to believe, but if you're not in a desperate struggle for your life right now, you soon will be. Before this week is over,*

temptation will strike. And if you resist, it will coil around your neck and start squeezing, demanding you either give up or find a way out. I want to show you what the Bible says about temptation and how we can..."

The other factor is energy, conveyed through the intensity of your voice and genuine emotions as you speak. In the diagram, the line represents energy. Many speakers—even seasoned professionals—let their intensity drop to zero, creating momentary voids between each element of their presentation. The audience will

> The other factor is energy, conveyed through the intensity of your voice and genuine emotions as you speak.

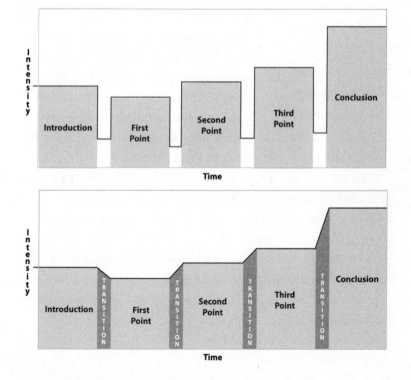

mirror your intensity; so, for the fleeting moment you withdraw, or fumble, or become distracted, your audience withdraws from you. Any lost connection must be reestablished as you continue. Better, keep your energy consistent as you move from one element to the next. That doesn't mean you have to keep talking in a steady stream. Note the pause in my example. You keep the energy consistent by maintaining eye contact and holding your current posture until you speak. Then, deliver the next sentence with the same volume and intensity as before. You can bring the audience down smoothly by lowering the volume and intensity of your voice as you speak.

To help with transitions, many people craft a good sentence, which they write in their notes, and then memorize it. They won't memorize anything other than the transition sentences because it's natural to maintain contact and energy throughout an introduction or within a major point. Transitions come so naturally to me now, I rarely think about it anymore. In fact, I frequently break the rules without losing connection with the audience. (Don't ask me how; I don't know.)

> To help with transitions, many people craft a good sentence, which they write in their notes, and then memorize it.

Take note of the diagram again. The transitions between elements help the audience subconsciously learn your pattern as a speaker so that, when you reach the end, the transition to the conclusion feels just like any other. They will know you're headed for the home stretch, but they stay with you. Very often, when I transition to the conclusion, people unconsciously close their Bibles and assume a different posture; they know we're coming in for a smooth landing (hopefully!).

Time to Conclude

Time is a constant concern for the preacher or speaker. You can lose yourself in a message as minutes pass like seconds. And you can sometimes draw the audience in so deeply they forget the clock as well. Nevertheless, time will become an issue sooner or later. Usually, you have an established parameter and it's reasonably firm. You might be able to push it a couple of minutes, but that's about all. Time is, perhaps, the least spiritually fulfilling factor in crafting a message, but it's nonetheless a crucial one. Therefore, if you don't plan properly, it will destroy your conclusion, taking the entire message down with it.

You can't "say it well" if you don't end it well. And for a sermon, in which motivation is such a critical factor, sufficient time needs to be devoted to the conclusion. After exegetical exposition has provided interesting data to support the desired response, and deriving timeless principles has demonstrated the relevance of the Scriptures, and your applications have described how to put this new information into action, you can't make a mad dash to an effective appeal to their will. You have spent a good amount of time filling their heads with knowledge—granted, with occasional appeals to the heart along the way—but now you must shift your focus from head to heart, from thinking to emotion, from the "how" of obedience to the "why." Again, that takes time.

> You can't "say it well" if you don't end it well.

From a quick survey of my sermon transcripts—actual data, not merely my plan or my recollection—I rarely devote less than 15 percent of my time to applying and concluding. More often than not, I plan for as much as 20 percent. That's anywhere from seven to nine minutes in a forty-five-minute Sunday morning message. Frankly, I had to do the math because, after fifty-plus years of preaching, I didn't know how much time I reserve for concluding; I simply go with my instincts. But that figure appears reasonable.

Other kinds of speeches don't need as much concentrated effort on appealing to the will, but no message is complete without one. Even if you're delivering a technical paper at a computer research symposium, people will remember your speech if you boil your information down to helpful principles, tell the audience how to use the information, and then urge them to follow through with action. For that kind of address, I think three to five minutes out of forty-five would be sufficient.

To protect the time reserved for conclusion, and until your instincts are honed, I encourage you to establish a time budget, devoting a set number of minutes to each major section of your message. A good rule of thumb for a sermon is what might be called the "25–50–25 rule." Break your allotted time into quarters. Devote a quarter of your time to establishing a rapport with the audience and introducing the subject. Use the next two quarters to deliver the body of the message, an explanation of your points. Then reserve the remaining quarter for applying and concluding. I realize that's 25 percent for a conclusion compared to my 15 to 20 percent figure above, but—trust me on this—time in front of an audience passes differently from time spent in the privacy of your study. It slows down in your head while the clock speeds up. By devoting a quarter of your time to the conclusion, you run less risk of skimping when the body of your talk inevitably runs long.

> Break your allotted time into quarters.

As you develop your own style and rhythm, you'll get a feel for your own pace. In the beginning, try the 25–50–25 rule.

I always rehearse my messages. Always aloud. I don't mean that I stand up and pretend there's an audience in front of me. But I speak audibly while I'm building the message at my desk, as I am writing my notes on my typewriter, and again when my notes are complete. You can think much faster than your mouth can move, so if you review the message merely in your head, you won't get a good sense of the time required to literally "say it well." Your ears need to hear your mouth speak your words. That's why I need privacy during this phase of preparation.

While I'm building and reviewing the message—aloud—I don't have to be as conscious of time for Sunday messages because the combination of routine and instinct keeps me well within bounds. But, if I'm to speak at an unfamiliar venue or for a different length of time, I keep a close eye on the clock when I review my notes. And I make sure I can deliver the entire message *with five minutes to spare*. Again, time slows down in your head and speeds up on the clock when you're speaking. Furthermore, you have to account for unplanned interruptions and audience reaction. If the audience laughs or applauds, for instance, you don't want to cut those precious seconds of connection short; so, leaving a five-minute buffer at the end will allow you to connect without rushing.

> I make sure I can deliver the entire message *with five minutes to spare.*

If I'm somewhere unfamiliar, I confirm with the program coordinator not only how many minutes I have, but the actual time I should be finished. (That alone may earn you an invitation to return. Time-conscious speakers are a godsend to event planners.) At Stonebriar Community Church, we have two identical services each Sunday morning, so the clock is a critical factor in maintaining everyone's sanity. If I overrun the first service, everything is impacted, even the traffic on the main road leading into our parking lot. So, I had a small digital clock installed in the top section of the pulpit of our church. Many venues have a clock posted at the back of the room. Some preachers and speakers place their watch on the pulpit or lectern. Before I begin, I make a mental note of where the *big hand* will be, or what the last two digits will read, when I must end. In the middle of a message, I can't devote brain cells to calculating time on the fly, so I need an instantaneous visual. Frankly, I am never *unaware* of my time.

> I am never *unaware* of my time.

I am told by those who are more technologically savvy than I that both Android and iPhone applications exist to help speakers budget their time and stay on target when speaking. You may find those helpful. I'll just stick with my watch...or my pulpit clock.

I also know where the big hand will be when I must begin applying and concluding. But, I'll be honest; my plans don't always work perfectly. Even on Sunday morning, when I have an established routine and I'm in my element, I sometimes see the number hit the fateful spot and I have more to say...sometimes much more. It happens to the best of us. That's when I have to make a tough decision on the fly.

You might discover partway through the message that you can't cover everything in your notes. You did your best, but you planned too much to say in too little time. If you forge ahead or try to rush your words, you'll botch the conclusion. So, you will have to—on your feet—cut something out. You may have planned to examine a parallel passage or a cross-referenced verse. Don't go there. Or you may have a great illustration for a particular point. Leave it out. Or worse, you might have to delete or combine a couple of points. Bypass them. Nobody knows you skipped over something except you. Trust me when I say,

> Better that the audience remembers the points you did cover because of a good conclusion than forget all of them because of a rushed closing.

those elements are expendable; your conclusion is not. Better that the audience remembers the points you did cover because of a good conclusion than forget all of them because of a rushed closing.

Wrapping Up

I know when I've hit on a great conclusion. No one fishes for his or her keys. No one eases toward the exit to beat the crowd to the restrooms or the parking lot. So, when I think about concluding a message, I try to think about what would interest me, what would keep me in my seat those last few moments.

As I scan my memory for the messages that have impacted me the most throughout the years, without exception, I recall the conclusion first. The conclusion then brings to mind the content of the message. It's almost like the conclusions are index tabs on those messages in the file system of my mind.

As I analyze just what makes these messages so memorable, I discover that the preachers or speakers who held my attention to the very end did so by going outside the realm of the obvious to say something unexpected. They offered a new perspective, a fresh look at an old issue. They pointed out something I would have missed, or helped me see life from an unexpected angle.

A good example is a message I heard in chapel as a first-year student at Dallas Seminary. Dr. Dwight Pentecost spoke that morning. He made it his purpose to encourage us, to refuel our tanks, to help us keep going through the difficulties of living in tiny, uncomfortable spaces, eating on a shoestring budget, and studying late into the night only to get up early the next morning. The central theme of his message was simple: *it's worth it.*

He closed his message with a personal story of his own trek through seminary. He and his wife, Dorothy (to whom he was married for sixty-two years before her death), had come to Dallas in the latter years of the Great Depression, just before the start of World War II. They lived in a makeshift trailer park next to the seminary, since student housing didn't yet exist and few could afford apartments. To say "times were tough" was an understatement.

One night during supper, his wife said something that changed his perspective, and he wanted to share it with us. She said, "Dwight, I've decided I'm no longer going to be discouraged. I've decided that as long as we live here, while we're preparing for ministry, we're going to live *an abnormal life*."

I don't know why, but those words completely shifted my paradigm. I realized that, sometimes, life takes on the "abnormal" when you're in transition, when you're moving between one kind of "normal" to another. Accepting and embracing "abnormal" helps you do what needs to be done without losing heart. I left the chapel service with a great weight lifted. And that night, I said to Cynthia, "You know, honey, what Dorothy Pentecost said to Dr. Pentecost is what we need to say to each other from time to time. This is just an abnormal period of time. We won't have much room to live in during these years in seminary, and we'll have just enough money to get by."

> I left the chapel service with a great weight lifted.

Dr. Pentecost may not even remember that specific chapel service. I'm sure in the thousands of messages he's delivered—in his nearly seventy years of ministry!—he won't remember that one in particular. But he concluded well *for me*. That little tidbit has served me well many times in the years after graduation. Every transitional period is an opportunity to say, "We're just going to live an abnormal life for a while." And that makes a big change just that much easier to endure.

From a speaker's point of view, providing a fresh angle on life in every message is impossible. You can't have a personal epiphany every week. But if you make it your habit to say something that isn't obvious, you will impact people

You can't have a personal epiphany every week.

without realizing it. Dr. Pentecost had no idea the positive effect he had on Cynthia and me that day until I told him many years later.

Generally speaking, the more unexpected the turn, the greater impact you will have. More than once, after preaching a gospel message, I have concluded with a fable I lifted from Peter Marshall:

It was an old legend of a merchant in Baghdad who one day sent his servant to the market. Before very long the servant came back, white and trembling, and in great agitation said to his master: "Down in the market place I was jostled by a woman in the crowd, and when I turned around I saw that it was Death that jostled me. She looked at me and made a threatening gesture. Master, please lend me your horse, for I must hasten away to avoid her. I will ride to Samarra and there I will hide, and Death will not find me."

The merchant lent him his horse and the servant galloped away in great haste. Later the merchant went down to the market place and saw Death standing in the crowd. He went over to her and he asked, "Why did you frighten my servant this morning? Why did you make that threatening gesture?"

Death responded, "That was not a threatening gesture. It was only a start of surprise. I was astonished to see him in Baghdad, for I have an appointment with him tonight in Samarra."

All of us have our own appointment in Samarra. Though we may try, the appointment will not be canceled.

Each time I have closed with that story, the audience literally gasped. The unexpected turn made its impression and their

| You must be careful not to introduce new information in your conclusion. |

response to the gospel let me know I had closed well.

While you want to provide a fresh viewpoint, and you want the audience to leave with a new perspective to ponder, you must be careful not to introduce new information in your conclusion. That might seem obvious, but you'd be surprised how quickly an offhand comment can open a can of worms you don't have time to close. For example, you've discussed the conflict between Cain and Abel, the potential dangers of lingering anger, how Cain should have responded to his resentment, and the tragic result of his growing hatred: murder. In your application, you have shown the audience how to deal with anger constructively, and now you want to urge them to resolve any conflicts in which they bear resentment. And, somewhere in the middle of your closing illustration, you mention Cain's wife.

Oops! Now you've lost them. They were ready to go straight to their estranged loved ones to make it right...and now they're wondering where Cain got his wife.

Plan your closing so that it ties up loose ends. You don't have to resolve every stray issue, but, for the sake of "saying it well," don't create new ones! Plan your exit and stick with the program. I generally close a message in one of three ways: a summary, a story, or a statement.

A summary covers your main points, principles, and applications in brief fashion, which is effective if remembering the information is important. I don't do this often because, as I stated earlier, people remember what is relevant to them. They will remember the points that impacted them personally. But if you want to aid memory, repetition and review can be helpful. Unfortunately, this can easily come across as pedantic unless you do something creative, like propose an analogy or paint a vivid word picture.

Analogies and metaphors can be extremely helpful as long as you don't—as my grandfather used to say—"make 'em walk on all fours." Be careful not to overwork word pictures. When used well, a creative summary not only aids the memory by providing an image, it shifts the audience from the rational side of their brains to the imaginative, emotional side. If they've been taking notes, they have your points written down for later review. An analogy simply engages parts of the brain that have been idle until the end. It can be simple or silly; whatever fits the subject matter best. For example, I might say, "Think of this as a train, and behind the engine we have five cars." Then I'll name the five cars and describe what's in them. "Oh, and there's a caboose..." That's where I might add the gospel to an otherwise unrelated topic.

Sometimes a good story can bring all of the points, principles, and applications together through illustration and, simultaneously, drive them deep into the audiences' hearts. Sometimes, when typing out my notes, I'll come to the end of the applications and I need a good closing. So, I'll close up all my books, return them to my library shelves, tidy up my desk, lay aside my notes, and pray. Then, I get out of my study. I've been so close to the trees, as it were, I need to back away to see the forest. I'll take a brief walk in the neighborhood or run some errands. I let my mind wander without ever drifting far from the message.

Sometimes sooner, sometimes much too late for comfort, the perfect story will occur to me. Usually it's something I've read. (Being well read helps a lot!) A human interest story from the news or in a magazine. A compelling description of an event in history. A great illustration used in someone else's book—I *always* give credit. A personal experience, or that of someone close. The beauty of a story is that it shows the application actively lived out by someone else. We

> The beauty of a story is that it shows the application actively lived out by someone else.

see the results and hopefully want to see those results repeated in our own lives.

I have also closed with a strong statement or a quote. But you can't just drop the line at the end; you have to set it up, usually with some information about the source. For example, I might want to end with this quote: "Friendship is a sheltering tree." It's a lovely line that might bring a message on God's unrelenting grace to a poignant close. But, only if I give the source and explain the context.

While attending school at Cambridge, Samuel Taylor Coleridge distinguished himself in three ways: voracious reading, prolific writing, and radical thinking. Eventually, his philosophical pursuits led him away from the faith of his father—a notable clergyman before his death—and away from Cambridge before graduating. He accumulated a large debt, pursued French philosophy, attempted to found a utopian society in Pennsylvania, married, divorced, became hopelessly addicted to opium, and eventually managed to estrange himself from everyone he knew, family and friends alike. One of the poet's most memorable lines comes from his epic "The Rime of the Ancient Mariner."

Alone, alone, all, all alone;
Alone on a wide, wide sea!
And never a saint took pity on
My soul in agony.[18]

Near the end of his life, Coleridge found refuge in the home of his sole friend, an apothecary named James Gillman. Despite Coleridge's ongoing addiction and repeated betrayals, Gillman cared for the pathetic poet for the rest of his life.

A few years before dying, Coleridge acknowledged the value of his sole friend when he wrote, "Friendship is a sheltering tree."[19]

The context gives this quote extra staying power in the minds of the audience, and hopefully it will be forever linked to the message on God's grace.

Keep Up the Good Word

Always infuse your conclusion with hope and encouragement. Don't beat the sheep. When I was a young preacher in New England, I beat the sheep until they were bloody. I'm embarrassed when I think about how I shamed them and chided them. That's a painful memory for me. Fortunately, that

> Don't beat the sheep.

came to an end a few months before I left for Irving. I noted to Cynthia that the people didn't seem very responsive to my preaching. She said, "I've noticed that, too. It may be because you're harsh when you're in the pulpit, which is strange because you're not like that normally. You're not like that with me or the children. But I don't hear a lot of encouragement from you when you're preaching, while you're generally encouraging most other times. Why don't you just be like you are at home when you're in the pulpit?"

I remember saying, "I can't do that."

"Why not?" she asked.

I couldn't answer at first. Upon reflection, I realized that I felt like I needed to model moral and spiritual leadership and that I had interpreted this responsibility as being "superior." At home and even with parishioners, I didn't see spiritual leadership that way.

I typically had no trouble acknowledging when I was wrong and I never took myself too seriously. But it never occurred to me that I should be that way while preaching.

So, the next Sunday I apologized to the congregation for being too harsh about their lack of response to helping out with vacation Bible school. "I want all of you to know that I was wrong for coming down on you so hard. I understand how busy you are and how you can't be here for everything. I apologize. I trust you will forgive me."

The response was incredible. That's when I began to discover the power of authenticity when preaching. I started using humor—poorly at first. And I poked fun at myself. I began to be myself in the pulpit, really for the first time. And because I'm all about encouragement and hope in my personal life, that began to come through more clearly in my preaching. As a result, the congregation began to respond, which stands to reason. We're wired to respond to the positive and to resist and avoid the negative. So, I determined never again to end on a negative note. Even if I must correct, reprove, or rebuke sin, I will conclude with hope and encouragement.

> That's when I began to discover the power of authenticity when preaching.

When a parent corrects a child, ending with the words, "And don't you ever do that again," doesn't help children do better next time. It frightens them. It causes them to become tentative. If they hear that often, they walk through life on eggshells. They become more confident, on the other hand, when a parent corrects the bad behavior and then goes on to explain how to do better next time: "What have we learned through this? Let's say from here on out you'll always do so-and-so instead. You're a great kid, so I know you can do better next time." That communicates hope. That says, "You're better than this."

If you must talk about something negative, be certain to end on a positive. Show
your listeners how the sovereignty and
goodness of God prevails over every circumstance, even past sin. Let them know
the Lord is *for* them, He wants them to do
well, and explain how the applications lifted from Scripture will
lead to a better future. People will come out of the woodwork to
hear that. Never wander too far from grace.

> If you must talk about
> something negative,
> be certain to end on a
> positive.

The Word of God is both encouraging and empowering. Our
messages, if they are lifted from Scripture, should be no less so.

Keep up the good Word. And never stop learning how to "say it
well."

Living It Well

O<small>n</small> August 5, 1979, I stepped behind the pulpit of our church in Fullerton, California, emotionally drained and completely distracted. I then stumbled my way through what felt like the worst sermon I had ever delivered. I had given my best effort, considering the circumstances. Still, anyone could see that my preparation was lacking and my delivery substandard. When it was finally over, the sanctuary emptied and I left for home. Once inside, I said to Cynthia, "That was the biggest flop of my entire preaching ministry." She tried to offer reassurance, but I wouldn't hear it. I couldn't.

I tried not to be too hard on myself. After all, the past ten days had been an emotional roller coaster through a parent's worst nightmare, starting with a phone call to my study on a Thursday afternoon. The voice on the other end said, "Pastor Swindoll, your daughter, Charissa, has been injured and the paramedics are here. We need to know which hospital you prefer." They told me she had been practicing with the cheerleaders, fell from the top of the pyramid, and landed on her head. I said, "Don't move her; I'll be there right away."

I arrived a very short time later—I don't want to admit how fast I drove. She lay on a gurney, strapped to a board with her head immobilized. With tears streaming from her eyes, she said, "Daddy, I can't feel anything." My heart thumped in my throat and my mind raced. I willed my face to show confidence as I kissed her and said, "I'm right here with you, sweetheart."

Within a minute or two, the paramedics were speeding toward the hospital, so fast, Cynthia and I couldn't keep up. By the time we arrived, they had wheeled Charissa to the X-ray room and began neurological tests. Meanwhile, time stopped for her mother and me. Without information from the doctors, our worst fears flooded our minds, including images of our good friend, Joni Eareckson Tada, whose tragic diving accident left her paralyzed from her shoulders down. We held each other, cried, and prayed the desperate groanings of desperate parents: "Oh, God, no...no, no, no...please, Lord, no...please help us, please..."

The attending physicians finally called us back late in the evening. One of them pointed to the X-ray images—which never make any sense to me—and confirmed that Charissa had fractured two vertebrae. "Fortunately," he said, "they are compression fractures of T7 and T8 with no indication of permanent nerve damage."

My head swam and I felt weak in the knees. Waves of relief and gratitude washed over Cynthia and me as we cried.

The doctor said the paralysis would persist in the short term, but that she would, most likely, experience a full recovery—with time. That night, Charissa began to feel tingling in her toes and, over the course of several anxious hours, slowly regained sensation everywhere else. By Saturday, we were able to take her home with a complicated contraption to keep her neck straight and her back braced.

While the drama of that weekend was a strain, I was in reasonably good spirits by Sunday—exhausted, but elated that Charissa would be fine. The message for Sunday was nearly complete by the time I received the emergency call on Thursday; so, I decided to preach rather than call for a last-minute replacement. (Finding someone on short notice to preach all five services was never an easy task.) We were midway through a sermon series titled *Gold in the Making*. My sermon title, already selected before the call on Thursday: "How to Enjoy a Shipwreck," was based on Acts 27. Paul's ministry had been interrupted by false accusations in Jerusalem, leading to a long imprisonment and endless legal battles. On his way to a hearing in Rome, a storm nearly sank the passenger ship, stranding the whole company on Malta.

I rode a wave of adrenaline going into Sunday. Buoyed by relief, I was able to stay focused. And, with Charissa's permission, I closed with the following:

You have a dream that's not fulfilled? Your Rome has wound up at Malta? Ditched on a beach with nothing to turn to?

The hope of our oldest daughter's life was to get to cheerleading camp next week. And when you're in senior high school, that really is important. And, of course, it then became important to us, because we care about what's important to our children. And so she's worked, labored feverishly and faithfully every week since school let out, in school, practicing with the squad and learning the tumbling routines and all that goes with that world. Camp is next week.

My phone rang on Thursday. And on the other end of the line was the principal of the school, who asked me to come quickly. And I arrived as I saw the paramedic trucks and the fire truck and all that out front. And I knew there had to be some grave problem. And I came to the patio of the school and I found her being wrapped up in a stretcher. She had in some of the routine of that particular yell slipped and landed on her head, and they feared a fracture.

We got her to the hospital locally. And she's been there so many times that people on duty say, "Oh, Charissa. How are you? Come on in." For some reason, she has gone through some tough times lately. Her back is broken. A couple of vertebra, numbers seven and eight, are fractured. And she certainly will not be at camp, and for eight to ten weeks will be recovering in a rather involved brace.

And as I helped her take it off last night and as she slipped in bed, she batted those big old eyes at me and said, "Daddy, why does this happen?" And, God, I really love her. I really love her. Cynthia really loves her. She's a very, very special gal. And I said, "I don't know." I couldn't lay a big trip like Acts 27 on her. All I could say is, "Honey, maybe it's so your daddy can learn somethin' through it." God knows I need to learn 'em. So she lives with broken dreams. And thank God she has full feeling and she'll be all right.

And maybe as she lives as an object lesson to all of us in the Swindoll family we will learn vicariously through her pain what it means to be beached at Malta.

I have always struggled to know how much of my personal life to include in a message. I want to be transparent, but I don't want to turn the pulpit into a therapist's couch. No matter how long you've been preaching or speaking, I think you'll always wrestle with this issue. Perhaps that's a good thing. The day I stop questioning whether to talk about myself in the pulpit is the day I have made the message about me. In this case, I decided to let the congregation know that the message I delivered was not for them only; it had hit perilously close to home that week. I felt good about that message and went home reasonably satisfied.

Surprised by Grace

A funny thing happens after a traumatic experience, even when it ends well. The emotional high of relief often leads to a very severe low. After the elation of hearing the good news, we took our daughter home, only to find that life had changed. When one member of a family hurts, the entire household suffers with her; so, all of us—not just Charissa—had to begin a process of healing. As Charissa's numbness gave way to pain, we hurt with her. As she faced the disappointment of a very different future than she had planned, we also had to make adjustments. Her restricted physical activity meant that everyone had to compensate. And throughout the process of healing—especially that first week—Charissa's back brace became a symbol of a difficult truth: the road to recovery would be long, difficult, and uncertain. Healing takes time.

As for me, I felt like I had been through a wringer. I maintained a confident exterior for the sake of my daughter, but in private moments, it was all I could do to keep going.

I worked on my message for the next week, but found it almost impossible to concentrate. After describing Paul's shipwreck on Malta, the author of Acts—Luke, a physician by training and trade—gives special attention to the theme of healing (Acts 28:1–10). Shipwreck…healing. I didn't miss the significance to us personally. Throughout the week, I did my best to study the passage and to form an outline, but it felt like trying to build a tower out of sand. By Saturday, I had very little to work with, not much more than a collection of loosely connected thoughts. I said to Cynthia, "I don't know that I can deliver, and it's too late to call on anybody."

She said, "Clyde Cook would do it for you. He'll understand the short notice."

"I can't do that. It wouldn't be fair to whomever I call. Besides, I'm healthy; I'm just broken."

Without batting an eye, she said something that would mark a fundamental shift in my ministry from that day forward. "Then… *deliver it broken.*"

Early Sunday morning, I was weary and distraught—I had been

up most of the night—and decided I would simply do my best to get through the morning without causing too much damage. I said, "Without going into all the details, I'm going to be straightforward about where I am emotionally and spiritually right now. I trust the Lord, but I'm discouraged, I'm fearful, and I don't have a lot of answers to explain what Charissa's going through and how it will affect our future."

Cynthia replied, "I think you should. This whole situation is on your heart, and that's where you have to speak from."

I shouldn't have been surprised by Cynthia's confidence, but I was. This woman who had been there through it all suggested I step up to the pulpit with my Bible open and admit I didn't have a lot of answers—a risky thing to do back in 1979. Vulnerability in the pulpit was virtually unheard of at that time. Furthermore, Insight for Living was broadcasting my messages and what I had to say wasn't going to fit the mold. Televangelists around that time were attracting large audiences with a very different message, an arguably more positive and appealing message for those in pain. Later, I dubbed their theology "The Four Spiritual Flaws."

Flaw 1: Because you are a Christian, all your problems are solved.

Flaw 2: All the problems you will ever have are addressed in the Bible.

Flaw 3: If you are having problems, you are unspiritual.

Flaw 4: Being exposed to sound biblical teaching automatically solves problems.

Those health-wealth, "word-faith" teachers of a false gospel had a simple, straightforward pitch: "Take the medicine I'm dispensing and all your problems will go away." I, on the other hand, wasn't offering any simple solutions. In fact, I wasn't offering any solutions at all. Personally, I had reached the absolute end of my rope. Candidly, I couldn't find any easy applications from my studies that would make Charissa feel better overnight or save her from a long recovery or spare her the disappointment of derailed plans.

I really didn't worry too much about what people outside our church thought. I did worry, instead, that I was failing in my duty as the spiritual leader of our church. It was my job to search the Scriptures and to present solutions to the difficult questions of life... and to "say it well." At the moment, however, I didn't have a lot of answers. I had some principles to share from Scripture, but no explanations. I refused to offer platitudes from Romans 8:28, and I couldn't pretend that what had happened wasn't difficult. At that point in time, all I could offer was unguarded, unvarnished candor. I didn't understand what the Lord was doing, but I trusted Him. I just hoped that would come through in the message.

After delivering the message titled "Time to Heal," I returned home, glad to have it in the past. I resolved to start the next week fresh and to redeem my failure with a well-crafted message.

On Monday, my assistant came into my office with a bewildered look on her face. "What on earth *happened* yesterday?"

She had been away that weekend, so she obviously didn't know how badly I had flopped. I expected a lot of people to be disappointed, but I didn't think they would complain in droves. Before I could apologize, she went on to inform me that the church office had been flooded with notes and telephone calls requesting a recording of the sermon. Many suggested I turn the message into a book. Many more wrote to tell me their own stories. The positive response took everyone by surprise, but no one more than me.

By the end of the year, people had requested that recording more than any other. In 1985, Word Books published my written adaptation of "Time to Heal" as the book *Recovery*. People continued to request the message for years after that unique Sunday. In fact, I've been told it became the most requested sermon I had preached in my twenty-three years of ministry in Fullerton.

My Turning Point

As I look back at the transcript of that particular sermon, I see that I never mentioned our daughter, Charissa, the slow progress of her recovery, or the personal anguish I felt. To be honest, that surprises me, because she was on my mind consistently throughout the message. I am told that my delivery wasn't as lifeless as I felt at the time, which also surprises me, because I wasn't able to speak above a whisper by the end. Objectively speaking, I broke almost every rule in the preacher's handbook of homiletics and I definitely failed to implement most of my own counsel in this book. Yet, somehow, people connected with me, and, amazingly, my message hit its mark. Why? What happened?

In a word: authenticity. While the details of my personal experience didn't find their way into the message, my personal anguish did. I didn't talk about my family specifically, yet I spoke every word with us in mind. I merely said what *I* needed to hear and allowed the congregation to listen in. And because I didn't have a lot of great answers for the problem of pain, I didn't try to offer any.

Ultimately, that message proved to be a defining moment in my ministry. I decided to make my preaching ministry about real life— more so than ever before. No straw-man issues. No platitudes. No easy answers. No skirting difficult or uncomfortable questions. In fact, I would go out of my way to discuss openly what everybody's thinking but no one's saying. I decided that life—as it is, not how we pretend it to be—would be the foundation of every message.

This was also a turning point in terms of style—if it could be called that. Feeling free to laugh in the pulpit helped me loosen up and be myself, but it was this experience that gave me the courage to be utterly and completely authentic. While there's never an excuse for neglecting preparation and it's never acceptable to give less than your best, authenticity covers a multitude of public-speaking sins. That morning, my congregation overlooked the glaring technical defects of "Time to Heal" because they saw their spiritual leader struggling with the same difficulties they face. They understood that I was looking to God's Word for hope and direction, and then speaking directly from my heart. They didn't see a larger-than-life human come down from some super-spiritual mountain with answers; they saw one like themselves, broken . . . seeking the Lord's wisdom in the midst of pain. And it resonated deeply.

While I hope my practical suggestions on preaching and public speaking prove valuable, trust me when I tell you that authenticity is the most effective tool of communication and no amount of technique can replace it. Becoming truly and transparently genuine in front of a crowd is risky because they might not see you as you want to be seen. But—as the saying goes—the greater the risk, the greater the reward. I encourage you to trust in the goodwill of your audience. More often than not, they will accept you, "warts and everything," and they will reward your courage with affection. When you "deliver it broken," they will love you.

If you can manage to be yourself in front of a group of strangers, you will discover, firsthand, that connection is the key to "saying it well." That's why I began this book not with a focus on developing the speaker's techniques but on developing the speaker himself or herself. I am convinced that "saying it well" begins with "living it well." Effective communication is a by-product of authenticity, which is the result of pursuing those three imperatives:

- Know who you are.
- Accept who you are.
- Be who you are.

To put it another way: discover your calling—learn who you are and what God has equipped you to do. Prepare for your calling— gain the knowledge and skills to pursue your calling with excellence. Pursue your calling—let it take you where it must. And throughout your journey, let your calling transform you. Live your calling with such integrity that you become the message. Then, when you share yourself authentically with an audience, you won't merely sway opinions with clever speech, you will deeply touch others with your words.

Appendix

GOD'S WILL, ~~God's~~ MY WAY
Ex.2:11-15/Acts 7:21-29   (#2)   PM 9/14/75

INTRO: One of the greatest battle Xians face is not
DOING the will of God...it's doing God's will,GOD'S WAY.
  We frequently discover what His will is for us---
  only to blow the whole thing accomplishing it
  OUR OWN WAY.   Let me give some examples:
  1) He tells us as parents--
        "Train up a child in the way he should go..."
  We roll up our sleeves and have at it--in our minds
  we know what God wants--but we carry it out OUR WAY-
---- We're TRAINING--but not HIS way-------------
  2) He calls us into His service--Xian work full time
     That's clear & unmistakeable.
  Before you know it, we're pursuing that plan with all
  the energy the flesh can muster. Insensitive to such
  matters as TIMING...WAITING...SEEKING HIS MIND AS FAR
  AS PLACE OF TRAINING.
NO! Instead we pull strings/force our way thru/compete
     for top spot...in OUR chosen area of service.
---We're gifted and capable--pursuing the plan OUR WAY!

  3) He assures us we're not to remain single.
     It's His will that we marry. Don't have gift of
  celibacy...not made to live alone...genuinely lonely!
  GREAT! We ask Him to get out of the way. When we
            get to the altar--we'll whistle!
  | Manipulation - - match-making - - gameplaying - -
  | panic - - rationalization - - compromise...
SUDDENLY--we find " (QUOTE) "MY LIFE'S PARTNER!!"
If it's any comfort to you--that battle is not new!!
  It goes all the way back to a very capable, highly-
    intelligent, polished & skilled man named Moses...
      Who spent 40 years UNLEARNING that lifestyle
  --------------- ----------- --------------
Last Sunday evening--Birth & Nursed in his own home...
Thru remarkable chain of events, he was protected from
death and allowed to be nursed & raised for few years
by his own mother. BUT FINALLY, HOUR OF TRUTH OCCURED.
  SEE EXODUS 2:10   Four penetrating words:
      "...he became her son..."
  (1) Pharaoh's daughter quickly gave him a new name
  (2) She ALSO had great plans for the boy.
ILLUS: Josephus, famous Jewish historian says:
  "Tradition is that she designed Moses for the throne,
  as the Pharaoh had no son..." (Antiquities ii,9,7)

-2-

I. EGYPTIAN LIFE STYLE
    (A) Nurtured in the Court [Ex.2:11a]
    Suddenly, the training began...a whole new frame of
refrence was built around the little boy...
    — The protective, quiet, humble hut of his mother,
        father, brother, and sister was only a memory.
    — He was given a stately suite--all his own.
        ——→tutored in court life & protocol
        ——→advised on cultural & traditional matters
        ——→instructed on the finest of taste in the arts
Note At that time, it's believed that land of Egypt--this
major area was populated by some 7 million people! No
doubt, he became the talk of the people--the object of
most conversations--the target of attention !!

TURN TO **ACTS 7**------let's start at v.21
    See "nurtured"? It means "nourish/educate/rear"
    She treated him as if he were her own offspring.

    (B) Educated in the Schools [Acts 7:22a]
        We dare not overlook this helpful detail given
here and no where else in all of Scripture!
    ("ALL") -- The schools of Egypt have been tagged
        ——→"The Oxford of the Ancient Egypt"
    First/foremost, learned the mysterious hieroglyph--
    Intensely complicated--sometime took lifetime to
    master. Language of pictorial symbols not characters
Educa. was carried to very great length, EDERSHEIM:
    Various sciences, mathmatics, astronomy, chemistry,
    medicine...theology, philosophy, knowledge of law.
    The arts were not omitted: music,sculpture,painting,
    broad knowledge of Egyptian literature--
    (No football scholarships...no majors in skindiving))
FURTHERMORE--there is no disagreement among scholars
that he distinguished himself as a military strategist.
                    mid-
He was, in his late 30s-- general in Egptian military--
and led smashing victory over ETHIOPIANS!

    (C) Respected in the Land   Acts 7:22b
    "Mighty" -- "man of power" -- INFLUENTIAL!
He was gifted and respected in WORDS and WORKS
Not an intellectual genius--w/o ability to communicate,
but a balanced product of the schools & learning.
ILLUS: A word is in order here. NEVER underestimate
the importance of solid, disciplined learning..but
do not think that that alone is the need of the hour!
Moses was BALANCED.   Now...let's go further.

-3-

II. OPERATION SELF WILL Ex.2:11b-15a/Acts 7:23-29a

Now the plot thickens in our story. Keep in mind that God had destined Moses to be His man effecting deliverance...the LEADER of the exodus.

A. God's Revelation (NOT RECORDED)

It is believed by many that the first time Moses knew God's will was when he stood before the burning bush at age 80/ THAT IS INCORRECT!

God revealed His plan to Moses sometime before he turned forty. We have NO record of such a revelation, but I want to show you why I believe he knew. In the event we are going to examine, we'll see a perfect example of a man who attempted to do GOD'S WILL/HIS WAY!

B. Moses' Response --Acts and Exodus/back/forth.

I want us to analyze precisely what occured from start to finish as Moses FORCED the situation and suffered the consequences:

1. Acts 7:23 "...it entered his mind..."

THE IDEA WAS INITIATED BY MOSES--not God.

You don't read here nor in Exodus that God prompted this encounter. Apparently Moses got "ANTSIE" ---

NOTE: He'd seen the Hebrews before...he'd been among them on other occasions--but this time, he planned to "make his move" and pull it off...

TURN BACK TO EXODUS 2:11 the makings of disaster, as far as the flesh is concer

Here he stood--vulnerable & "antsie"--anxious to get the ball rolling & "do great things for God"

THEN it happened! IT WAS PREMATURE

2. Exo.2:12 "...looked this way & that & saw no one around, he struck down..."

I might also add, he "struck out"

THE PROCEDURE WAS ENERGIZED BY THE FLESH

Careful here! There was nothing illicit nor sinful in his passion for his people--resentment against a tyrannical people... HE WAS SINCERE! (but)

IT ROBBED HIM OF WISDOM--DIVINE PERSPECTIVE!

He was driven by false sense of dedication.

He committed himself to the TASK instead of the LORD who, alone, must motivate such actions!

Note that he was TERRIBLY man-conscious-------

"looked this way & that..." (not up!)

Rolled up his sleeves--"If ever I'm needed, it's now!

DEDICATED TO WILL OF GOD--not OGD WHOSE WILL IT WAS!

-4-

<u>APPLICA</u>: Let me level a warning. <u>This is ESPECIALLY</u>
<u>easy for those who are CAPABLE</u> and <u>GIFTED</u>. Often, the
better educated you are--the more difficult it is.

(That's why I took time to emphasize his educa.)
Strong, natural leaders fight this fleshly urge more
than any of us want to admit.

<u>LOOK ALSO</u>--- "...he hid him in the sand."

He attempted to cover up the raw, ugly truth. He
had a corpse on his hands--no other way to view it.
<u>THE FLESH NEVER LIKES TO FACE THE UGLY TRUTH OF</u>
<u>WHAT IT HAS CREATED</u>-------

③ Back to <u>Acts 7:24-25</u>   "...he supposed his breth-
ren understood...they did not"
[THE ACT LED TO CONFUSION AND FAILURE]

He was genuinely of the opinion they'd rally behind
him...they didn't. Things didn't fall into place.

HE KNEW GOD'S PLAN WAS TO USE HIM MIGHTILY------ (will
· But--------he set out to do it HIS WAY.

If you'll be kind enough to go back once again to the
Exodus passage, I'll show you something on this same
point.

Ex.2:13-14a "...went out next day..."
WHY? To carry out his plan to deliver! He wanted
to get a following--gather a crowd around himself. He
even tried to take charge again--forced himself into
the situation.
BUT OTHERS COULD SEE GOD'S HAND WASN'T IN IT.

----Note: Not that he wasn't gifted or even capable.
It just wasn't God's method of working.

Why, <u>Moses couldn't even bury an Egyptian</u>--one crummy
<u>taskmaster</u>! Probably <u>left his toes sticking out sand</u>.

--Later on, remember what God buried? The
entire ARMY of Egyptians at the Red Sea--

The difference? GOD'S WILL------GOD'S WAY.

Listen, <u>when God is in something</u>, <u>IT FLOWS</u>--doesn't
have to be FORCED...PUSHED...PRIED LOOSE...SHOVED THRU

"I try...I fail. I trust...He succeeds!"

④ Exo.2:14b [THE PLAN CREATED UNBEARABLE CONDITIONS]
Not merely "unfortunate event"---Moses was AFRAID
Can you imagine HIS confusion? His misery? Inner ache?

"Matter has become known"
You see--he began to be "found out!"

-5-

<u>LISTEN</u>: When <u>you work</u> something out <u>your own</u> way,
invariably <u>you must</u> <u>"cover up"</u> certain things...
you must <u>"hide the true evidence"</u>...and you live
in the misery of fear--that you'll be discovered.

Believe me------<u>you will be!</u> UNBEARABLE SITUATION!
Flesh doesn't lead to a tie...or a standoff. It
ultimately leads to our becoming demoralized---
depressed--totally defeated-- AWFUL REPERCUSSIONS!

(C) Other's Reaction?

➤ 1. First, <u>Moses</u> himself----"afraid" which
made him unfit for his regular responsibilities

➤ 2. Second, <u>others unnamed</u>--no doubt caused to
stumble because of this scandal.

➤ 3. <u>Pharaoh himself</u>---TRIED TO KILL HIM!
"Moses fled..." What a scene, friends.
Forty-year-old man, ready for the throne, <u>highly</u>
<u>qualified</u>------COMPLETELY USELESS.

• Educated & gifted---------DISARMED
• Able to speak in public/sway them-----SILENT
• A man of power in DEEDS------------FORGOTTEN

<u>What a conclusion:</u> "settled in land of Median, he
sat down by a well..."

<u>CULMINATION:</u> THE PRIDE OF EGYPT--LICKING HIS WOUNDS!!

I suggest <u>two final principles</u> in this serious
and exposing study of God's Word this evening:

(1) WHEN SELF-LIFE HAS RUN ITS COURSE--
We settle in a desert. (Note 15:a)
<u>ILLUS:</u> The bleakest, most harsh soil on face of the
earth--is in this very area. Dry, partched, hot, only
stringy bushes and large rocks dwell together.
THERE HE SAT------THERE WE SIT!

(2.) WHEN THE SELF-LIFE SITS DOWN---
The well of a new life is near.
Something <u>much worse than being at the end of</u> a
<u>SELF-DRIVEN life...it's being in the midst of</u> it!
God offers great hope to those at THE END of it.
A well of fresh, new, cool water .

--------And tragic part of it all is that it took
. Moses 40 years to find it. How about you?

SEE F.B. MEYER QUOTE--------------➤ CARD.

GOD'S WILL, MY WAY*

Exodus 2:11-15; Acts 7:21-29

Last week we studied the events that surrounded the birth and childhood of Moses. We witnessed how God protected him from death and allowed him to be nursed and trained in his home by his faithful mother, Jochebed. Tonight, the scene changes. His surroundings are altered in a dramatic way as he is adopted by an Egyptian princess . . . trained in the finest of schools . . . and groomed for a high-ranking position in the court of Pharaoh. But all that crumbles to dust as he carries out a self-made plan in the flesh--then runs for his life, a beaten, disillusioned man. Although forty years old, highly gifted, immensely wealthy, and a man of the schools, he wasn't ready for the place of leadership in God's plan for his life.

I.   EGYPTIAN LIFE-STYLE   Exodus 2:11a; Acts 7:21-22

    A. Nurtured in the Court

    B. Educated in the Schools

    C. Respected in the Land

II. OPERATION SELF-WILL   Exodus 2:11b-15a; Acts 7:23-29a

    A. God's Revelation *(not recorded)*

    B. Moses' Response

       1. IDEA WAS INITIATED BY MOSES...NOT GOD.

       2. PROCEDURE WAS ENERGIZED BY FLESH.

       3. LET (E) TO CONFUSION & FAILURE.

       4. PLAN CREATED UNBEARABLE CONDITIONS.

    C. Others' Reactions

III. CULMINATION: DISCOURAGEMENT AND DEFEAT   Exodus 2:15b; Acts 7:29b

    A. WHEN SELF-LIFE RUNS ITS COURSE WE SETTLE IN A DESERT.

    B. WHEN SELF-LIFE SITS DOWN THE WELL OF NEW LIFE IS NEAR.

Second in a series of biographical studies on Moses: God's Man for a Crisis. Cassette tapes are available in the tape room. Copyright, 1975, Charles R. Swindoll 9/14/75-PM

PANORAMA OF MOSES' LIFE

NOTE: *Acts 7:23 and 30 along with Deuteronomy 34:7 confirm that Moses' life was divided into three forty-year segments.*

THE FIRST FORTY YEARS

. . . thinking he was somebody . . .

— EGYPT —

· Nursed at home

· Schooled . . . skilled

· Self-willed, impatient

· Driven from home

Exodus 1:1-2:15...Acts 7:20-29a

THE SECOND FORTY YEARS

. . . learning he was nobody . . .

— DESERT —

· A father, shepherd, servant

· Alone . . . broken

· Humble . . . sensitive

· Useful to God

Exodus 2:16-7:5...Acts 7:29b-34

THE THIRD FORTY YEARS

. . . discovering what God could do with a nobody . . .

— HEBREW PEOPLE —

· Deliverance

· The Law

· The Tabernacle

· Wanderings

Exodus 7:6 - Deuteronomy 34:12

Notes

1. Dietrich Bonhoeffer, quoted in Eric Metaxas, *Bonhoeffer: Pastor, Martyr, Prophet, Spy* (Nashville: Thomas Nelson, 2010), 446.

2. Hermon Eldredge, "Tip-Toe Preaching," *The Herald of Gospel Liberty*, 110, 1–26 (1918): 443.

3. A. W. Tozer, *Rut, Rot or Revival*, 1st ed. (Camp Hill, PA: WingSpread, 2006), 163.

4. T. S. Eliot, quoted in Michael Grant, *T. S. Eliot*, vol. 2 (New York: Routledge, 1997), 572.

5. John Henry Jowett, *The Preacher, His Life and Work: Yale Lectures* (New York: George H. Doran Company, 1912), 114.

6. When a participle is used in combination with a regular verb in this particular construction, the participle takes on the characteristics of the main verb. In other words, "go" in the Greek sentence is a participle, but it's translated as an imperative like the main verb, "make."

7. Metaxas, *Bonhoeffer*, 272.

8. Richard Chenevix Trench, *Notes on the Parables of Our Lord* (New York: D. Appleton & Company, 1854), 265.

9. *Merriam-Webster's Collegiate Dictionary*, 11th ed., 253.

10. Hartley Coleridge, *The Worthies of Yorkshire and Lancashire* (London: Whittaker and Co. et al., 1836), 322.

11. Warren W. Wiersbe, *The Wiersbe Bible Commentary: The Complete New Testament* (Colorado Springs: David C. Cook, 2007), 162.

12. "I am proud to be accused of having introduced Yury Gagarin to Orthodoxy," *Interfax*, last modified April 12, 2006, http://www.interfax-religion.com/?act=interview&div=24, accessed August 2, 2011.

13. A. W. Tozer and David E. Fessenden, *The Attributes of God,* vol. 2,. *Deeper into the Father's Heart* (Camp Hill, PA: WingSpread, 2001), 151–52.

14. Yogi Berra, *The Yogi Book* (New York: Workman Publishing Company, Inc., 2010), 92.

15. Harry Emerson Fosdick, *The Living of These Days: An Autobiography* (New York: Harper and Brothers, 1956), 99.

16. William E. Sangster, *The Craft of Sermon Construction* (Grand Rapids: Baker, 1972), 150.

17. Yogi Berra, *When You Come to a Fork in the Road, Take It!* (New York: Hyperion, 2001), 53.

18. Samuel Taylor Coleridge, "The Rime of the Ancient Mariner," *The Collected Works of Samuel Taylor Coleridge: Poetical Works I, Poems (Reading Text),* vol. 1, ed. J.C.C. Mays (Princeton: Princeton University Press, 2001), 391.

19. Coleridge, "Youth and Age," 1,012.